English Studies/Culture Studies

ENGLISH *Studies /* CULTURE *Studies*

Institutionalizing Dissent

Edited by
Isaiah Smithson and Nancy Ruff

University of Illinois Press
Urbana and Chicago

© 1994 by the Board of Trustees of the University of Illinois
Manufactured in the United States of America
1 2 3 4 5 C P 5 4 3 2 1

This book is printed on acid-free paper.

Library of Congress Cataloging-in-Publication Data
English studies/culture studies : institutionalizing dissent / edited
 by Isaiah Smithson and Nancy Ruff.
     p.   cm.
   Includes bibliographical references and index.
   ISBN 0-252-02108-8 (cloth). — ISBN 0-252-06398-8 (paper)
   1. English philology—Study and teaching (Higher)—United States.
2. Culture—Study and teaching (Higher)—United States. 3. Language
and culture—United States. I. Smithson, Isaiah, 1943– .
II. Ruff, Nancy, 1956– .
PE68.U5E57   1994
420'.71—dc20   93-48766
                                                                CIP

In Memoriam

Alvin Sullivan, 1942–91

Leo Ingrande, 1929–92

Eric Ruff, 1955–92

Contents

1   Introduction: Institutionalizing Culture Studies
    Isaiah Smithson

    PART 1: *Dissenting Voices within Culture Studies*

25 A Dialogue on Institutionalizing Cultural Studies
    *Gerald Graff, Janice Radway, Gita Rajan, and
    Robert Con Davis*

43 Cultural Studies versus the New Historicism
    Patrick Brantlinger

59 Can Cultural Studies Speak Spanish?
    George Mariscal

76 Passing as Pedagogy: Feminism in(to) Cultural Studies
    Pamela L. Caughie

94 Elder Wisdom: Native American Culture Studies
    Lee Francis

108 Griots, Bluesicians, Dues-Payers, and Pedagogues: An African-American, Autobiographical, 1960s' View of Culture Studies
    Eugene B. Redmond

127 Asian Immigrant: Confessions of a "Yellow Man"
    Sheng-mei Ma

    PART 2: *The Impact of Culture Studies on the Institutions of English Studies*

143 Rhetoric Returns to Syracuse: Curricular Reform in
    English Studies
    Steven Mailloux

157 Institutional Identity at the State University of New York at
    Albany: The New Ph.D. in English
    Warren Ginsberg

167 Burning the Commodity at Both Ends: Cultural Studies and Rhetoric in the First-Year Curriculum at Carnegie-Mellon University
Kristina Straub

180 *The Heath Anthology* and Cultural Boundaries
Paul Lauter

191 Always Already Cultural Studies: Academic Conferences and a Manifesto
Cary Nelson

207 Works Cited

221 Contributors

225 Index

☐ Introduction: Institutionalizing Culture Studies

Isaiah Smithson

Referring to change within "criticism and the American university" in recent decades, Jonathan Culler distinguishes "two general models at work.... The first makes the university the transmitter of a cultural heritage, gives it the ideological function of reproducing culture and the social order. The second model makes the university a site for the production of knowledge" (33). While the first model entrusts criticism with the responsibility for "elucidating the masterpieces of [a] cultural heritage," the second envisions criticism as a source of "critical progress or innovation" and as a means with which to "advance one's understanding of cultural phenomena" (35). *English Studies/Culture Studies: Institutionalizing Dissent* brings together essays by scholar-teachers working primarily within the second model—educators committed to creating, as well as transmitting, knowledge; to increasing understanding of the relations among texts, writers, readers, and cultures; and—equally important—to prompting dissent and effecting social change through this increased understanding. The collection represents some of the transformations in pedagogy, curriculum, research, and dissemination of knowledge that are redefining English studies so that, in universities in the United States, it is becoming inseparable from the study of culture.

The phrase "English studies/culture studies" denotes a shift from the New Critical concept of the text and reader as separable from each other and their culture to an affirmation that texts, writers, readers, and culture are intertwined, simultaneously constituting and reflecting one another. Scholar-teachers involved in this shift toward English studies/culture studies—toward culture studies—maintain that literary texts are always cultural texts and that readers read differently according to the cultures from which they derive their identities. Thus, they see themselves and their students as interrogating cultural phenomena rather than elucidating literary masterpieces.

Their teaching and research assume not only that the objects of knowledge—such as art, religion, politics, economics, and means of representation—are tied intimately to specific cultures, but also that knowledge itself is defined, produced, disseminated, and evaluated differently in specific cultures. And these educators are aware that in the United States there are several cultural heritages whose objects and ways of knowing are to be studied. They recognize that, given the changing demographics, the United States is undergoing transformation from a nation that has one dominant culture and several subcultures to a society comprised of several cultures, each expressing differences and none necessarily assuming a hegemonic position. Accordingly, teachers working within culture studies accept that they are working with multiple, expanding canons and with students who are increasingly aware of the ethnic heritages that make up the United States. These educators are aware that, in their classrooms, they and their students are participating in, are affected by, and are influencing social change occurring throughout the United States.

The shift within English studies toward culture studies has various and sometimes conflicting intellectual sources. Marxism, feminism, and cultural critique are major influences. Multiculturalism and university ethnic studies programs are additional significant sources of ideas and information. And the British cultural studies movement is yet another significant influence behind changing conceptions of English studies in the United States. It is because the intellectual traditions and current theories affecting English studies are diverse and sometimes conflictive that the term *culture studies* has been adopted for the title of this collection. Some teachers and scholars in the United States work consciously out of the British cultural studies tradition and are comfortable with the term *cultural studies*. Others have their roots in multiculturalism or other traditions and seem unaware of, or uninterested in, the Birmingham Centre movement. Thus, "culture studies," Gayatri Spivak's term, seems a useful way to refer to the several theories of culture that influence the direction of English studies.[1]

The interfusion of English studies and culture studies occurs not only in teaching and individual research. Culture studies is also being institutionalized within revised department curricula, academic conferences, interdisciplinary and traditional English studies journals, and university and textbook presses. The academic institutions that comprise English studies are changing: Culture studies, which began in opposition to an older, institutionalized form of English studies, is itself being institutionalized. Profound change requires its own institutionalization. If culture studies were dependent solely on a small number of individuals for its definition, continuation, and expansion—rather than on academic institutions—concern with culture would remain a controversial logo sewn on the surface rather than become a part of the fabric of English studies. Within this institutionalization, though, lies a danger. The institutionalization of culture studies confronts several problems, many of which will be discussed in this Introduction and in the chapters to follow. Foremost among the problems is the likelihood that the original conceptions of culture studies will lose their oppositional edge, become distorted, be absorbed, and die the subtle death that institutions can casually impose on dissent.

English Studies/Culture Studies

English Studies

"English studies" denotes a discipline with a long, complicated history. Studies by William Parker, Arthur Applebee, Richard Ohmann, Brian Doyle, Terry Eagleton, Gerald Graff, and others establish two relevant points. First, "English studies" has always denoted a contest as much as it has a content. Disputing, revising, and transforming the principles, theories, methods, subjects, and goals of English studies—activities common in the 1990s—are not new to English studies. During the middle of the nineteenth century in the United States, English studies included spelling, grammar, rhetoric, logic, oratory, reading, and history; the study of English and American literature had no significant role as yet, while reference to the themes, grammar, and rhetorical principles of ancient Greek and Latin texts permeated curricula. It was primarily in the second half of the century that the study of English literature began to appear in several universities. The teaching of composition became an integral part of English studies in the late nineteenth century. Inclusion of American literature became common in the early twentieth century, its significance boosted by the patriotism of World War I (Graff, *Professing Literature* 212). Serious study of modern literature—American and British—developed as late as the first half of the twentieth century. During some periods in some universities, English studies has included not only literature and composition, but also journalism, speech, drama, and linguistics.

The nineteenth-century study of literature was given respectability by the importation of rigorous (but often irrelevant) German philology, while the twentieth century has seen the ascendance of dozens of teaching and research theories: New Criticism, writing as process, and discourse analysis, to name only a few. Indeed, in the 1980s and 1990s, "theory"—the myriad, sophisticated ways English studies is aware of itself—dominates the discipline. Each revision of English studies has occurred over several years, none has occurred without profound disagreement, and defining "English studies" continues. As one historian comments, English studies "has never finally settled down. . . . its history has been more complex and extensive than that of most other academic disciplines" (Palmer 1).

Histories of English studies establish, second, that English studies has always been intimately connected with culture. In the past, English studies has often conformed to the first model defined by Culler: It has attempted to transmit a carefully chosen cultural heritage through elucidation of canonized texts, and it has concerned itself with the canon of the dominant culture within Britain or America, not with the texts of several cultures making up a single nation. English studies emerged in eighteenth- and nineteenth-century England, in part as a means of encouraging national unity. Consisting primarily of English language, literature, and history, English studies sought to engender national pride, maintain a particular definition of the English "character," instill respect for a specific social order, and impose a particular set of values onto growing sectors of the population whose literacy, income, political power, and importance to the economy and labor force were increasing. "The criteria of what counted as literature"—whether philosophy, history, essays, letters, or poetry—were "frankly ideological: writing which embodied the values and 'tastes' of a particular social class" (Eagleton, *Literary Theory* 17). In spite of doubts about the effectiveness of English studies as an instrument of "social control" (Graff, *Professing Literature* 12–15), and in spite of past and present opposition to this role within the profession, twentieth-century English studies in the United States is still called upon to instill cultural coherence. Writing in 1976, Ohmann observed, "Society needs help from the schools to justify its present divisions. . . . There is pressure—indirect but heavy—on teachers of literature to join in this effort. The ruling classes want a culture, including a literature and a criticism, that supports the social order" (25).

Culture Studies

In the 1990s, in keeping with the second model described by Culler, English studies is resisting this pressure and beginning to affirm the diversity of cultures in the United States, to study the texts of several ethnic groups, and to critique the cultural biases subsumed within institutions, including colleges and universities. Instead of emphasizing the restricted cultural narrative typical of earlier English studies in England and the United States, it envisions, as Spivak notes, "a confrontational teaching," an "arena of cultural explanations that question the explanations of culture" (*Other Worlds* 117). In the 1990s, English studies/culture studies investigates—at least—how literary canons are formed; the conventions that have defined some texts as "literary"; why some histories and interpretations prevail while others struggle to get into print; the differences made by gender, sexual orientation, ethnic background, and political and economic power in the writing, publication, and reading of texts; writers, texts, and readers as cultural commodities; the roles of educational and other institutions in defining objects, methods, and values of education; and the relations among educational institutions, governments, business interests, and other cultural components.

English teachers investigating relations among texts, writers, readers, and cultures encounter a vast web of interconnections. One of the first attempts to define "culture" for English cultural scholarship was E. B. Tylor's 1871 *Primitive Culture;* its opening sentence explains that culture is "that complex whole which includes knowledge, belief, art, morals, law, custom, and any other capabilities and habits acquired by man as a member of society." In subsequent decades, the concept of culture has become even more inclusive. Most modern scholars would include language, economics, politics, education, science, "popular" culture, and modes of representation among the "other capabilities" that make up the "complex whole" referred to by Tylor. And most modern scholars (noting the inadequacy of Tylor's generic "man") would include gender, sexual orientation, ethnicity, race, and socioeconomic power as cultural components. Thus, when English studies investigates the cultural derivation, relations, and significance of its texts, it seems to encounter no boundaries. Cultural intertextuality is, evidently, infinite.

Raymond Williams offers an approach to culture that is more recent than Tylor's but no less daunting. In one of his many discussions of culture, Williams isolates three definitions within cultural analysis: the "ideal," "documentary," and "social." While the ideal conceives of culture as a "timeless order" of selected "absolute" and "universal" "works" and "values" ("the best that has been thought and written"), the documentary envisions culture as the complete record of actual texts, paintings, sculptures, and other artifacts of "intellectual and imaginative work." The social conceives of culture as "a particular way of life, which expresses certain meanings and values not only in art and learning but also in institutions and ordinary behaviour" (*Long Revolution* 41). Williams realizes these three conceptions overlap and describes them not to argue for the superiority of one of them but to insist that "any adequate theory of culture" must include all three (43). Even including all three conceptions is not sufficient: "It is with the relations between them, the particular forms of the whole organization," that cultural analysis is "especially concerned." Williams views cultural analysis as "the study of relationships between elements in a whole way of life" (46). He rejects cultural histories that assume economics, politics, and social organizations to be the "core," histories that include "art and theory" only as "marginal illustration" or as "'correlation.'" But he also rejects studies of literature, science, or philosophy that reduce economics, politics, and social organizations to "background elements" (46). The "whole life" of cultures is approached only by attention to relations among myriad elements (63).[2]

Tylor's "complex whole" and Williams's "whole life" illustrate the scope, complexity, and attention to relationality encountered in culture studies. English teachers and students working within culture studies may build on Tylor's definition, use terminology specific to *The Long Revolution,* or adopt other cultural theories developed out of Kantian critique, Marxism, the Birmingham Centre tradition, feminism, multiculturalism, or other intellectual movements available from thought of the twentieth, nineteenth, and eighteenth centuries, even from ancient Sophist thought. Regardless of the lineage, these teachers and students find themselves engaged in an interdisciplinary study of infinite, interlocking relations among "literary" texts and the cultures these texts simultaneously are created by and help to create. Each analysis within English studies/culture studies necessarily remains incomplete; each chosen object of study is inescapably overdetermined by other possible objects of study. Although culture studies is, thus, challenging, it is also compelling. Teachers and students engage in this complex, extensive criticism because it allows a more comprehensive analysis of texts, because it offers tools and a vocabulary for expressing dissent, and because it can lead to social change.

Culture, Nature, Essence, Dissent, and Change

Culture, Nature, and Essence

"English studies/culture studies," as the phrase indicates, relies on the concept of culture, not on such foundational concepts as nature and essence, as the means for its analyses. Traditionally, categories such as nature and essence denote that which is perceived as given and unyielding in experience; phenomena safely classified under "nature" or "essence" are immune to change and to human intervention. However, "culture," as used in culture studies, signifies that which can change and grow through effective critique and political action. The term *culture,* even when applied to human societies, has never lost contact with its original sense of a soil, plant, or growth that can be cultivated. Accordingly, many teachers and students who find themselves dissenting from traditional forms of English studies and are committed to social change are drawn to culture studies.

Jacques Derrida's now-famous criticism of Claude Lévi-Strauss's opposition of culture and nature is emblematic for culture studies. Derrida asserts that "the opposition between nature and culture . . . is congenital to philosophy . . . even older than Plato . . . passed on to us by a whole historical chain which opposes 'nature' to the law, to education, to art, to technics—and also to liberty" ("Structure, Sign, and Play" 252). Working within this "historical chain," Lévi-Strauss sees the incest prohibition within kinship systems as an important anomaly, a "scandal," for it seems to participate in both nature (that which is "*universal* and spontaneous, not depending on any particular culture or on any determinate norm") and culture (that which "depends on a system of *norms* regulating society and is therefore capable of *varying* from one social structure to another") (253). In incest prohibitions, Lévi-Strauss discovers what he perceives to be a scandalous contradiction, a violation of categories, a phenomenon forbidden by nature *and* culture. However, Derrida counters by pointing out that it is in this instance that "the limit of nature/culture opposition makes itself felt" (254). "Obviously there is no scandal except in the *interior* of a system of concepts sanctioning the difference between nature and culture," he asserts (253). Lévi-Strauss can be appalled by a scandalous exception to the nature/culture division only because he has accepted the prevalent division as somehow "given," instead of as historically constructed in the past and liable to reconstruction in the present. Nature, culture, and the relations between them are defined and redefined throughout human history. The real scandal is that nature has been presented by Lévi-Strauss and others as universally unchanging in spite of its always having been constructed and redefined by cultures.

The culture-nature dichotomy that Derrida examines is not a remote, metaphysical conundrum; it has significant social implications. Eagleton observes that "it is one of the functions of ideology to 'naturalize' social reality, to make it seem as innocent and unchangeable as Nature itself. Ideology seeks to convert culture into Nature" (*Literary Theory* 135). One specific example of this attempted conversion has been elaborated throughout modern feminist theory:

> The subjection of women . . . is brought about not by their "natural" inferiority but by their classification as intrinsically inferior by a male-dominated culture they cannot avoid living in. The rival forces which compete discursively for the possession of "woman" used to be called "nature" and "custom." Nowadays the pair is labeled Nature and Culture. . . . it is characteristic of Culture to be passed off as Nature, especially by dominant groups who resort to this tactic in order to police human behavior and keep other groups subordinate. (Ruthven 44–45)

Educators involved in culture studies are as suspicious of appeals to essence as they are of claims made in the name of nature, as is illustrated by discussion within African-American criticism. Hazel Carby argues that there are "major problems" with asserting the "existence of an essential black female experience and an exclusive black female language in which this experience is embodied" (9). "Black feminist criticism cannot afford to be essentialist and ahistorical," for such criticism can easily lead to a "political cul de sac" (10, 9). Carby advocates, instead, cultural critique that "works within the theoretical premises of societies 'structured in dominance' by class, by race, and by gender" (17). Similarly, Henry Louis Gates, Jr., objects to "belief in an essence called 'blackness'" and insists that "blackness is *produced* in the text only through a complex process of signification" (7, 316). Just as Carby concludes that "black feminist criticism should be regarded . . . as a sign that should be interrogated" (15), Gates maintains that "blackness exists, but 'only' as a function of its signifiers" (316) and that what is needed is a "critique of the structure of the sign itself" (315).

Naturalist and essentialist assumptions are issues not just in literary theory. They pervade the academy. These assumptions are most evident in literary canons, which take some texts "synecdochally" to be the "*essence* of the culture" (Giroux et al. 477). However, they are present in several more subtle ways. Giroux et al. point out that "most of us think of academic disciplines as the reflection of more or less 'natural' categories" even though the academic division of the pursuit of knowledge "reflects cultural, social, and institutional demands" (473–74). And Mas'ud Zavarzadeh and Donald Morton argue that the traditional humanities curriculum operates through a "strategy of essentialization" ("Theory" 1, 9). According to Zavarzadeh and Morton, the "dominant curriculum is . . . an ideological operation, the purpose of which is to maintain the existing system." The humanities curriculum maintains this status quo by regarding the "individual and his consciousness as manifestations of a human essence that is timeless, ahistorical, transcultural"; by conceiving of "reason . . . as a timeless essence through which the subject has access to the 'truth,' which is seen as pancultural"; by assuming that "literature is a discourse inherently different from other discourses of culture"; by asserting firmly "that there is a core truth in the text itself"; and, finally, by relying on a view of language that asserts the "stability/naturalness of language" instead of asserting that language is a "system of differentiation" ("Theory" 2–9).[3]

Dissent and Change

Teachers and students involved in the institutionalization of English studies are increasingly carrying out cultural analysis modeled—in very different ways—by Derrida, Eagleton, Ruthven, Carby, Gates, Giroux et al., and Zavarzadeh and Morton. Whether the topic is language; the construction of readers, writers, and texts; canon formation; curriculum; institutions; or the social position of women, African Americans, and other marginalized groups, these teachers and students are exploring the cultural relations of texts rather than settling for what are ultimately naturalist and essentialist explanations. The goal of this culturally based interrogation is not merely description of cultural intertextuality. Expressing political dissent and achieving social change are also primary goals. Carby's concern with avoiding a "political cul-de-sac" and Zavarzadeh and Morton's identification of the humanities as an "ideological operation" are typical expressions of this insistence on the social, political implications of literary study. Sometimes the change sought is increased awareness—helping students (and colleagues) understand that, and how, social relations and institutions are formed not by nature, but by power and ideology. In other cases, the change envisioned is in behavior—helping students acquire the tools needed to question the explanations of culture given by their own institutions (including universities) or helping students (and colleagues) honor rather than suppress cultural differences.

Most often, it is difficult to separate the goals of increased awareness and altered behavior. For example, the "archival work"—the actual recovery of cultural history, texts, and artifacts carried out by ethnic and women's studies programs—and the "theoretical reflection" that accompanies this recovery of cultural identity inevitably encourage material change (JanMohamed and Lloyd 6). In the United States, culture studies is being institutionalized not to transmit the essence of the dominant culture and not as a means of spreading the notion that the dominant culture is somehow "natural." Culture studies is committed to understanding how texts acquire meaning, examining the relations among texts and the nation's several cultures, expressing dissent based on these investigations, and fostering social change.

Obstacles to Institutionalizing Culture Studies

Michel Foucault observes that the "university stands for the institutional apparatus through which society ensures its uneventful reproduction" (224). Louis Althusser maintains that educational institutions have the "dominant role" among what he terms "ideological State apparatuses" (152, 155).[4] According to Althusser, educational institutions are more influential than political, religious, and telecommunications institutions, even more influential than the family, in society's reproduction of itself. He also maintains that although schools may seem to present a "neutral environment" (156), may indeed seem to be "'natural'" (157), they necessarily reflect the values of the dominant social group and are the site of "struggle" between dominant and exploited groups (147). Given that formal education influences all members of a society, that schools cannot be neutral and certainly are not natural phenomena, and that struggle and debate are endemic to education, the ideas, points of view, and methods presented in classrooms are crucial. Depending on their educational experience, students gain different knowledge, adopt different ways of thinking, and relate to one another differently. Correspondingly, societies possess different knowledge and adopt different ways of thinking and relating depending on their educational "apparatuses," or institutions. Because English studies is and always has been a major component within educational institutions in the United States, the forms it takes, the methods it practices, and the goals it seeks are vital.

The Example of New Criticism

The importance of the forms, methods, and goals of English studies is illustrated by New Criticism, a dominant form of English studies during much of the twentieth century. The history of New Criticism illustrates how thoroughly particular conceptions of English studies can be institutionalized and how influential—for good or bad—a firmly institutionalized conception of English studies can be. Although New Criticism is a form of English studies mostly antithetical to culture studies, its past offers insight into the future of culture studies. New Criticism's institutional history suggests the obstacles that culture studies must confront as it supplements or succeeds traditional forms of English studies and, in turn, becomes institutionalized.

According to Cleanth Brooks, New Criticism conceives of a poem or story as an esthetic object whose "essential structure" is to be explicated (199, 203, 211). The structure is discussed in terms of "ambiguity," "paradox," and "irony" (passim), and close attention to this structure usually reveals "coherence" or "unity of experience" (206, 214). The poem's relation to the culture and history instrumental in its production is ignored, given only passing attention, or denied. Brooks cautions against bringing poetry "into unreal competition with" other cultural forms such as "science or philosophy or theology" (201). History, also, is down-played; W. K. Wimsatt categorizes history as "external evidence," evidence qualitatively different from and clearly inferior to the "internal evidence" that is the poem itself ("Intentional Fallacy" passim).

New Criticism was easily institutionalized during the 1940s and 1950s, primarily because it emphasized what is termed "close reading" and separating art from the rest of the world. In its simplest (perhaps distorted) form, it provided an attractive model for studying literature because it concentrated on single works (usually a poem), seemed to require no knowledge of historical context or of an author's biography or other works, and did not force readers to consider complex, ambiguous relations between literature and social experience. New Criticism was also attractive to teachers because it provided them with a ready means of scholarly publication; explication of a text was sufficient rationale for an article. Beginning in the late 1930s, New Criticism provided widely used textbooks (including *An Approach to Literature, Understanding Poetry, Understanding Fiction,* and *Understanding Drama*); journals (*The Kenyon Review* and *Sewanee Review*); several individual volumes (such as John Crowe Ransom's *The World's Body*); a handbook for the study of literature (*Theory of Literature*); and a history of criticism (*Literary Criticism: A Short History*) through which New Critical principles were elaborated, illustrated, and institutionalized. The textbooks in particular had a substantial and long-term influence. Beginning in the 1940s and continuing for more than two decades, *Understanding Poetry,* edited by Brooks and Robert Penn Warren, was almost as common as freshman composition in the undergraduate's experience. While instilling the value of close reading, this and the other New Critical textbooks also inculcated specific attitudes with respect to the relation of poetry to the rest of the world. Although the criticism, poetry, and fiction of Ransom, Allen Tate, Robert Penn Warren, and Brooks often contain commentary on or allusion to agrarian, industrial, religious, and other cultural forces, the textbook advice offered by Brooks, Robert Penn Warren, Austin Warren, René Wellek, and Wimsatt consistently directs teachers and students away from cultural concerns.

It is difficult to overestimate the pervasive influence New Criticism had and continues to have on English studies—on several generations of teachers and students. "Before long," notes Eagleton, "New Criticism seemed the most *natural* thing in the literary critical world; indeed it was difficult to imagine that there had ever been anything else" (*Literary Theory* 49–50 [italics added]). In the 1990s, English departments still have many teachers practicing New Criticism (teachers who often claim they do not teach "theory"). There are also many students in the 1990s who do not realize that the method of "close reading," study of imagery, explication of brief texts, searching for "unity of experience," and giving little attention to cultural intertextuality constitutes only one of many ways to approach literature. As William Cain summarizes the situation, "It is not simply that the New Criticism has become institutionalized, but that it has gained acceptance as the institution itself" (105).

Cain maintains that, because of its avoidance of "culturally oriented" criticism, the New Critical form of English studies "omits too much" (xvii). Culture studies seeks to rectify this omission. Foucault and Althusser are correct: Academic institutions traditionally embody the presuppositions, values, discourses, and epistemologies of the dominant culture only. Therefore, in the United States in the 1990s—where there are many marginalized cultures—academic institutions necessarily fail to represent a large portion of the population. English studies is not an exception; insofar as its curricula concentrate on a narrow literary tradition, ignore cultural intertextuality, and disregard literary theory, its classrooms fail to engage all students and to develop a sufficiently complex concept of culture. As the United States increasingly becomes aware of its cultural diversity, this type of English studies "omits too much." The institutionalization of culture studies is an attempt to transform English studies, acknowledging all groups and literatures in the United States and including the study of relations among individuals, texts, and ethnic groups. However, in doing so, this new form of English studies encounters serious obstacles not encountered by New Criticism. Some of these diverse problems are described in the following discussion. Unless these problems (and others discussed elsewhere in this collection) are resolved, culture studies will not be institutionalized successfully within higher education.

The Expanded Text

Instead of offering students and teacher-scholars the isolated New Critical text, culture studies expands the notion of text. Instead of encouraging readers to avoid investigation of the world external to the "literary" text, it encourages them to envision the text as part of a complex network leading to and from diverse cultural phenomena in and out of the academy. As Tylor's and Williams's definitions of "culture" illustrate, textual relations and the scope of English studies seem unlimited. When teachers and students seek to investigate intertextual relations within one culture, their task is imposing. How much greater is the problem for English teachers and students in the United States, whose province is the texts of the several cultures making up the nation? Culture studies is correct to claim that all texts are cultural texts and that all writers and readers write and read differently according to the cultures that produce them. However, given the breadth and complexity of culture in general, and cultures in the United States in particular, culture studies is faced with a serious question of how competently teachers and students can investigate the implications of these claims. At the least, culture studies requires teachers who have far greater backgrounds than the teaching of New Critical reading requires.

Addressing Nonacademic Audiences

Because culture studies is oppositional and seeks to intervene in cultural practice, it faces another difficulty not encountered by New Critical English studies. Culture studies produces knowledge that is more intrusive and less palatable than the knowledge created by the narrowly esthetic readings developed in New Critical classrooms. The knowledge generated has social implications that are often uncomfortable and that can easily be perceived as offensive; after all, students, teachers, and the public are necessarily members of the social groups and forces whose texts are analyzed. Culture studies calls on teachers to be "resisting intellectuals" who offer "students forms of oppositional discourse and critical social practices at odds with the hegemonic role of the university and the society" (Giroux et al. 480); encourages teachers to think of "reading and writing as potentially subversive and liberatory activities" (Trimbur 11); and describes the study of culture as a means of "intervening in the ways 'texts' and 'discourses' are produced within, inserted into, and operate in the everyday lives of human beings" (Grossberg, "Formations" 122).

If teachers occupying this "subversive" and "liberatory" position wish to gain something other than a hostile response, improved communications are needed among university faculty, students, parents, high school teachers, and the rest of the public. It is time, as Marianna Torgovnick advises, to "widen the circle of groups we professors think important" (8). Faculty supporting culture studies will have to move beyond speaking and writing for one another at conferences and in professional journals. They will have to write jargon-free prose for magazines and newspapers, appear on talk radio, and engage in other forms of public exchange, not only to define the role of educators in a free, equitable society but also to argue for two important educational principles: first, that good education is sometimes disturbing—education limited to what the dominant culture already accepts comfortably is not sound education—and, second, that all education—even education that is opposed to or is seemingly indifferent to culture studies—always expresses a political point of view. If educators do not speak—and listen—to this larger audience, the content, methods, and objectives of culture studies are likely to be ignored, misunderstood, or seen as intolerant attempts to enforce political correctness.

Funding Culture Studies

English studies, ethnic studies, women's studies, and other participants in culture studies compete for the same scarce institutional resources.

Even though faculty in ethnic and women's studies programs have extensive experience in, and excellent credentials for, culture studies going back at least to the 1960s, English departments often have an advantage in budget competitions. English studies has been institutionalized in the form of departments for almost a century, is responsible for highly visible university writing programs, and includes many white (male) faculty. Accordingly, when bidding for university resources, English departments sometimes have an unmerited advantage over more recently developed, more loosely organized, less readily categorized, interdisciplinary women's and ethnic studies programs. In times of financial crisis, the budgets of interdisciplinary programs are more vulnerable than departmental budgets. If English studies/culture studies is institutionalized successfully, there is a real danger that funds that could go into culture studies carried out by ethnic and women's studies programs would be allotted instead to English departments. The objective of English studies/culture studies is to supplement and cooperate in the work being done in the established interdisciplinary programs, not to replace it. English studies that investigates cultural intertextuality needs the cooperation of other programs carrying out cultural research and needs to learn from scholars in these programs. Cultural analysis and social change will not be increased if English studies tries to do the work now effectively done by ethnic and women's studies programs and if English studies receives the budget allocations now received by these programs.

Marginalization within English Departments

English studies faculty committed to culture studies need not look outside their own English departments—at poor communication with the nonacademic community or budget threats to ethnic and women's studies programs—to encounter another obstacle to institutionalizing culture studies. Most English departments that would extend their critiques of texts to include political imbalances that make up the texts' social context have marginalization and exploitation closer to home that require attention. A 1992 article comments on Graff's *Professing Literature,* "throughout the book, he defines 'English departments' solely in terms of literary studies, currently the most powerful, but not the only discourse in the discipline. As a result, his argument upholds a pervasive kind of oppression within English departments: the marginalization of composition and rhetoric studies" (Friend 278). In the 1985 Chair's Address to the Annual Convention of the Conference on College Composition and Communication (CCCC),[5] Maxine Hairston spoke of literature specialists as the "intimate enemy" faced by composition specialists: "They are uninterested in what we have learned about teaching writing. . . . Some of them openly dismiss our research and scholarship as trivial" (277, 276); "the hardest work of the department, teaching freshman writing, remains at the bottom of the social and political scale" (275; see Slevin also).[6]

Within this general marginalization of rhetoric and composition teachers is embedded a more specific, more important marginalization: widespread exploitation of the temporary, part-time faculty who teach freshman writing. While tenured and tenure-track English faculty teach the graduate, upper-level, and some freshman classes, most freshman writing classes are taught by "anonymous, underpaid, and conveniently invisible adjunct faculty" (Hairston 275). According to the Executive Committee of the Conference on College Composition and Communication, "More than half the English faculty in community colleges, and nearly one-third of the English faculty at four-year colleges and universities, work on part-time and/or temporary appointments. Almost universally, they are teachers of writing, a fact which many consider the worst scandal in higher education today" (330). These teachers—mostly women and referred to as "call staff," "gypsies," "academic nomads," and "academic migrant laborers"—usually have at least an M.A. in English and extensive experience in innumerable freshman writing courses, yet they typically receive no job security, no health benefits, no retirement benefits, low pay, haphazard hiring and retention reviews, and minimal social recognition by their "colleagues." As long as these disturbing marginalizations continue *inside* English departments, they restrict the moral authority that English faculty can muster when criticizing power, gender, and economic imbalances in institutions *outside* the university.[7]

Underrepresentation of Women and Ethnic Groups

Yet another serious problem in the institutionalization of culture studies arises out of the scant representation of some ethnic groups on college campuses. If the nation's cultures are inadequately represented in classrooms, "culture studies" becomes a vacant phrase. Classes in which European-American teachers and students discuss Native-American, African-American, or Vietnamese-American cultural texts are well intended and may do some good. However, culture studies will thrive only in classrooms populated by teachers and students who have actually experienced and gained their identities from the diverse cultures making up the United States. As the diversity of ethnic background, gender identification, and sexual orientation within a classroom increases, so does the quality of the intellectual exchange with respect to culture. Yet, according to studies carried out by the American Council on Education (Carter and Wilson), the National Research Council (Thurgood and Weinman), and the Department of Education (Schantz), colleges and universities are making little progress in increasing the presence and influence of minority students and faculty.

The following are just three sobering sets of statistics with respect to demographics in higher education. First, in spite of the increased *numbers* of minority students entering college, the *percentage rates* for college participation have not increased for blacks and Hispanics, while both indicators have increased for whites.[8] From 1980 to 1990, the numbers of blacks and Hispanics who enrolled in college increased, but the college participation rate for blacks between eighteen and twenty-four remained at 28 percent, 29 percent for Hispanics of the same age. However, college participation rates for whites between eighteen and twenty-four, instead of remaining the same, rose from 33 percent in 1981 to 40 percent in 1989 (Schantz iii). Second, in 1979, African Americans held 4.3 percent of all full-time university and college faculty positions; in 1989, they held 4.5 percent (Carter and Wilson 22). There was no appreciable increase over this ten-year period, the most recent decade for which statistics are available. Nearly half of these positions are held at historically black colleges and universities; only 2.3 percent of full-time faculty at predominantly white colleges are African American. Third, "As of 1989, more than half (51.4 percent) of the higher education labor force was female, compared with 46 percent in 1975 and 48 percent in 1979. However, regarding full-time faculty positions, little progress was made: only 30.3 percent of current full-time faculty positions are held by women" (Carter and Wilson 21). Dozens of other statistics also illustrate higher education's dramatic disparities with respect to ethnic group and gender. Until higher education in the United States can offer a more supportive atmosphere to all students, increase the proportion of nonwhite and women faculty, and thereby increase the range of cultural voices on campuses, culture studies will be severely compromised.

Problematic Roles of Culture Studies Teachers

Continuing underrepresentation in higher education gives rise to a related problem. Given the absence of full cultural representation among faculty and students, English teachers involved in culture studies must question themselves closely. Well-intentioned professionals who have not thoroughly examined their roles in culture studies can do damage. "Often contemporary white scholars writing about black people assume positions of familiarity, as though their work were not coming into being in a cultural context of white supremacy, as though it were in no way shaped and informed by that context," notes bell hooks (124). She warns that "participants in contemporary discussions of culture" who are not acutely aware of "the location from which they write in a culture of domination can easily make of this potentially radical discipline a new ethnographic terrain, a field of study where old practices are simultaneously critiqued, re-enacted and sustained" (125). Gregory Jay, who is Euro-American, adds, "Before we get too busy celebrating our position at the forefront of the liberation of the culture, we must recognize that *we* are often the problem. It is our racism, our sexual prejudices, our class anxieties, our empowered desires that we must confront and resist" ("End of 'American' Literature" 265). Not only white teachers but also teachers who are members of marginalized groups must be aware of their "location" in a "cultural context." "I may be serving as a collaborator with a racist structure," hooks says, "I must interrogate my role as educator. Am I teaching white students to become contemporary 'interpreters' of black experience? Am I educating the colonizer/oppressor class so that they can better exert control?" (132).

Culture Studies' Self-Critique

All teachers involved in culture studies must question not only their roles in predominantly white universities; they, and their students, must also be the means through which the institutionalization of culture studies itself undergoes self-interrogation. Culture studies is both a means of cultural investigation and a cultural phenomenon requiring analysis. If culture studies fails to be constantly self-reflective, it will not occupy a position of dissent, it will lose its identity to the academic structure it intends to change, and it will not redefine the scope and approach of English studies. This potential loss of oppositional identity is another obstacle confronting the institutionalization of culture studies. Graff argues that this was the fate of New Criticism: "It was only as the New Criticism became institutionalized in college curricula and pedagogy after World War II that its method of 'close reading' became detached from the theoretical and cultural programs which had originally inspired the method with larger purposes" ("Future of Theory" 253). Giroux et al. offer American studies as another "cautionary example," arguing that movements that "begin with a critical perspective" often "retreat from radical critique as they become more successful" (476). Given this history, they argue for "counter-institutions" (483) in contrast to traditional academic institutions. There is good reason for this profound mistrust of institutionalization of educational movements. Because the pressure to compromise with higher education's dominant ideology is subtle, constant, and usually effective, institutionalizing culture studies involves serious, complex risks.

Culture studies recognizes that individuals, texts, epistemologies, academic institutions, political power, and hundreds of other phenomena are culturally constituted—and that these, in turn, constitute the "complex whole" that is culture. Culture studies also recognizes that objects, subjects, and relations are always in motion, always overdetermined, and always unfinished. And scholar-teachers involved in culture studies acknowledge that their work is never done out of a firm foundation, always operates in a fluid context, never achieves final stability, always requires self-interrogation, and usually entails dissent. Culture studies cannot become separated from these theoretical concerns and remain culture studies; having no essence, it must constantly be reconstituted by cultural information, queries, doubts, and problems. It must avoid, on the one hand, the experience of New Criticism and American studies, movements that lost their identity to academic institutions in the process of being integrated into them. On the other hand, it must also avoid the fate of concepts like "multiculturalism" and "cultural diversity," ideas that have never actually been institutionalized, once-meaningful phrases that have been reduced to slogans by some administrators and faculty as they have signaled to legislators that their university is now "doing the right thing." Culture studies will not always be able to define itself by its opposition to the educational status quo. If, in the future, culture studies successfully redefines English studies and institutionalizes a culture-based, politically concerned conception of English studies, culture studies itself will become the status quo. The objective is to transform existing institutions without being transformed by them.

Although culture studies may someday be as thoroughly institutionalized as New Criticism has been, its institutionalization will have to be unlike earlier forms of English studies, and its relation to the rest of higher education will have to remain uneasy. Just as the cultures studied constantly evolve and exhibit differences along with unity, so culture studies itself will have to remain protean and be characterized by conflicting views. Culture studies must not only maintain dissent against policies, attitudes, and theories within higher education that, for example, hold to a narrow canon, deny the relations between classroom texts and political power, and fail to create an environment supportive of all ethnic groups and those with different sexual orientations. Culture studies must *also* stimulate and respect internal dissent; teacher-scholars involved in culture studies must openly disagree with one another, resisting the tendency to affirm mere orthodoxy. The constant self-critique must include awareness both of dissent from higher education and dissent within culture studies itself. Indeed, the degree to which external and internal dissent characterize culture studies will be a measure of its ability to survive institutionalization. The subtitle of this collection, *Institutionalizing Dissent,* denotes what is perhaps an oxymoron: the difficulty, almost impossibility, of maintaining profound dissent within academic institutions. Nevertheless, the essays in this collection explore the concept of institutionalized dissent through both external and internal dissent.

Institutionalizing Dissent: The Essays in This Volume

The essays included in *English Studies/Culture Studies: Institutionalizing Dissent* concern the changes occurring within academic institutions as culture studies becomes interwoven into the fabric of the teaching, learning, and research that make up English studies in the United States. (Nine of the twelve essays have been written exclusively for this collection, and three are extensive revisions of work that has appeared elsewhere.) The essays analyze some of the history that has already been made as English studies and culture studies have become interfused; describe some of the changes occurring as culture studies begins to be integrated into academic institutions such as department and class curricula, freshman writing programs, textbook anthologies, professional conferences, and academic journals; pose several of the problems, controversies, and benefits developing within these institutions; and consider how culture studies can be institutionalized without losing itself in the process.

The dialogue and six essays making up the first part of the collection, "Dissenting Voices within Culture Studies," exemplify both external and internal dissent. They are composed by scholar-teachers who work in Spanish studies, women's studies, Native-American studies, black studies, and Asian-American studies, as well as English studies. (Unfortunately, the collection lacks essays written from the perspectives of gay and lesbian studies.) The scope of the essays is broad; their authors examine such issues as the philosophical basis for cultural studies' political critique, models for culture studies pedagogy, and the ambivalent relations between ethnic and gender studies programs on the one hand, and culture studies on the other. The tone of the work is often questioning, sometimes overtly skeptical. For example, Patrick Brantlinger characterizes cultural studies (and New Historicism) as "escapes" from poststructuralism's "more radical implications," approaches that omit the "work of hard economic and social analysis." George Mariscal observes, "Some of us who write on Hispanic topics approach with caution any totalizing project with anglophone origins," including "cultural studies." And Lee Francis notes that although "mainstream scholars are able to cite a dozen or more feminist, African-American, and European 'authorities,'" they seem not to be aware of a centuries-long tradition of Native-American speaking and writing on U.S. history, culture, and internal relations. The dialogue featuring Gerald Graff, Janice Radway, Gita Rajan, and Robert Con Davis, and the essays by Pamela Caughie, Eugene B. Redmond, and Sheng-mei Ma, are equally doubtful in tone. However, while each of the first six pieces poses serious questions for culture studies, each also expresses hope and, in offering deft critiques, each contributes to culture studies' growing sophistication.

The five essays constituting the second part of the collection, "The Impact of Culture Studies on the Institutions of English Studies," delineate dissent embodied in three significant institutional forms of English studies: curricula, literary anthologies, and scholarly conferences. Their scope is, for the most part, more narrow than the scope of preceding essays; they describe some of the changes and conflicts that have arisen as culture studies redefines the institutional expressions of English studies. Steven Mailloux discusses the history leading to revision of an undergraduate English major program, Warren Ginsberg describes the revision of a Ph.D. program, and Kristina Straub analyzes the transformation of a sequence of lower-level undergraduate courses so that they "include both cultural studies and rhetorical assumptions about the nature of meaning production and consumption." Ginsberg's, Mailloux's, and Straub's essays provide a dramatic sense of the intellectual exchange that fuels profound curriculum change and of the possibilities available once departments and individuals begin to question traditional forms of English studies.

The final two essays deal with forms of English studies related to curricula and classes. Paul Lauter narrates the history of *The Heath Anthology of American Literature,* which, since its appearance in 1990, has widened the scope of what is taught in survey courses and increased the cultural consciousness of teachers and students. Cary Nelson's essay could as easily have been placed in this collection's first section, "Dissenting Voices," as in the second. Although it does analyze the relations between cultural studies and a particular academic institution—academic conferences—it is also a statement of dissent. Nelson focuses on conferences primarily to emphasize a distinction between what he defines as "cultural studies" and what he observes as its "recent commodification in English studies." He resents the current attempt in the United States "to depoliticize a concept whose whole prior history has been preeminently political and oppositional." Although acknowledging that no one can "police" the "cultural studies field," Nelson offers "a first draft of one version of a cultural studies manifesto"—an extended definition of "cultural studies" that sometimes contradicts and sometimes affirms the description of "culture studies" offered in this introduction.

Conclusion

Nelson's essay provides an apt conclusion to *English Studies/Culture Studies: Institutionalizing Dissent.* The dissent exhibited in this essay mirrors the dissent expressed back and forth among the other essays in the collection, back and forth among all practitioners within culture studies, and back and forth between those committed to culture studies and those critical of the movement. Within this collection, Nelson criticizes Radway and Davis, Francis criticizes Brantlinger, and Caughie criticizes Graff. And these are just the dissents marked by use of the names of scholars associated with particular views. Less overtly, threads of disagreement weave in and out of several of the essays. For example, without referring to one another by name, Nelson, Mariscal, Brantlinger, Radway, and Graff give significantly different depictions of cultural, or culture, studies. In addition, almost everyone included in this collection offers opinions dissenting from opinions expressed in this Introduction.

Although twelve essays and an introduction are hereby gathered between two covers, their authors cannot even settle on whether to use "cultural studies" or "culture studies" to designate the educational phenomenon being debated. In the book's introductory exchange, Radway insists that "cultural studies certainly is not a unitary thing. It's not even a single movement. . . . it might perhaps better be called 'culture studies' as a way of emphasizing its multiple embodiments." She goes on to voice her approval of the "contentious, contestatory nature" of this movement and to praise its "generative contentiousness." This collection means to contribute to the "generative contentiousness" of culture studies as culture studies and English studies work out their complex relations within academic institutions.

Notes

I wish to thank friends who read and offered suggestions on this introduction: Susan Gabriel, Nancy Ruff, Jeffrey Skoblow, and Jack Voller (all of Southern Illinois University at Edwardsville), and Robert Con Davis (University of Oklahoma). I wish also to thank friends and colleagues who provided valuable information and advice in the initial stages of this project: Nancy Armstrong (Brown University), Linda Brodkey and Barbara Harlow (University of Texas at Austin), Robert Con Davis and Ronald Schleifer (University of Oklahoma), Lawrence Grossberg and Cary Nelson (University of Illinois), and Steven Mailloux (University of California at Irvine).

1. The phrase *culture studies,* as employed by Spivak in "The Making of Americans, the Teaching of English, and the Future of Culture Studies," includes "transnational culture studies" as well as culture studies within the United States.

2. Williams offered several more discussions of culture over a period of about thirty years. See, for example, *Culture, Culture and Society, Keywords, Marxism and Literature,* and *The Sociology of Culture.*

3. For a view of essentialism that differs from mine (and from Zavarzadeh and Morton's), that sees cultural constructionism as ultimately embedded in essentialism, see Fuss.

4. Althusser distinguishes between "(Repressive) State Apparatuses" and "Ideological State Apparatuses." Although the two are interdependent, the first (e.g., the police, prisons, and government) function primarily through violence and repression, whereas the second (e.g., churches, trade unions, the family, and schools) function primarily through ideology (145). Sometimes Althusser capitalizes these terms, sometimes he does not.

5. The CCCC, which came into existence in 1949 and began to publish *College Composition and Communication* in 1950, is sometimes perceived as the "MLA" of rhetoricians and composition teachers.

6. The "marginalization" observed by Hairston and Friend in the 1980s and 1990s is not new: Francis J. Child, Boylston Professor of Rhetoric and Oratory at Harvard University from 1851 to 1876 and, beginning in 1876, the first Harvard English professor to be exempted from teaching freshmen, is famous within the history of English studies for championing literary studies and his concomitant disdain of rhetoric and composition (see Berlin, Halloran).

7. Misuse of adjunct faculty has been recognized in 1982 in the Modern Language Association's "Statement on the Use of Part-Time Faculty" (*Profession 82*, 52) and in the "Wyoming Resolution" published by the Conference on College Composition and Communication in 1989 (*College Composition and Communication* 40:61–72, 329–36). These statements are motivated as much by concern with "potential damage to academic programs" [MLA] or "commitment to quality education" [CCCC] as by concern for the women and men serving as part-time teachers.

8. College participation rates are a measure of the presence of high school graduates in institutions of higher education in these cases, according to racial and ethnic categories.

PART 1: *Dissenting Voices within Cultural Studies*

☐ A Dialogue on Institutionalizing Cultural Studies

Gerald Graff, Janice Radway, Gita Rajan, and Robert Con Davis

The following dialogue includes Gerald Graff (University of Chicago), Janice Radway (Duke University), Gita Rajan (University of New Orleans), and Robert Con Davis (University of Oklahoma). The exchange is edited by Davis (referred to as "R.C." by the other three). The four were chosen for this dialogue because of their diverse approaches to connecting English studies with cultural inquiry. Davis approaches cultural analysis through psychoanalysis, American studies, and classical studies. Graff is known for his research on the history of English studies as an institution. Radway worked first in American studies and popular culture studies before beginning to work on theories of cultural studies. And Rajan approaches English studies and cultural inquiry through a postcolonial critique. Their objective in this exchange is to assess the status of cultural inquiry, discuss some of its current controversies, and speculate on its future.

ROBERT CON DAVIS: When Isaiah Smithson and I were putting together this group, we approached you three because of your immersion in pedagogical reform under the general umbrella of cultural studies. Also, while you are involved in cultural studies, you have also worked on bridging the connection between cultural studies and English studies—on situating literary study within cultural inquiry.

I would like to begin by saying that I see cultural studies as having arrived at a second stage in the United States. We are almost past the point at which it is interesting to keep repeating the rudiments of what cultural studies is and where it came from. Cultural studies has become a fact of our nation's education. It is more appropriate now to talk about the early track record and the functioning of cultural studies *as an institutional program.* I don't want to suggest that there is an orthodoxy for cultural studies, a single route to the study of culture. This would be especially misleading since—as this collection illustrates—there's so much dissent within the ranks, disputes between the philosophical and political left and right, between the theoretical and the more overtly political, and between cultural studies and ethnic studies programs. I'd like to hear your sense of how cultural studies is being implemented in the 1990s in the United States.

GERALD GRAFF: I think that, in some ways, the cultural studies project revives a nineteenth-century philological ideal that existed before it was trivialized by positivistic specialization—that is, the ideal of studying the history of civilization as an organic whole. Yet, a precondition of the cultural studies project was the postmodern decentering of organic totalities and hierarchies, and the consequent blurring of distinctions between high and popular culture. This blurring of cultural levels reflected the general democratization of higher education after World War II, which eventually brought over half the eligible population of the United States into college. Suddenly, and for the first time, academic "high culture" was itself a form of "popular culture," disseminated to millions of people.

For some time, however, the antiquarian and specialized forms of academic study remained remote from the interests and understandings of lay people and undergraduates. It was unclear how academic knowledge production—especially in the humanities—related to the needs of the expanding constituency of nonacademics. Before the great university boom of the 1940s and 1950s, people had wondered why academic humanists should need to do "research" at all, but this research seemed to do no great harm when the average college enrolled only a few thousand students and the average humanities department consisted of two or three professors and a handful of graduate students. With the rise of the postwar "multiversity," the gulf between the interests of the academy and those of the larger society was magnified, with the humanities in particular thrown on the defensive. The academic humanities were part of an expanding postwar culture-industry, yet hardly anyone outside humanities departments had a clear idea what they did—as is still largely the case.

We should keep this historical context in mind in considering today's wave of attacks from the right against the recent overt politicizing of culture. These attacks would not have such broad appeal if they did not tap into a much older set of confusions and suspicions that took root long before any feminist or cultural studies programs were dreamed of. The current attack on politicized teaching and scholarship is overlaid on longstanding uncertainties about what academic humanists do when they aren't correcting grammatical and spelling errors and why their work deserves to be supported by taxpayers, donors, and tuition-paying students.

To a large extent, "cultural studies" has been called forth by the long-perceived cultural irrelevance of traditional humanistic work. Yet, clearly, its ways of making the humanities "relevant," which have entailed radical social engagements and the blurring of traditional levels of culture, are obviously not what most critics of humanistic irrelevance had in mind.

On top of that, the new ways of making the humanities socially relevant tend to be practiced in vocabularies that few outside the university (or inside) can understand. In fact, the blurring of the distinction between high and popular culture has been accompanied by a rigidification of the distinction between professional and lay ways of thinking and speaking. This poses a central problem for cultural studies, which on the one hand closes the gap between high and popular culture but on the other seems to keep the academy as circumscribed as ever.

DAVIS: The debates in the media about multiculturalism and so-called political correctness and all the misinformation about academic work attest to how poorly those in other sectors understand the academy. Are you saying, however, that the social function of academic work is not taken seriously by the nonacademic culture?

GRAFF: In a way, sure. But I'm trying to highlight something else—that the academy has yet to come to terms with the fact that, once it became a mass institution, it perforce became an agent of cultural popularization. Even cultural studies practitioners tend to think of popularization as inherently vulgar. Like other disciplines, cultural studies acts as if it has to legitimate itself by distancing itself from "mere" popularization. It's feared that to popularize cultural studies would be to let it be "co-opted" by the dominant institutions and discourses—as if that would necessarily be a bad thing! For whatever reasons, proponents of cultural studies often end up being as reluctant as traditional humanists to accept a popularizing function. But what else is a teacher but a popularizer, especially in a democratic educational system with a constituency of millions of students?

Of course, some cultural studies practitioners eagerly accept a popularizing role even as they continue to write in specialized vocabularies. These are the current exponents of radical pedagogy, who would turn cultural studies into a staging ground for social transformation along the lines suggested by Paulo Freire, Henry Giroux, and others. I have problems with this version of cultural studies, but perhaps we could return to them later.

JANICE RADWAY: I agree with Jerry, especially his framing of education within postmodern "image" culture. But I prefer to emphasize that cultural studies can be traced to the polysemy of the very word *culture,* as well as to the ambiguity of its referent. Both conditions have been carefully described by Raymond Williams in *Keywords.* In addition to tracing the complex etymology of the word, he discriminates among three "active categories of usage." Modern users, Williams argues, employ the word *culture* to refer, first, "to a general process of intellectual, spiritual and aesthetic development"; second, "to a particular way of life, whether of a people, a period, a group, or humanity in general"; and, third, "to the works and practices of intellectual and especially artistic activity." Contemporary cultural studies, it seems to me, has developed as a historically specific attempt to think about the nature of the relationship between culture as a way of life and culture as artistic and intellectual representation. The interesting question, I think, is what sets cultural studies apart from other, older efforts to negotiate this relationship? What differentiates cultural studies from, say, philology, biographical criticism, the sociology of art, or American studies? For me, the self-consciously interested, committed, wholly political nature of cultural studies marks it off from its predecessors. Indeed, it is cultural studies' self-construction *as political practice* that I find most exciting.

DAVIS: But certainly other cultural theories in the twentieth century were and are politically committed. Various kinds of Marxist criticism predate cultural studies, and political practice is intrinsically related to Jean-Paul Sartre's understanding of culture. With respect to cultural studies, its sense of political practice is situated within the critique of the subject that cultural studies gets primarily from psychoanalysis. The issue of political practice is crucial, but it is politics reconceived within the Lacanian and poststructuralist critique of the subject.

RADWAY: Well, yes and no. I would say that some cultural studies is congruent with the Lacanian view of the subject, but not all of it. My view of cultural studies is much less restrictive on the issue of the subject.

DAVIS: All right. Gita, you've focused on the specifically ideological dimension of cultural studies in your work.

GITA RAJAN: Yes, but I want to go back to the initial question and say that your query has an ironic twist. Cultural critique is the nebulous area that cultural studies is appropriating now, and cultural critique has always been part of the liberal humanist tradition. That's why we have voices from England such as Wollstonecraft, Mill, the Pankhurst sisters, Macaulay, and even Arnold, and, in the United States, Stanton, Anthony, Truth, Douglass,

Webb, Turner, and Mencken. These are just some people in the Western tradition who have addressed the definition of culture and acculturation quite critically. While one strain in the study of culture has maintained the elitist and hegemonic trend, there has always been another, subversive strain questioning the assumptions behind defining culture in these arbitrary terms, pointing out its male- and race-centered biases. As Stuart Hall maintains, cultural studies has a traceable genealogy because of its "unbroken continuities." The list I mention serves as one marker for areas in cultural studies like race, gender, and identity studies, or—to take it even further—as what James Clifford at a recent conference referred to as the politics of "post-identity" in cultural studies.

DAVIS: Yes. It was that tradition of "critique" that Ron Schleifer and I tried to trace in *Criticism and Culture: The Role of Critique in Modern Literary Theory*. We were told by some professional philosophers that there was no such tradition or set of conventions for "critique," but we discovered that many philosophers, writers, and literary theorists did know about, even assumed, such a tradition. We argued for seeing the tradition of cultural critique as a multifaceted set of cultural developments. But I'm not sure that I know what you mean, Gita, by "post-identity" in current varieties of cultural critique.

RAJAN: Clifford meant the reexamination of "identity," a basic construct in cultural studies, such that boundaries of self-other are renegotiated. He and Hall argue along similar lines; Hall, too, says we must be recognized as "social subjects" who live in particular social and cultural systems. Cultural studies itself has this sort of identity. Simultaneous with the orthodoxy of cultural criticism and commentary is a subversive but persistent and often unacknowledged strain. The movement in the United States, for example, in addition to expanding canons and increasing interdisciplinary study, has called negative attention to itself by systematically debunking the truth claims behind the Western, humanist myth. With the aid of critical theory, the current movement has vocalized its objections in a sophisticated, if sometimes jargonistic, discourse. This movement has never had—until the most recent discussions of an "oppositional" tradition—any clear, or clearly recognized, sense of "identity," even though it has had and continues to have an impact. I think this is what Clifford has in mind.

RADWAY: I would like to interject something here with respect to what Rajan calls cultural studies' "subversive strain." I think that the thoroughly politicized character of some strains of cultural studies is a function of its appearance in the post-World War II world. Its self-consciously interested nature is itself a product of the cultural consequences of late capitalism, that is, of the institution of an international consumer economy and media culture. This is not the place to tell my own idiosyncratic history of cultural studies. But I do want to note that I think it important to resist the now-common tendency to locate the sole origins of contemporary cultural studies in the classrooms and corridors of Birmingham. Certainly, a clear line of descent can be drawn from the early work at the Centre for Contemporary Cultural Studies to a particular body of work carried out now under the rubric of cultural studies. But it is my belief that the Birmingham project constituted only one efflorescence of a complex, diffuse, conflicted set of social practices.

DAVIS: I agree that it is a mistake to overplay the importance of innovations at the Birmingham Centre. Doing so also distorts the separate and ongoing developments of cultural studies in the United States. A lot has happened in cultural studies here, and Birmingham has not always been either the inspiration or the paradigm for those developments. Jan, by "efflorescence" are you talking about the global phenomenon of postmodern culture, or are you speaking about more local shifts in economic development and class structure?

RADWAY: I'm still talking about political intervention. The historical conditions I speak of were themselves enormously complicated, but they were all deeply affected, I think, by the triumph of a consumer economy complete with its own supporting epistemologies and subjectivities. This historical moment produced a series of *multiple* efforts to resurrect, if not to construct, an oppositional political agent, someone not wholly integrated into capitalism's imperialist, racist, patriarchal, and heterosexist vision of a consumerist utopia, nor represented by that social formation's repressive and highly mass-mediated forces. This response occurred differently and unevenly in the New Left (of which Birmingham was one academic arm), in the civil rights movement, in the women's movement, in anticolonial and anti-imperialist movements, and in the gay/lesbian civil rights movement. Each of these movements adopted multiple strategies and practices and defined its targets in specific ways, but all of them attempted to survey the nature of the connection between power, culture, and representation so as to challenge the way their own subjects had been positioned or actually subjected by those relations. All seem to share an interested, politicized commitment both to the analysis and to the dismantling of practices and patterns of representation that serve oppressive forms.

DAVIS: We're all working out of a sense of cultural studies as part of a sometimes unacknowledged and quite varied, even veiled, tradition of cultural critique. Gita was describing such a tradition, and that's what I see, too.

RADWAY: Yes, I suppose so. Cultural studies certainly is not a unitary thing. It's not even a single movement. Rather, it is an expansive set of differentially sited political practices focusing on questions of representation. I agree with the editors of this collection that it might perhaps better be called "culture studies" as a way of emphasizing its multiple embodiments. Despite the fact that many of these practices now operate under the sign of cultural studies, they have not always been compatible. I would assert that many of them were initially constructed as contestatory, even contradictory. In many cases, they still are, despite increased efforts to explore the intersections among these multiple practices. In fact, I like the contentious, contestatory nature of these practices. The contentiousness is productive, because it exposes the complexity of power and demonstrates that no single framework for analysis is wholly adequate to understanding, let alone for intervening in, that complexity. Thus, culture studies together foreground the situated, interested, and contingent nature of knowledge production.

DAVIS: Let's talk more specifically about cultural studies, or culture studies, within an institutional context. We're all fairly immersed in cultural studies theory and in attempts at pedagogical reform and reorientation. We are from four schools that represent a huge range in the United States academy—Duke University, the University of Chicago, the University of Oklahoma, and the University of New Orleans. It could be argued that our diversity as a group gives us some authority to talk about what may happen yet in cultural studies. What are you willing to project as the future of cultural studies in the United States, in any institutional context you can imagine? How deep will its influence go?

RADWAY: It's difficult to say how influential cultural studies will be, since it is now under attack from both the right and the left. The right accuses it of "bias" and charges it with the imposition of "political correctness." Some on the left, however, lump all forms of cultural studies together and dismiss the imagined result as a form of pollyanna populism, foolishly seeking out even the minutest traces of opposition or resistance within the texture of daily life. I worry that in responding to the former, that is, to the William Bennetts, Lynne Cheneys, and Arthur Schlesingers of the contemporary scene, advocates of cultural studies will suppress their own internal dissent in order to present a united front to the right so as to stave off their efforts to muzzle those associated with cultural studies. I am afraid this will suppress the generative contentiousness of cultural studies and that it will result, secondarily, in a willingness to give up on a fruitful line of thinking before fully exploring its limitations or its potential. Caught up in their own fight against powerful forces that would deliberately suppress their opportunity to speak, students of cultural studies may forego subtlety in the way they conceive and model power relations and, thereby, choose to ignore work that has suggested that determination, or more properly, hegemony, is never complete.

Although I agree that some work on the resistance involved in media use is incautious and too optimistic, I also believe that the lessons taught by this strain of work must not be dismissed out of hand. To do so is to return too easily to a vision of the modern individual as completely co-opted by consumer and media culture and, therefore, incapable of opposition to the powers of repression. This results in a static, airless vision of the cultural formation as well as a theoretical cynicism and pessimism that is in no way politically empowering.

GRAFF: Perhaps it's not what you have in mind, Janice, in worrying about cultural studies advocates suppressing "their own internal dissent in order to present a united front to the right," but I am not altogether convinced that it's a good thing for "cultural studies" to become a code word for various kinds of leftist or oppositional studies—which is what troubles me most about the Freire-Giroux model.

DAVIS: Yes, but Jerry don't you think cultural studies must also be willing to undertake a serious critique of the relations of power in culture, especially its own cultural relations? Its origins in England and in the various cultural projects Gita spoke of suggest precisely that kind of critique of existing institutions, even an oppositional critique of its own opposed social functions.

GRAFF: Yes, this kind of critique should certainly be a *part* of cultural studies, but not to the exclusion of other different perspectives, including liberal and conservative ones. In my view, cultural studies should mean a democratic debate about "culture," one that includes all major voices, not just the rainbow coalition of oppositional critics. I'm opposed to cultural studies being defined in a way that says, in effect, "No Arnoldians need apply." Gita rightly points out that the social critique embedded in current cultural studies has always been part of the liberal humanist tradition—and, I would add, the conservative humanist tradition as well.

Why then should liberal and conservative conceptions of culture be excluded from cultural studies, especially if cultural studies claims to be democratic?

DAVIS: I'm not sure I see the conflict. The interests of democracy should not obscure the point that no cultural studies practice is ever taken up from "the view from nowhere." "Democracy" doesn't mean running after some impossible neutrality. In academic terms, I think "democracy" just means that you never think you've reached the end of the debate—you keep talking. I don't see that there's any damage done to democracy if we try to recognize the real concerns and the social contexts of academic inquiry. That recognition inevitably entails seeing and being responsible for the dimension of power inherent to any inquiry we take up.

GRAFF: Sure, but who is the "we" in that sentence? I'm not talking about some kind of pseudo-neutrality. I'm just saying that I don't see cultural studies as inherently "oppositional." Conceiving cultural studies as an expression of nothing but oppositional discourses seems to be not only undemocratic but also seriously mistaken from a political and tactical point of view. It perpetuates progressive academics' bad habit (although one that is hardly peculiar to us) of speaking only or mainly to our own kind. In pedagogy, this often means that we either preach to the already converted among the student body or else we intimidate resistant students into sullen silence.

DAVIS: You're talking about so-called political correctness?

GRAFF: Well, yes. The critics of "political correctness" have greatly exaggerated the extent of this intimidation, but they have not made it up (indeed, they stole the phrase from us). Students and parents have every right to ask what justifies some teachers and scholars in mobilizing the university as an instrument of a particular vision of social transformation. It's no excuse to point out, rightly enough, that conservative assumptions have always had intimidating force—two wrongs don't make a right. My sense, by the way, from recent conferences I've attended, is that teachers on the left are increasingly reassessing these questions in the wake of resistance from their students.

It's true that in one sense, as R.C. says, there is no orthodoxy in so diverse a movement as cultural studies. But there *is* a certain orthodoxy when cultural studies is looked at from the point of view of people who don't take for granted—and who may not even find intelligible—the idea that cultural meanings are "culturally constructed" rather than natural or universal, that knowledge is implicated in forms of power and domination, that texts are sites of struggle in which subject positions are negotiated, and so forth.

In other words, the often fierce internal conflicts inside the rainbow coalition exist within a framework of shared assumptions that are felt to be so obvious and uncontroversial that they go without saying. It's just these shared assumptions that strike conservatives, liberals, and other outsiders as offensive, foolish, or bizarre. The fact that there may be quite serious differences, after all, between the views of, say, Lynne Cheney, William Bennett, and Pat Buchanan doesn't prevent us from talking about a relative consensus on the right. So it's not surprising that people are not impressed when we assure them that feminists, deconstructionists, Marxists, postcolonialists, and ethnic and gay studies people don't always get along.

DAVIS: Then you're not talking about the nature of cultural inquiry—whether it's ideologically based or not—so much as suggesting an appropriate strategy for dealing with the players actually on the current scene?

GRAFF: Precisely, though political strategy need not be at odds with cultural inquiry and pedagogy. It seems to me that the culture war has made it urgent for the left to develop a strategy to win over those at present in the middle—those who may at the moment be persuaded by conservative critiques of education but who are not necessarily conservatives. If this is the case, there is a problem with any conception of cultural studies that in its very founding excludes people who don't already agree with the premise that culture is unavoidably political and ideological.

DAVIS: So, for a change, intellectuals and teachers might actually try to be effective in the culture instead of choosing to be privately "right" among themselves?

GRAFF: Yes. Furthermore, the ghettoization that results when cultural studies is defined in an exclusionary way also makes for bad pedagogy. It's bad pedagogy when students always experience traditional and oppositional teachers in separate rooms, with no opportunity to see their differences transacted in the open. I've lately begun to feel that assigning attacks on the academic left by Lynne Cheney and Robert Kimball has a more "radical" effect on my students than assigning Terry Eagleton or bell hooks. Since my students' assumptions about literature and reading are usually much closer to Cheney's and Kimball's than they are to Eagleton's and hooks's, having these assumptions objectified in the reading material helps disarm any suspicion that I'm trying to brainwash them. It also makes it possible for them to see what is at stake in the challenge to their assumptions posed by Eagleton and hooks, who are likely to be simply incomprehensible otherwise. If we assume that oppositional viewpoints are defined dialogically by their relation to what they oppose, then oppositional critics *need* their opponents in order to become intelligible to students.

Then, too, as Janice's comment implies, when cultural studies teaching is not in dialogue with traditionalist teaching, positions more readily become hardened and reified. The lack of dialogue encourages an essentialist identity politics, in which it becomes difficult to discover the many points at which the "right" and the "left" converge or inhabit each other's positions.

In short, we need an alternative to the idea that the way to bring about social change through education is to directly radicalize our students—something which too often means "empowering" them whether they want to be empowered or not. I think the political goal of cultural studies should be not to radicalize students but to make the politics of culture a central and regular object of discussion across the whole university—as it has not been since the sixties—and let students make their own informed choices. A university in which serious political debate was continuously and publicly at the center of academic life would be a very radical departure from what we have—more radical, even, perhaps, than replacing Matthew Arnold with Paulo Freire.

DAVIS: I'd like to go back and follow up on Jan's comment for a second. Jan, you seem quite optimistic about the institutional inroads and current good effect of the cultural studies project. You see good things in store for cultural studies.

RADWAY: Yes, a cautious yes. Despite the attacks on cultural studies, scholars and teachers who associate themselves with cultural studies have already exerted significant pressure within the humanities, and perhaps to a lesser extent in the social sciences, on traditional curricula and modes of constructing research. Given the fact that many of these individuals have been able to attain tenure, I think they may continue to function as a troubling presence in an institution that still organizes its business around the concepts of objectivity, universal truth, and bias-free research. I guess Jerry's strategy for being persuasive could come in here as a smart way of approaching the culture war. In any case, cultural studies could well continue to disturb the peace, that is, to the extent that its practitioners insist on the connection between knowledge and power, demonstrating that all forms of knowledge production are not only situated and, therefore, interested, but also contingent and, thus, limited as well.

DAVIS: Could you be a little more specific about the site of cultural disturbance?

RADWAY: Sure. The struggle will be over the extent to which the connection between knowledge and power is allowed to challenge the institutional practices of the academy, as well as over the nature of the speech students of cultural studies can engage in within the classroom. Much is at stake for the right in their current project to brand those who do cultural studies as "ideological" and "biased." They must do so if they are to preserve the illusion that their own work is wholly objective, universally "true," and beyond question. To acknowledge the possibility that culture and knowledge production are situated would be to admit that they, too, are engaged in advocacy, a move that would expose the interested, even the coercive, nature of their project.

Their aim is to stifle dissent under the happy banner of national consensus and a common democratic culture. The right must not only prevent cultural studies from formally introducing subordinate and marginalized knowledges into the required, officially legitimated curriculum (hence the concern with introductory courses, with core or survey courses, and with general education requirements for undergraduates), but it must also label any speech associated with cultural studies that takes place within the traditionally protected preserve of the individual classroom not only biased but also fascist, un-American, and subversive. The hope, of course, is that even those protected by tenure will be silenced by the patriotic clamor of aroused students, parents, and trustees.

RAJAN: Because the right will resist cultural studies in precisely the way Jan is describing, there must be effective organization among everyone on the cultural left. One reason that I am optimistic about this struggle is that cultural studies is not an invention of the 1990s. However much the opponents might like to argue that cultural studies was invented by angry feminists or disgruntled ethnics on the campuses of Michigan, or Brown, or Duke (see Dinesh D'Souza for such claims), there is no gain saying the fact that history shows that cultural studies has always been part—a too-often unacknowledged part—of the humanist tradition. This is the substratum on which we can build—a shared tradition of liberal humanism. For example, there was a Gorgias before Plato, a Sappho or a Douglass before Bloom or Bennett. Even Matthew Arnold, who is held up like a beacon by the opponents of cultural studies, formulated a cultural critique within his own intellectual milieu.

DAVIS: As I said, too, it is important to see cultural studies as an important part of a tradition of cultural critique. The enemies of cultural studies always miss, or want to miss, that point. Nevertheless, you will grant that the movement under the explicit name of "cultural studies" evinces some differences from what came before it?

RAJAN: Yes. Contemporary cultural studies is a particularly energetic field, and people like Stuart Hall pioneered this field in Britain, making it inclusive, bringing together disciplines like literature, media and communication study, sociology, philosophy, politics, and history through cultural markers like race, gender, and class. The Open University that Hall has been associated with is a great model. People from various disciplines not only taught together simultaneously but also published collaboratively. In my position as observer (a foreigner still not very high on the professional ladder), I see that cultural studies has given English academics a chance to regroup, garner state and private funds to finance their research endeavors, and, most importantly (and this is not said often enough), attract nontraditional students back to the classroom.

DAVIS: You three are upbeat and hopeful about the institutional future of cultural studies—or culture studies—in English studies in particular and the United States in general. Other people tell me about their concern over a movement with such a strong theoretical base. Who but a few can understand cultural studies well enough to do good work in it? Don't such theory-driven approaches lead away from the texts that actual students can read? How can theorists in the academy focus on the material conditions of third world poverty? You all know the objections I'm talking about. Am I simply asking questions here that elicit optimistic answers, or are you really hopeful that cultural studies will have a significant impact on the academy and the culture, say, over the next ten years?

RAJAN: I think it's your questions. [She laughs.] I want to be optimistic and say that cultural studies will affect English studies and prosper in the United States primarily because it is such an exciting area of research. But I have to wonder how much the economic climate as a whole and financial insolvency, particularly in the liberal arts, will destroy its potential. Since cultural studies is such a new field, at least under the present rubric, and deals with issues not explicitly connected to specific disciplines (for example, third world film as text), and has such wide-ranging implications beyond the classroom, we will need very strong proponents and very persuasive administrators to support cultural studies. It will be very tempting for departments to lay aside this field which seems to have no direct bearing on established degree programs and no interest in covering canonical material that defines today's accepted education. The weaker schools will lose out in this battle, and the stronger ones will emerge, slightly compromised but basically intact in proposing a whole, new, revitalized curriculum.

We must have the courage to envision a twenty-first-century model of education. The whole concept of the twenty-first century sounds like a jingle, but we must not trivialize or pass up this opportunity to build for the future. To speak of the "United States" academy is shortsighted even now. It is documented that the configuration of this nation's classrooms is shifting rapidly and will continue to do so. We must envision a global classroom, explore the conditions of possibility for a *post-something* perspective, an examination of this *something,* without *misnaming, misclassifying,* or *misappropriating* its substance. I speak here as a postcolonial scholar, and many of us can attest to how clearly phenomena in the West are repeatedly *othered.* This is what we must avoid over the next decade or so. What about you, R.C., are you optimistic about cultural studies?

DAVIS: Me? Yes, in a certain sense. Some very good things have come already from changes made under the heading of "cultural studies." Over the last several years, I've visited many colleges and universities in the United States, and I've already seen significant curricular changes as a result of the interest in cultural studies. In many of these schools it does not seem to matter that faculty are following one line of thought or another. Many people making changes might even be hard-pressed to say exactly what is meant by "cultural studies." Perhaps it's common to intellectuals in the United States to bypass theory in this way and go for what will work. Often "cultural studies" gets translated simply as a call for more interdisciplinarity, more non-Western concerns, and more gender study. That trio of changes may not be "cultural studies" according to Stuart Hall or any of us, but they constitute major changes in higher education in the United States. If cultural studies never, ever means more than these changes in many schools, it will certainly have been a useful project. I'll be happy to say that I had a hand in it.

On the other hand, I'm skeptical that we should even want to be talking about "cultural" or "culture" studies in ten or twenty years. By that time, we should have been led to practices, probably quite different from what we're doing now, that will respond to social and educational conditions that we can't even guess about at present. "Cultural studies," or "culture studies," is not a jewel that we should be trying to enshrine for the ages. It's merely a strategy that makes sense now. In its lifetime, I fully expect that it will give shape to the achieving of certain valuable ends.

But beyond that kind of significant but passing effect, we shouldn't try to make too much of the movement. We certainly don't want to make the future promise to imitate what we're doing in our educational practices of the 1990s.

RADWAY: I, too, must separate my sense of cultural studies' current good effect and what its fortunes will be over the next ten years. I think the next several years will be characterized by efforts from many quarters to police cultural studies and to discipline it, albeit along contradictory lines. The right will attempt to quarantine it by marginalizing it as disruptive, as foreign, as an attack on democratic ideals. Some within cultural studies itself will attempt to define it rigorously, to purify it, to weed out all those who are practicing it without the proper political credentials in an effort to strengthen it for the battle with the right. While I see the need to affirm political commitments and resolve, I fear that such a move will suppress internal dissent and lead to the ossification of disciplinary orthodoxy. This would be detrimental to the fluid, unstable, and wholly generative character of cultural studies as it has developed so heterogeneously and divergently in the past. People associated with cultural studies should resist the tendency to issue intellectual passports, to identify "authentic" cultural studies work as opposed to work that merely "passes."

DAVIS: Are you speaking about Cary Nelson's comments [included in this collection] on the cultural-studies conference at Oklahoma versus the earlier one at Illinois?

RADWAY: That's only one reference. What is needed in cultural studies generally is a multiplicitous, polyphonic, disputatious discussion of the complex ways in which cultural representation is mobilized in the interests of power. On this stage of events, it simply won't do to assume that once one or two ruses of representation are exposed, the whole edifice of repression will come tumbling down. Power is more extensive, ingenious, and dispersed than that.

DAVIS: Jan, do you see any institutionalized form of cultural studies, at your own institution or elsewhere, that could be effective in the critique of the "whole edifice of repression"?

RADWAY: I've really been trying to argue in the other direction. I am very suspicious of efforts to institutionalize cultural studies within the current structure of the academy. I don't see how it can be done without either gutting cultural studies of its disruptive potential or entirely changing the disciplinary divisions and legitimating ideologies presently underwriting most academic research. Much more preliminary work needs to be done before a vision of knowledge production as an interested and contingent form of cultural practice can be embodied in curricular reforms and institutional reorganization. I would rather see practitioners of cultural studies forge political alliances across disciplinary boundaries and even over the walls surrounding our academic quadrangles. We need sustained and collectively produced accounts of the way material, social, and cultural practices interact to produce familiar forms of political domination. We need to know, for instance, what the connections might be among changing patterns of the organization of work; changing constructions of masculinity, femininity, and the notion of the family; the racist, homophobic, and xenophobic reaction to the AIDS crisis; the popularity of Madonna; and the Jesse Helms-led campaign to control and police artistic funding and production. We need to ask how all of these interact to produce certain kinds of political subjects with both limitations and hidden potentials. Cultural constellations and questions like this one are so complicated that their complexity is, in fact, out-distancing any single researcher's capacity to understand them. I would like to see a good deal more collaborative work that takes on these very large problems and, as practice itself, challenges the hegemony of the autonomous liberal subject.

DAVIS: All of this will have to happen within the educational and research institution as we know it.

RADWAY: Perhaps, but intervention needs to be carried out elsewhere as well—in practices of cultural representation in the media, for example. I would also like to see more work on the question of disciplinarity itself in the academy, on its supporting ideologies, on its consequence and effects. In addition, I hope greater efforts to pursue interdisciplinary connections and alliances will develop. I would like to see this occur in the formulation of research agendas, in imaginative pedagogical practice within single classrooms (such as team-teaching), and in the creation of seminars both for faculty and graduate students. Although I am under no illusion that interdisciplinarity is a panacea, I do believe that it can serve as a starting point from which to question business as usual in the knowledge-production business.

DAVIS: Gita, you and I have talked a lot about cultural studies and cultural and social responsibility. You object to programs semiotic in orientation that pursue largely popular-culture topics in the United States and call that "cultural studies." We all admit that this is a problem, a potential weakness of cultural studies as it is sometimes practiced here. What should our colleagues be doing right now, either nationally or locally?

RAJAN: Well, I first need to talk about your question, R.C. [All laugh.] I don't like it, and I'll give you a Janus-faced reply. Are you not already hierarchizing cultural studies with this question—the West and then other nationalities? As numerous other postcolonial scholars have pointed out, every inquiry in the United States, however genuine, sounds as though the West *is* the subject. Cultural theorists are now remarking on the disproportionate influence that the West exerts in the global forum. Is that not what cultural studies is trying to overcome? Does not cultural studies force its students to challenge the semiosis of power behind established categories, even ones like nationalities? The critique of culture, especially with the kind of theoretical language that we all use, makes us aware of our political locations—as in the discourse communities and class-situations we inhabit, antiracist/imperialist viewpoints, perspectives on gender differences, etc.

There is no purity of origin. Would you be able to ask your question of a fellow U.S. citizen? The injunction to speak from my place and for my homeland arises from an ideology of self/other, originary/supplementary, first/next. But that ideology, that kind of cultural reductionism, has been exposed. The very method of information processing nowadays allows us to function synchronically. All of us "do" mostly the same kind of work with a similar vocabulary, perhaps with different emphases.

DAVIS: I thought Janus had *two* faces. My question is getting hung out to dry on the first face only! [All laugh.]

RAJAN: Just wait. Now to the other face of Janus! I'll answer the question within the boundary of nationhood, which means I'll have to bring postcoloniality into cultural studies. The complexity of postcolonial studies today depends upon examining the historiography of each land. This isn't an essentialist position, but rather a culture-specific requirement, one that demands the examination of legal, political, socioeconomic issues, nationalist reform movements, all of which affect the texture of each country's culture in very different ways. For example, the cultural practice of *sati,* or "bride burning," in India has caught the interest of Western theorists, but abstract formulations about women's silence or oppression will not prove useful. That will become a different kind of colonization, a neocolonization. What is needed is a sustained inquiry into the whole network of related cultural issues that are particular to India by theorists/critics capable of grasping the issue in its entirety.

This is the kind of cultural inquiry that Indian scholars in India are engaged in. They are more *activist,* more sociopolitical in their "take" on cultural studies. Jan's point about the implicitly and explicitly political nature of cultural studies governs the work of Indian scholars working from India, scholars who are self-consciously using discourse to intervene into "knowledge" about cultural issues. This is very refreshing. One important difference in their work is their refusal to use abstract theoretical language which does not engage the issue at hand. This is what I meant earlier about the apolitical nature of theoretical language in the United States in general. But, otherwise, we are working in and around the same area.

Finally. . . .

DAVIS: *Two* faces, I thought you were talking about the *two* faces of Janus.

RAJAN: Finally, the enunciation of cultural difference, going beyond a certain essentialist boundary, can be productive only in collaboration. Cultural studies must incorporate difference structurally, allow space for various cultures and varying perspectives to be legitimized through dialogics, and not through strict hierarchy. We need to think of ourselves as Gramsci's organic intellectuals and keep our particular struggles alive.

DAVIS: Well, I think the dialogics of this discussion and the enunciation of difference here must be collaboration in the best sense. [All laugh.] I'm particularly struck that the areas of difference among us mirror the differences evident in the national debate about culture studies, cultural studies, and multiculturalism. The advantage in our exchange is that we're taking the time to look at our own internal dissent and see some of the implications, instead of losing track of one another's claims and getting confused about what is at stake in our counterclaims. These differences don't seem to be failings of cultural studies as a project so much as signs of vitality in an ongoing and productive debate.

☐ Cultural Studies versus the New Historicism

Patrick Brantlinger

The "versus" in the title of this essay may suggest that cultural studies and the New Historicism are the main rivals whose conflict will answer the question, After poststructuralism, what next? But there are at least two problems with this agonistic fantasy. First, cultural studies and the New Historicism have much in common: They share many of the same assumptions and methods, and at least some of the same practitioners. Second, the idea that either or both movements may be the successors of poststructuralism is problematic, if only because both have been heavily influenced by poststructuralism, especially by Michel Foucault. Yet in his 1986 essay "What Is Cultural Studies Anyway?" Richard Johnson suggested that it might be a "post-poststructuralist" movement. It remains to ask, though, whether this new post-something delivers the mail in such a completely new way as to displace, dismantle, deconstruct, or even just somewhat disrupt the previous delivery system.[1]

The "New" Historicism clearly promises novelty, although not necessarily in relation to poststructuralism—perhaps only in relation to an old historicism which, in most of its variants, looks like Hegelian idealism, Whig liberalism, or Marxist materialism. Cultural studies, too, does not always seem especially new or novel. It often blends Marxist ideological critique, of either an Althusserian or a Gramscian sort, with an ethnography of everyday life under capitalism, or else with culture-and-society analysis modeled upon the work of Raymond Williams. And it sometimes appears to be completely innocent of poststructuralism. Thus the new mail promised by both cultural studies and the New Historicism may be destined never quite to arrive, at least in terms of answering the question, What will succeed poststructuralism?

Rather than being advances beyond poststructuralism, the New Historicism and cultural studies are either adaptations of it or escapes from its more radical implications. A few of my English department and MLA colleagues have welcomed New Historicism as a retreat from what they see as the ravages of literary-critical deconstruction. They find comfort and reassurance in the very word *historicism,* involving as it does the claim that we can know the past even if we cannot actually retreat to it.[2] For these same colleagues, though, cultural studies still appears to be less a solution than part of the problem. This is so partly because its practitioners tend to stress *contemporary* culture instead of the past—often using that panic-inducing term *postmodernism*—and tend also to deal in mass or popular culture. Their work is often accompanied by the claim or perhaps disclaimer that, in our postmodern condition, there is nothing but mass culture (see, for instance, Denning and Baudrillard). New Historicists such as Stephen Greenblatt and Louis Montrose have continued to focus upon (mostly) canonical works of literature (Shakespeare, for example), while culturalists such as Stuart Hall and Dick Hebdige have tended instead to focus on questions of ideology and social class in relation partly to the contemporary mass media (rock music and youth "subcultures," for example).

Although not alternatives to poststructuralism, cultural studies and the New Historicism are its necessary corollaries—two branch post offices established because the Grand Central PO had too much mail to deliver. Poststructuralism had to deliver, especially on the very truth-claims it appeared to deny, and so cultural studies and the New Historicism have arisen in part to recall, with qualifications, the forms of truth-claiming representation necessary for any communication whatsoever to take place. Although no longer understood as substitutes for "the real" in any absolute sense, "culture" and "history" are the messy, totalizing words that reopen the questions of reference and reality by refusing to reduce them to language and textuality. If this is correct, both movements are in some sense retreats from the ultimate poststructuralist abyss—from, as Michael Holquist puts it, "the perpetual elusiveness of meaning as it fades away in the phantom relay of the signifying chain" (165). They are also in different ways responses to the crisis of Marxism or historical materialism, a crisis that, on the theoretical level, has itself been partly caused by poststructuralism and by the postmodern attack on "metanarratives" (see, for example, Aronowitz, Lyotard, and Habermas [*Philosophical Discourse*]). Or we could say that both cultural studies and the New Historicism are attempts to fuse elements of poststructuralism (especially Foucault) with something like "the best that has been thought and spoken" in Western Marxism (see Anderson, Ryan, and Norris).

In terms of their institutionalization—their accommodation to established disciplines and the powers-that-be of higher education—the two movements cannot be reconciled so easily. The New Historicism has grown up inside (mostly) North American English departments as, according to Simpson, "the most fashionable literary-critical movement since feminism" (*Subject* 12). Cultural studies began in Britain—first at the Centre for Contemporary Cultural Studies at the University of Birmingham and later at the Open University—as an alternative, radical form of higher education. The New Historicism is not really much of a force beyond English and other language/literature departments. (Historians lodged in history departments, for instance, have not paid much attention to it.) Cultural studies has from the outset attracted malcontents from various academic disciplines (English, history, sociology, and education, for example), in part because it has offered a concerted critique of the present constitution of the academic disciplines.

Cultural studies focuses on the question of how to use aspects of recent Marxist cultural theory to analyze and, hopefully, influence contemporary cultural, political, and economic formations, especially those centered around gender, class, and race. The New Historicism, in at least partial contrast, seems to circle around the question of how to do advanced literary criticism and/or cultural history by using some of the insights generated by poststructuralism and recent Marxist cultural theory.

But, granting that the New Historicism is more literary, more willingly or complicitly "academic," and less overtly radical than cultural studies, how much of a contrast is there between the basic assumptions of the two movements? Are cultural studies and the New Historicism competing theories and methodologies, or are they one thing with two names? Moreover, in relation to poststructuralism, just what do they deliver?

The New Historicism: Marxism or Cultural Poetics?

Some New Historicists claim allegiance to cultural studies; it is less clear that most practitioners of cultural studies would or could call themselves New Historicists. For one thing, culturalists are not always either literary critics or historians; they are just as apt to be sociologists or mass media and film theorists. But Alan Sinfield and Jonathan Dollimore—the editors of one of the key texts in the emergence of the New Historicism, *Political Shakespeare: New Essays on Cultural Materialism*—claim a dual allegiance. Their volume contains perhaps the most frequently cited example of New Historicist work, Stephen Greenblatt's "Invisible Bullets" essay; their volume also contains an afterword by one of the founding fathers of British cultural studies, Raymond Williams. Similarly, when in *Learning to Curse* Greenblatt asks how he became a New Historicist, he points to the year he spent at Cambridge as a graduate student and the impact Williams's teaching made upon him. In place of Yale New Criticism, Williams offered a thoughtful version of Marxist literary and cultural analysis: "In Williams' lectures all that had been carefully excluded from the literary criticism in which I had been trained [at Yale]—who controlled access to the printing press, who owned the land and the factories, whose voices were being repressed as well as represented in literary texts, what social strategies were being served by the aesthetic values we constructed—came pressing back in upon the act of interpretation" (2).

Greenblatt's autobiographical sketch complicates the brief, critical comparison of the two movements offered by Robert Young in *White Mythologies*. Writing about "the tactical use of Foucault . . . in current forms of criticism," Young spies a difference between the New Historicism and "cultural materialism" (or cultural studies): "The former is identified closely with Foucault, while the latter owes its allegiance to Raymond Williams, and really only amounts to a way of describing British ex-Marxists" (88). For Young, one obvious similarity between New Historicism and cultural studies is that both forms of critical/theoretical practice want also to be forms of radical political practice—to change the world, not just to interpret it. From his poststructuralist perspective, Young maintains an ironic distance from both movements. His assertion that "the British cultural materialists quickly adopted a name which tactfully removes the suggestion of Marxism as such" (89) is matched, if not exactly balanced, by his claim that the cultural materialists are, after all, more common-sensical, more Foucauldian, and more effective about politics than "the more fastidious" and "more strictly academic new historicists, whose own politics remain more carefully hidden" (90). (Antony Easthope offers a related comparison, 119–123.)

Because one of Young's main targets is the old-style, orthodox Marxist metanarrative of history, he is inconsistent in criticizing perhaps former or perhaps post-Marxists for distancing themselves from that very metanarrative. Is post-Marxism less honorable in its postal politics than poststructuralism? Is it a sign of weak-kneed apostasy to arrive at Young's recognition that "Marxism's universalizing narrative of the unfolding of a rational system of world history is simply a negative form of the history of European imperialism" (2)? Indeed, if the New Historicism *is* new, it is so largely through its claim to offer a version of "historicism" while rejecting the teleological, imperializing assumptions of nineteenth-century forms of historicism, including Marxism. "Historicism" in general can be defined as any attempt to theorize history—to find the pattern, hidden unity, direction, or goal in the totality of human time and experience. But the New Historicism registers skepticism, at least, that there is any pattern or direction to find, and/or that the necessarily linguistic tools of the historian can adequately represent that totality.

Much of Greenblatt's work is antihistoricist, at least in the sense that it is anti-imperialist. Like "Invisible Bullets," most of the essays in *Learning to Curse* and *Marvelous Possessions* open onto the terrain of cultural conflict and genocide that constitutes early American history. If Greenblatt's work is taken as paradigmatic of the New Historicism, that movement is partly an attack on the logocentric, ethnocentric tales called national histories that European victors have told themselves throughout centuries of imperial domination of the rest of the world.[3] But on what grounds is the New Historicist attack made? Because the Marxist metanarrative of the past is just as Eurocentric as other versions of historicism, what allows for the narration of *different,* non-Eurocentric versions of the past? Greenblatt's replies to this question have led him from the qualified sort of literary-critical Marxism he learned from Williams, through what he used to call the New Historicism, to what he now calls "cultural poetics" (*Learning* 146–60).

One virtue of substituting "cultural poetics" for Marxism or for "historical materialism" may lie in its acknowledgment that, as Jacques Derrida says, "There is nothing outside the text." But this virtue is just as readily understood as a problem. After poststructuralism, the only "materialism" possible seems to be one that is discursive or cultural. "Cultural poetics" is a tautological phrase—"culture" equals "poetics"—that expresses the poststructuralist view that language can refer only to other language. It also represents a foreshortening of the old Marxist base/superstructure paradigm: The "material" or economic base has withered away; now there is only superstructure, culture, "poetics." What sorts of explanations can cultural poetics produce except poetic ones? Rejecting the New Historicism in favor of "Marxist or dialectical materialism," Simpson writes that only such materialism "consistently offers . . . ways to explain how both representations and reality are necessary to an account of the production and reproduction of cultural life, without either flattening out the analytical model into a tautological indifference (representation is all there is) or simplifying the relation between cause and effect to the point that it is easily ridiculed by anyone armed with a few apt deconstructive nostrums" (*Subject* 7–8).

Lacking the explanatory power that referring cultural phenomena to the material or economic base seems to afford, cultural poetics appears to grant its practitioners complete license to reconstruct any story about the past that they choose. Arbitrariness has been a charge leveled against the New Historicism from the beginning. Greenblatt is the first to concede that "in American universities critical affiliations like new historicism or deconstruction or now even Marxism are not linked to systematic thought" (*Learning* 3). He continues, "It is possible in the United States to describe oneself . . . as a Marxist literary critic without believing in the class struggle as the principal motor force in history; without believing in the theory of surplus value; without believing in the determining power of economic base over ideological superstructure; without believing in the inevitability . . . of capitalism's collapse" (3). Greenblatt is referring to his own "critical affiliation" in this passage. He implies that his New Historicism is a version of Marxist literary criticism minus belief in any of the ideas that could still make it recognizably Marxist.

Greenblatt's apparent willingness to call himself a sort of a Marxist while rejecting most of the beliefs that would qualify him as a Marxist helps to explain Catherine Gallagher's remark that "new historicism confronts Marxism now partly as an amplified record of Marxism's own edgiest, uneasiest voices" ("Marxism" 47). As Gallagher also observes, "The new historicist, unlike the Marxist, is under no nominal compulsion to achieve consistency" (46). But if that is the case, the New Historicism must either come to look very much like the old historicism, in the sense of liberal historiography and literary history, or it must, through adopting Foucault's genealogical procedures and philosophical nominalism, reject historicism altogether. The New Historicism evades this theoretical problem in part by stressing the contingent in history and, therefore, the impossibility of systematizing it.

Cut loose from its moorings in some sense of systematic representation and historical causality, the ship of the New Historicism drifts anywhere and everywhere, from anecdote to anecdote (*Learning* 5). But the move from metanarratives to anecdotes solves nothing because most of the same epistemological claims are at stake in both micro and macro forms of narration. Are they rooted in documentable evidence? What do they explain? What do they represent? What explains them? Why does the New Historicist choose to retell them? And so forth. Arguments around representation are too familiar to rehearse here (but see Thomas, *The New Historicism* 3–23). In relation to causality, however, Frank Lentricchia notes that for there to be "historicism" at all there must be some "principle of causality." He quotes Williams: "'A Marxism without some concept of determination is in effect worthless. A Marxism with many of the concepts of determination it now has is quite radically disabled.'" Lentricchia then writes, "Substitute historicism for Marxism and perhaps Stephen Greenblatt for Raymond Williams, and you have a description of the theoretical quandary within which some recent historically minded critics, with strong and problematical relations to Michel Foucault, and who tend to specialize in the English Renaissance, now find themselves" ("Foucault's Legacy" 232).

Greenblatt's efforts to solve this "theoretical quandary" are fascinating albeit ultimately unsatisfactory. The final two essays in *Learning to Curse* are as close to programmatic statements as any New Historicist has yet written, but the first—"Towards a Poetics of Culture"—involves the rejection of *both* Marxist *and* poststructuralist theory as "eschatological," "utopian," (149), or teleological in the bad old historicist sense. Greenblatt discovers the old Marxist metanarrative in Frederic Jameson's *The Political Unconscious* and dismisses it as having "the resonance of an allegory of the fall of man" (148).[4] Lumping both Jameson's Marxism and Lyotard's poststructuralism under the unifying term *theory,* Greenblatt accuses both of an "effacement of contradiction [which] is not the consequence of an accidental lapse but rather the logical outcome of theory's search for the obstacle that blocks the realization of its eschatological vision" (151).

But how is the "cultural poetics" Greenblatt would substitute for an "eschatological" Marxism and an equally eschatological poststructuralism an improvement? By implication, at least, cultural poetics would recognize the complexity or contradictoriness of capitalism as a world-historical process. Capitalism must be viewed, writes Greenblatt, "not as a unitary demonic principle, but as a complex historical movement in a world without paradisal origins or chiliastic expectations" (151). In particular, in understanding the relationship between art and society, *complexity* must be an operative word, and in Greenblatt's essays the nature of that complexity is conveyed especially by quasi-economic terms such as *negotiation* and *circulation:* "The work of art is the product of a negotiation between a creator or class of creators . . . and the institutions and practices of society. In order to achieve the negotiation, artists need to create a currency that is valid for a meaningful, mutually profitable exchange" (*Learning* 158). Greenblatt adds that "the society's dominant currencies, money and prestige, are invariably involved," and also that the "terms 'currency' and 'negotiation' are the signs of our manipulation and adjustment of the relative systems" (158). They are also the signs of, at best, a very weak "principle of causality" or "determination."

Greenblatt does not privilege the economic as final cause or outer limit, as in all variants of the Marxist base-superstructure paradigm, but rather treats it merely as the source of metaphors by which "exchanges" take place between a society's institutions and its artistic creators. These exchanges can be described on a case-by-case or, perhaps, anecdotal basis, rather like the ethnographic "thick description" that is a main methodology of cultural studies, and they can also be ascribed to the vast and vague set of economic developments and processes Greenblatt is still willing to call "capitalism" from the Renaissance forward. However, they cannot be understood more systematically, theoretically, or teleologically as *leading somewhere*—as the inexorable, world-unifying, or world-massifying march of economic and cultural modernization (and now postmodernism).

A similar rejection of theory occurs in a different way in the last essay in *Learning to Curse,* "Resonance and Wonder." Here Greenblatt cites one of the definitions of "historicism" given by the *American Heritage Dictionary:* "The belief that processes are at work in history that man can do little to alter." Greenblatt responds, "New historicism, by contrast, eschews the use of the term 'man'; interest lies not in the abstract universal but in particular, contingent cases, the selves fashioned and acting according to the generative rules and conflicts of a given culture. And these selves, conditioned by the expectations of their class, gender, religion, race and national identity, are constantly effecting changes in the course of history" (164).[5] That is to say, individuals may be "conditioned" by circumstances, but they have just as much to do with the making of the circumstances as vice versa. This tautological proposition leads Greenblatt next to assert "the new historicism's insistence on the pervasiveness of agency" (165). The idea here appears to be that everywhere one looks in history there are people—selves or individual agents—doing things that affect the course of history. This idea, in turn, seems to be a variant of Foucault's famous proposition that "power breeds resistance," which means that "power" (hence, "agency") is everywhere in society—it is just that some agents have more of it than others. According to Louis Althusser, for instance, an ideological state apparatus is an agency for self-fashioning over which the selves fashioned have little or no control. But Greenblatt's agents seem to be the selves or unit-individuals that make up the stock and trade of American individualism.

In a single loop, Greenblatt maintains contact with one of his power sources, Foucault, while also giving expression to what Brook Thomas calls the New Historicism's "unacknowledged link to American progressivism" ("The New Historicism" 197).[6] The New Historicism, according to Thomas, takes its place alongside other manifestations of neo-pragmatism in the United States and thereby "reaffirms the liberal tradition of American progressivism and its sense of temporality" (197). It thus also reaffirms that tradition's sense of individual agency—exactly the antithesis of Foucault's or Althusser's position with regard to the pervasiveness of *de*individualized power (for example, discipline as the tyranny of "the Norm"), at least in modern and now postmodern social formations. Rather than echoing Foucault's insistence upon the impending dissolution of the modern abstraction, "man," the New Historicism resuscitates that humanist category through "self-fashioning."

Cultural Studies and the Search for "Resistance"

Against the anti-individualistic tendencies of both Marxism and poststructuralism, Greenblatt covertly reinvents individual agency. In contrast, cultural studies maintains a more radical but nonetheless traditional emphasis on collective agency, which often takes the form of an appraisal of the potential for political resistance in various marginalized groups and cultural phenomena. Of course, the search for resistance is a much-diminished version of the traditional Marxist goal of revolution. As a derivative of British democratic socialism, cultural studies no doubt remains consonant with earlier forms of Marxism, but, as Young suggests, may for that very reason fit less comfortably than the New Historicism does with poststructuralism (90). In any event, the cultural studies movement, partly because of its British origin, has been much more directly political than has New Historicism. The key figures in the early history of the cultural studies movement—Richard Hoggart, E. P. Thompson, Raymond Williams, and Stuart Hall—have all been political activists, influential outside the academy as well as inside.

Nevertheless, Young is not the only critic who has suggested that cultural studies involves a sort of watered down Marxism. Following Dick Hebdige's *Subculture,* some practitioners of cultural studies have been prone to discover and celebrate moments of resistance or even subversion in mass cultural forms (for example, rock music and television) *without* Hebdige's ironic awareness that "power breeds resistance," which it is the very purpose of power to contain. Thus Judith Williamson complains about "left-wing academics [who] are busy picking out strands of 'subversion' in every piece of pop culture from Street Style to Soap Opera" ("Problems" 14; see also Morris).

The discovery of "critical and resistant elements" in the production and consumption of mass culture is analogous to Greenblatt's discovery of agency everywhere. Where before there appeared to be just domination, the ideological impositions of what Theodor Adorno and Max Horkheimer called the "culture industry," suddenly—in the work of John Fiske, Iain Chambers, and others—complex negotiations over meanings and values appear to be going on between producers and consumers, or between the managers of the culture industries and their mass audiences. In a Raymond Williams–like move, "the masses" of powerless, robotized "subjects" feared by Adorno and Horkheimer and anatomized by Althusser turn out to be everyday gals and guys, pretty much just like you and me. Hey, we don't own corporations, but we know what we like in the way of TV shows, movies, and music, and we make our own sense of these mass cultural forms when we consume them. *This is the meaning of those forms:* We, the people, confer meaning and value on the products of the culture industries.

In analyses of mass media effects and audiences undertaken by Fiske and Chambers, social class as a problematic does not disappear as it does in much empiricist and functionalist American media research. But it is nevertheless true that, as in much Western Marxist and now post-Marxist work, class is no longer the dominant or even clearly the main analytical category. Thus Fiske writes that his pluralization of the term *audiences* at least "recognizes that we are not a homogeneous society, but that our social system is crisscrossed by axes of class, gender, race, age, nationality, region, politics, religion, and so on" (*Television Culture* 17). Fiske recognizes the complexity of social processes under capitalist conditions much as Greenblatt does, although the risk of doing so lies in failing to explain that complexity and relying instead on something like (mere) "thick description." Similarly, Chambers notes that "connections between popular tastes and a white, urban, male working class can no longer be assumed. Popular culture . . . flows across the older lines of class. But then the idea that popular culture is simply a synonym for working-class leisure has always been a simplification" (*Popular Culture* 59–60). The very recognition of these complications—the plurality of audiences, the multiple differentiating factors that work against massification (or proletarianization), the apparent classlessness of popular culture—erodes the old Marxist forms of class analysis and leads Fiske and Chambers to a position similar to that of the New Historicism. Because of their affirmative, often appreciative, stance toward the products of the culture industries as well as toward the audiences those industries target, Fiske and Chambers arrive at something close to Greenblatt's pragmatic liberalism.

The work of Fiske and Chambers shows how cultural studies loops back toward a populist individualism that, whether in the British or the American setting, is related only tangentially to Marxism. Here, for example, is Fiske writing about Antonio Gramsci's model of hegemony:

> This definition of culture as a constant site of struggle between those with and those without power underpins the most interesting current work in cultural studies. Earlier work in the tradition tended to show how the dominant ideology reproduced itself invisibly and inevitably in the forms of popular television. [Stuart] Hall's influential essay, "Decoding and Encoding" is often seen as a turning point in British cultural studies, for it opened up the idea that television programs [and other forms of culture] do not have a single meaning, but are relatively open texts, capable of being read in different ways by different people. (260)

From this position, however, as Fiske well knows, the temptation of the culturalist is to forego the analysis of differential power—how the struggle proceeds—for the bland assertion that everyone takes away from popular culture the meanings she or he wants, so that in the mere recognition of difference all social divisions appear miraculously healed.

Continuing his account of Hall's "Encoding and Decoding," Fiske arrives at a word that once again connects cultural studies with the New Historicism: "Reading or viewing television, then, becomes a process of negotiation between the viewer and the text. Use of the word 'negotiation' is significant" (260). The danger here, however, is not so much the New Historicist one of letting metaphors like *negotiation, exchange,* and *circulation* do the work of hard economic and social class analysis; rather, it is the suggestion that the viewers of television shows, for example, have as active a role to play in the negotiation or social construction of meanings from those shows as their producers do. Where has the initial sense of *unequal* power relations in Fiske's statement gone? Consumers are never active in the same way as producers, nor can workers be active—or even negotiate on equal terms—with owners and capitalists. Fiske borrows some of his terminology from Michel de Certeau's *Practice of Everyday Life,* so he is aware that, for de Certeau, the "poacher" or consumer of meanings always operates from a position of weakness—she may have "tactics" of resistance at her disposal, but not the grand "strategies" that are the preserve of the media managers.

Insofar as cultural studies has tended to emphasize consumption over production—to pay attention to the ways audiences construct meanings rather than to the ways the culture industries do so—there has been an imbalance. Older or more traditional forms of economic and ownership analysis need to be recalled—for example, Herbert I. Schiller's *The Mind Managers* or Ben Bagdikian's *The Media Monopoly.* It is symptomatic of the current overemphasis in cultural studies on audience participation (again, compare "agency" in the New Historicism) that Fiske, in *Television Culture,* does not cite either Schiller or Bagdikian. Moreover, following the 1984 translation of Pierre Bourdieu's magisterial *Distinction: A Social Critique of the Judgment of Taste,* it is hard to see how there could be any dispute about the centrality of class to all questions about hierarchy, power, and esthetic judgment in all modern cultures and societies. Yet class, especially in discourse in the United States, is almost always the first item to get elided in discussions of patterns of mass consumption and mass culture. In many situations in the United States, it makes more sense to talk about the homeless than about the proletariat; Britain at least continues to have a Labour party.

Cultural History and Cultural Critique in Higher Education

In relation to literary-critical paradigms, both cultural studies and the New Historicism start from the poststructuralist deconstruction of the boundaries between literature and other forms of textuality and between high culture and "low," popular, or mass culture. This is not to say that these boundaries no longer exist. They are real enough, but they are recognized as social, ideological constructions. Easthope locates the emergence of cultural studies in the crisis and collapse of the modernist (read: New Critical) paradigm of literary study and of literature as a high cultural form of discourse, absolutely separable from low, popular, or mass cultural forms (3–21; see also Grossberg, Nelson, and Treichler, *Cultural Studies*).

The New Historicism can also be understood as emerging from the disintegration of the humanistic, Arnoldian paradigm of literary study. But the shift away from literature—based on the recognition that any definition of "literary" as opposed to "ordinary" language will be arbitrary and on the even more obvious recognition that literature is only one of the many sites of cultural self-fashioning—makes any institutionalization of either movement problematic within already established college and university literature departments. The various terms so far suggested to take its place pedagogically—*rhetoric, literacy, discourse analysis, cultural literacy,* and *cultural history*—are all bigger and vaguer than *literature,* thanks to decades of fine-honing and canonization that have focused that term on a select set of supposedly high-cultural texts and writers. Further, now that literature is no longer a privileged category—now that it seems to be merged with other, larger, messier categories such as *culture* and *history*—literary-critical studies in university settings must necessarily, as Catherine Belsey argues, move in the direction of a "cultural history" at least similar to the New Historicism, even though most varieties of current historiography are perhaps clearer, open to more precise definition: social, intellectual, or literary history. Belsey writes that the "cultural history I should like to see us produce would refuse nothing. While of course any specific investigation would find a specific focus, both chronologically and textually, no moment, no epoch, no genre and no form of signifying practice would be excluded a priori from the field of enquiry. Cultural history would have no place for a canon, and no interest in ranking works in order of merit" (160). There may be different sorts of merit, however, including merit as historical evidence rather than as literary or cultural value. But Belsey's rejection of literary criticism in favor of cultural history opens the way to another point, one again informed by poststructuralism: the relation between signifying systems (cultures or ideologies) and what Greenblatt calls "self-fashioning."

Both the New Historicism and cultural studies focus upon the social and cultural processes that produce us as individuals—the social construction of subjectivities. Self-fashioning, informed by Greenblatt's stress on agency, seems antithetical to the complete subjection of the subject to ideology in

Althusser. But the spectrum between Greenblatt's assertion of the pervasiveness of agency and Althusser's Marxist-structuralist determinism suggests the range that theories about the subject now span, whether those theories are identified with the New Historicism, with cultural studies, or with versions of poststructuralism and feminism.[7] In pedagogical terms, a cultural history focused upon the social construction of past forms of subjectivity can open a space for a more radical, provocative, and usefully disturbing exploration of the contemporary, postmodern forms of self-fashioning to which we and our students are subject, in part through schooling but in part also through the mass media.

Bringing the New Historicism and cultural studies together, no matter under what departmental or disciplinary rubric, could produce a curriculum with both a historical and a contemporary dimension. In such a curriculum, the question of how individuals—including teachers and students—are constituted socially would inform all aspects of teaching and learning, just as self-knowledge has supposedly always been the main goal of a liberal arts education. To take that goal seriously entails precisely the kinds of research and teaching that are now often labeled "New Historicism" and "cultural studies." Whatever chance institutionalized teachers have of helping themselves and students achieve greater self-understanding depends upon how well they understand the social processes that shape them and that have resulted in the postmodern condition (on which, see Harvey). Literature, as identified with high culture and higher education, may be merely tangential to those processes, at best a mere record or reflection of them, and yet may still be of great significance as one of the principal sites where those processes are explored. Popular or mass culture, on the other hand, in part because it is popular or mass, is in some sense an aspect of those processes or one of those processes.

Graeme Turner writes, "Popular culture is a site where the construction of everyday life may be examined. The point of doing this is not only academic—that is, as an attempt to understand a process or practice—it is also political, to examine the power relations that constitute this form of everyday life and thus to reveal the configuration of interests its construction serves" (5–6). If subjectivity is understood as a near-synonym for the individual's experience of the ordinary, the analysis of everyday life—as in the work of Bourdieu and de Certeau—is also identical to the analysis of the social construction of the subject. Further, popular or mass culture is more than just any old "site where the construction of everyday life may be examined." If, indeed, as Denning, Baudrillard, and others have contended, postmodernity is characterized by the complete triumph of mass over all other forms of culture, then the postmodern signifying systems within which our individual identities or subjectivities are forged are nothing more nor less than what Turner blandly calls "popular culture."

Just because high may be collapsing into mass culture, and just because the old Marxist base-superstructure paradigm may be defunct while forms of poststructuralism have arisen that treat all social phenomena as discourse, does not mean that social conflict has vanished. A starting point for both the New Historicism and cultural studies is recognition of the *differential* power relations in history and society, and also among individuals, some of whom have far more agency than others. Who dominates, who is dominated—the old Hegelian Master and Slave paradigm—this does not vanish as the central issue just because the "economic mode of production" or "class conflict" can no longer be invoked as the exclusive motor of history, nor because we have now arrived at our postmodern senses and realize that "there is nothing outside the text."

Perhaps there is nothing outside the yellow submarine of textuality or of culture but the ocean. But we can see the ocean through the portholes, we can analyze it, and we would be foolish not to: One name for it is "material causation." Poststructuralism tends too frequently to sever the chord that ties the balloon of language, textuality, or culture to what Marx called "the real foundations." Those real foundations are not some mysterious, inaccessible reality beyond the grasp of language. On the contrary, discourse at least implicitly names its real foundations in every utterance, in every cultural form. Television shows, for example, do not just emanate from the airwaves as free-floating texts or simulations. They have institutional, technological, and economic forces underlying them that are, in fact, much more than static foundations—that produce them and their patterns of representation far more actively than their audiences can be said to bestow meanings upon them.

On the other hand, as Hebdige notes, merely negative, merely intellectual critiques of the power relations in everyday life and the formation of our—and our students'—subjectivities may not be sufficient, even when reinfused (as I am recommending) by a strong dose of what used to be called "materialism." Such critiques themselves begin to look like idle or indulgent forms of idealism. Hebdige advocates a redefinition of "the function(s) of critique" that would involve concentrating "on the problematic of affect." This move would constitute "a break with those forms of (interpretive, functionalist, [post]structuralist) cultural critique which are bound into the problematic of meaning. It would involve a shift away from semiotics to pragmatics, from the analysis of the putative relations between cultural practices and social formations, between 'texts' and 'readers' towards a critical engagement with those processes through which libidinal and 'information' flows are organised" (*Hiding* 223). Maybe. But I still contend that any new version of a "politics of desire" such as Hebdige is advocating will simply spin off into celebrations of whatever happens to be desired (whatever produces the appropriate affect) unless it continues to be rigorously theorized through the older forms of critique, including those aspects of Marxism that are still essential for understanding ideologies and ideological state apparatuses.

What, then, of the future of cultural studies and the New Historicism in higher education? My answer is, quite simply, that they seem to be the future. In other words, they provide at least the *beginnings* of answers to the questions, What comes after poststructuralism, and, more pointedly, what shapes should the academic study of literatures and languages take after poststructuralism? Other, related forms of research are also on the increase: women's studies, African-American studies, postcolonial literature courses and programs, and multiculturalism. All these forms of academic work/political practice are responses to the widely acknowledged crisis in the humanities and social sciences (see Brantlinger 1–33). All of them move in the direction of a greater democratization of higher education, because the "decentering" of knowledges and of "the subject" (or subjectivities) by poststructuralisms means not just crisis in the negative sense, but an opening up of new possibilities.

Above all, both the New Historicism and cultural studies make way for new voices—for the voices of "others" previously excluded from academic canons and contexts and from roles of power in the organization of Western societies. The political goals of both the New Historicism and cultural studies are, in the words of Edward Said, "noncoercive knowledge produced in the interests of human freedom" (*World, Text, Critic* 29). And as Hebdige eloquently writes, "There are many good things to be grown in the autumn of the patriarch, many good things to be found in the ruins, in the collapse of the older explanatory systems, in the splintering of the masterly overview and the totalising aspiration" (*Hiding* 225). Cultural studies and the New Historicism are, I believe, among those "good things."

Notes

An earlier version of this essay appeared in *Surfaces* 2, no. 4 (1992), an electronic journal published by the Université de Montréal.

1. On the "postal politics" of poststructuralism and of Derridean postcards, see Bennington.

2. Compare David Simpson's warning against "the kind of 'new historicism'

that looks to history as to a safe and approved harbor, a place where one may sleep peacefully, lulled by anecdotal stories, after tossing on the stormy seas of deconstructive and theoretical Marxist uncertainty" ("Raymond Williams" 9).

3. Greenblatt may be more idiosyncratic than paradigmatic, but he is widely viewed as having founded or invented New Historicism. Some of the foibles or weaknesses I attribute to him, and therefore to the New Historicism, may be less in evidence among other cultural historians who are more or less connected to the New Historicism—Natalie Zemon Davis, Lynn Hunt, and Thomas Laqueur, among others.

4. Having rejected Marxism even in its postmodern, Jamesonian guise, Greenblatt turns next to Lyotard's postmodern poststructuralism. Greenblatt finds in Lyotard the mirror opposite of Jameson's "allegory of the fall," but with nearly identical results: For both, "history functions . . . as a convenient anecdotal ornament upon a theoretical structure, and capitalism appears not as a complex social and economic development in the West but as a malign philosophical principle" (151).

5. The concept of self-fashioning comes from Greenblatt's *Renaissance Self-Fashioning*.

6. A version of the essay reappears in Thomas's *The New Historicism and Other Old Subjects,* the fullest account (and critique) to date of the New Historicism.

7. For recent analyses of "the subject," see Cadova et al. and Zizek.

☐ Can Cultural Studies Speak Spanish?

George Mariscal

> What shall we do with such a miserable conglomerate of undesirable peoples based on an effete civilization?
> —George Ticknor, founder of Spanish studies at Harvard University, on the eve of the Mexican War[1]

As a beginning graduate student in comparative literature at the University of California at Irvine, I was told by a senior faculty member that I could not receive credit for Spanish as one of my required languages because "there is no significant corpus of literature in Spanish. We accept only French or German." In the mid-1970s my experience was not an isolated one. At some University of California campuses, Spanish was simply not accepted; at other institutions across the country (Yale University, for example), one had to file a special petition in order to receive credit for it. Writings in Spanish did not emit the same amount of high cultural sheen that French, German, and even certain periods of Italian literature exuded for the academy in the United States.

To understand fully the history that produced this situation, it is necessary to go back several centuries in order to locate the beginnings of what has come to be called the "Black Legend." During the sixteenth century, a project was begun in English writing to construct a Spain so different, so other to what Elizabethans valued, that Spanish culture became a simple inversion of English culture (see Gibson and Maltby). This political agenda realized through writing functioned in tandem with shifts in the centers of economic power (Seville to London to Amsterdam) and worked to construct an imaginary identity called "spanishness." It also contributed to the process by which "englishness" was invented, and it was an early manifestation of such future cultural-economic projects as nineteenth-century theories of racism and the contemporary international North-South dichotomy.

The potency of the opposition Spain/England (and later, Spain/Europe) was so great that it has survived through countless historical periods and in countless national contexts. My anecdote from graduate school indicates one way it has functioned at a micro level of knowledge production. At the level of state policy-making, it would be transported to the

American continents and made to serve the imperialist ambitions of the United States in 1898; modified by the insertion of Mexico in the place of Spain, it would be made to serve related U.S. ambitions from 1848 to the present. As George Ticknor's question suggests, Mexico and other former colonies were thought to be the progeny of decadent Spain. Thus, for elites in the United States, the center and its margins became interchangeable. It is because of the power of this opposition and the tendency for entities named "Spain," "Mexico," and "Latin America" to function as essential categories in anglophone thought that some of us who write on Hispanic topics are cautious about approaching any totalizing project with anglophone origins. This caution extends to cultural studies, now being institutionalized in university settings traditionally hostile to Spanish-speaking cultures.

The conventional model of humanistic study, with its privileging of only select sectors of European culture, has always depended to a great extent on the alterity of Spain. "Africa begins at the Pyrenees" was a phrase often repeated without the slightest bit of irony, thereby casting Spanish and African people into the domain of the uncivilized. If the moment of modernity was marked by the installation of Reason as the guardian of Western values, aristocratic and Catholic Spain was written as hopelessly (and conveniently) mired in the mud of theocratic and pre-Enlightenment consciousness. With the paradigm of Enlightenment rationality and progress presumably in shambles after successive attacks by poststructuralism, postcolonialism, feminism, and those writings associated with cultural studies, Spain is admitted into the Western tradition, but only to become the embodiment of the worst features of that now problematized tradition. In an article in *Critical Inquiry,* for example, Marc Schell, a winner of the prestigious MacArthur fellowship, reproduces most of the major elements of the Black Legend as it has been elaborated since the sixteenth century. For Schell, Spain is marked by two predominant institutions—the Inquisition and the bullfight. Taking a late seventeenth-century, anti-Spanish treatise as his starting point, Schell informs us that the Inquisition's obsession with blood purity led logically to the rise of the bullfight and ultimately to Spain's "national ideology." He goes on to make a series of absurd generalizations, such as "pure blood is still cherished among modern Spaniards," and "the killing of bulls in urban arenas was developed to its still-present zenith" (312, 316). Consumer-oriented Spaniards interested in soccer, rock music, or international politics (the majority of the population) would have trouble recognizing themselves as aristocratic aficionados of animal-baiting.[2]

Schell's othering of Spain is not surprising. What is somewhat shocking is his willingness to make sweeping assertions about an entire culture even as he admits to have drawn his information from the *National Geographic,* popular bullfighting manuals, falangist magazines of the 1950s, and occasional remarks by right-wing aristocratic kooks. It is only in a short footnote (316n27) that he even hints at the complex ideological struggle that took place in early modern Spain, a heated battle that produced a Bartolomé de las Casas, to name only one writer without whose influence subsequent discourses of toleration might not have emerged. The will to essentialize is simply too strong for Schell to resist; his liberal narrative about the birth of tolerance depends upon a fanatical and bloodthirsty Spain as much as did the jingoistic pamphlets of the sixteenth-century English ideologues.

The role played by Spain in recent New Historicist studies of early modern culture is less offensive but no less characterized by an uncritical simplification of complex historical processes. Even the elegant and measured arguments of Stephen Greenblatt display an unwillingness to understand early modern Spanish culture and Spain's colonial project on their own terms. In Greenblatt's hands, for example, the text read by Spaniards to indigenous people in America as a kind of Miranda clause (the *Requerimiento*) is a "diabolical and, in its way, sophisticated document," "a strange blend of ritual, cynicism, legal fiction, and perverse idealism" (*Learning to Curse* 29). Clearly, Spanish colonialism produced a great deal of violence and suffering. The counterdemonstrations in reaction to the 1992 "discovery celebrations" reminded us of this. But a text such as the *Requerimiento,* which mapped the contradictions of Castilian society as it outlined the "rights" and responsibilities of the colonized, is only "diabolical" and "strange" because the critic fails to subject it to the refined analytical tools he uses elsewhere.

Because the document is Spanish (and thus outside Greenblatt's field of expertise as well as vulnerable to the kind of caricaturization found in Schell's work) it does not merit a sustained reading, but rather is reduced to two adjectives typical of the colonizers' discourse in the original encounter with native people. In fact, there is little that is diabolical about the *Requerimiento* once one knows something about the ideological struggle between Catholic universalism and the rigid hierarchies of gender, blood, and religion that constituted sixteenth-century Iberian culture. Greenblatt unwittingly confuses early modern Catholicism's belief in a common origin (but not in an innate equality) for all people ("all men have the same Father") with liberal humanism's appeal to a basic unity of humanity ("all men are created equal"). This confusion forces him to cast Spain as strange in comparison to other European nations that were no less committed to the exploitation of native populations (although they were perhaps less legalistic).

It is not my contention that the essays by Schell and Greenblatt are in any way affiliated with other work being carried out under the rubric of cultural studies. But the two myths they deploy—monolithic Spain and/or Spain as Other to Europe—are at the core of a great deal of Anglo-American literary criticism. As the intersection of disciplines broadly construed as cultural studies becomes institutionalized and co-opted by the powerful ideologies of liberal pluralism and esthetic formalism, we must ask ourselves to what extent and to what end the new field of knowledge might appropriate and misrepresent the objects of its analysis, especially objects such as previously marginalized "third world" and "minority" cultures.

Ethnic Identity, Myth, and Academic Appropriation

> We are the holy relics,
> the scattered bones of a saint,
> the best loved bones of Spain.
> We seek each other.
> —Gloria Anzaldúa, "Holy Relics"
>   (*Borderlands* 154)

If one kind of cultural studies project is to dismantle the ways in which anglophone criticism and historiography have represented Hispanic traditions, a complementary project would be one that interrogates foundational narratives within those traditions and the oppositions they produce. The case of Chicano studies is an interesting one, for what was an almost invisible area of the curriculum has become an integral part of projects whose aim is to rethink the humanities. In this section of my essay, I want briefly to outline the relationship among claims of ethnic authenticity, the appropriations of that imagined authenticity, and the role of cultural criticism in the refashioning of a progressive agenda.

In her meditation on the sixteenth-century Castilian mystic and activist Teresa de Avila, the Chicana writer Gloria Anzaldúa explains that Latino culture is a field of diverse cultures apparently rooted in the common ground of language and religion. The search for pure origins, however, whether they be European or pre-Columbian, is inevitably condemned to failure, for each move back in time discovers little more than a pile of scattered and unmatched bone fragments. Acts of analysis in the service of cultural nationalism have little to do with getting back to a past source and a great deal to do with the construction of new identities in the present.

Anzaldúa's writings are a case in point. For all its emphasis on hybridity and *mestizaje,* Anzaldúa's work depends to a great degree on a series of othered groups, ranging from the Spaniard (who in this scenario functions in ways related to how that group has functioned for Anglo identity but now in a predominantly nationalist context) to Aztec patriarchs to the Chicana or Chicano who is perceived to be insufficiently Mexican. What Anzaldúa wants to construct is a myth about the feminine and matriarchal origins of pre-Columbian society so as to be able to intervene in contemporary discussions of ethnicity and gender. But in order to do so, she must first deny certain groups the authenticity she claims for herself: "Unlike Chicanas and other women of color who grew up white or have recently returned to their native cultural roots, I was totally immersed in mine" (21). The "return to native cultural roots" is cast as less authentic than an original oneness with them. With one decisive phrase, Anzaldúa takes a "browner than thou" position and says, "I'm too complex for you to understand me," not only to a majority of her potential allies in the struggle against discrimination but also to members of her own community. The concept "growing up white" further complicates the ambiguity because "whiteness" itself is a socially constructed category riddled with class and gender divisions.

Despite the presence of traditional othering mechanisms, Anzaldúa's writing is occasionally powerful where it is historical, that is, where it reveals how history is not given, but collectively made. Academic appropriations of her work, however, drive it back into the familiar territory of middle-class individualism. The liberal academy has taken up the identity myths of various disempowered groups (often in the name of cultural studies) and made them speak the language of the unique and self-determining individual. Establishment academics and administrators interested in pushing depoliticized notions of difference and diversity have suddenly discovered those groups that previously had been constructed as an undifferentiated mass (Mexicanos, Chicanos, Salvadoreños, et al. = Hispanics). The last will be first, but only in theory. Disempowered people of color become either the ego-ideal or the object of ethnographic fascination for a new intellectual bourgeoisie that theorizes race and minority discourse from such privileged sites as institutes, foundations, and academic conferences. The will to speak with authority about economic and racial realities from outside those realities—to speak for the other—reinscribes the worst features of liberal pluralism and reduces cultural studies to Madison Avenue marketing strategies. From here to the corporate slogan "making diversity work" (used by one San Diego-based company) is not too far a leap. The question becomes, For *whom* is it working?

The drive toward multiculturalism and an increased emphasis on multiple subject positions follows close on the heels of the so-called death of the bourgeois individual. In the context of the United States, however, very few people outside select literature departments believe that individualism is a thing of the past. As in an earlier moment liberal feminism constructed a female version of the self-possessed individual (critiqued by Norma Alarcón),[3] other formerly excluded groups clamor for what they never had and never will have in the postmodern dispensation. At every level of daily life, the conventional middle-class self, reproduced daily in the imagination of the mass media and certified by "living examples" such as Supreme Court Justice Clarence Thomas, continues to flourish. In the universities, the increasing presence of "multiply-inscribed" people of color in the 1970s may have momentarily challenged the reign of the Individual, perhaps to a greater extent than did French poststructuralism. But even radically recast subjectivities (decentered and provisional) have been steadily transformed into one more version of the deeply interiorized and unique person. The myth of individualism proves to be as adaptive as the capitalist system that underwrites it.

The current situation has been willfully misunderstood by right-wing ideologues who, in their lingering cold war paranoia, represent the call for multiculturalism as a takeover of the university by radical interest groups. In reality, the subject positions for which women of color, Chicanos, and others have struggled are taken up and promoted by those already in power; the disempowered groups retain their subordinate position. Thus the cultural production of Chicanos, African Americans, and others becomes the focus of institutional practices uninterested in, if not hostile to, the political and potentially system-threatening dimension of that production. In its extreme form, elite intellectuals who think that to be Chicano or African American means nothing more than to be a victim have transformed this appropriation into a discourse of victimization. (A similar move is often made with regard to working-class people when their resourcefulness and ability to act on behalf of clearly perceived interests is subsumed by a fascination, from afar, with suffering and violence.) The sentimentalizing and estheticizing of minority status and political struggle generate more scholarly papers, make academic careers, and obfuscate the need for praxis designed to reach beyond university walls (see Fregoso and Chabram).

Like the myth of individualism, the idea of a metaphysical home or a physical homeland is a powerful ideological instrument. It has functioned in certain kinds of feminist theory and is certainly at work in any ethnicity-based politics. In the context of the United States, its appeal slides easily into ideologies of nationalism and patriotism. The pressure to belong, to not be different, is difficult to resist. This is why some Chicano entertainers who have gained national visibility can insist that they be allowed to draw on ethnic material, yet simultaneously claim, "I'm not a Chicano; I'm an American." The possibility that one could simultaneously occupy both categories is unthinkable, and for many the myth of the melting pot is still attractive. It is not clear to what extent alternative myths have been able to displace it. The idea of Aztlán (the mythic Chicano homeland in the southwestern United States) was critical to the development of the Chicano movement in the early 1970s. The concept of the borderlands, as it has been elaborated by a number of Chicano writers, is a more useful tool for the 1990s.[4] But it, too, can be made to accommodate old-fashioned pluralism. José David Saldívar tells us, "Finally, cultural studies, a border zone of conjunctures, must aspire to be regionally focused and broadly comparative, a form of living and of travel in our global borderlands" (264).[5] The emphasis here on daily life and physical movement coincides with what I will propose at the conclusion of this essay. But the notion that cultural studies or any other theoretical practice is a border zone sterilizes the reality of border life and converts it into an uneasy metaphor susceptible to further appropriation. Thus the rather vulgar suggestion made at a session of the 1990 Modern Language Association convention that the MLA's smorgasbord of panels was an instantiation of "the border."

The point about both of these mythic entities—the individual and home—is that, like all appeals to an original identity based on blood, nation, or gender, they are necessarily made through writing and the myth-making power of figurative language. The Chicano poet Alurista, a central protagonist in the Chicano movement of the late 1960s and early 1970s, reminded us of this fact when, in 1981, he recalled, "There was a real need for all of us to find a way, a metaphor . . . that would serve as a unifying tool to look at each other as brothers and sisters. . . . Our unity is not bound to homogeneity. . . . The myth of Aztlán, as I saw it in the 1960s, was just a way to identify a people, a land, and a consciousness that said, 'Struggle. Do not be afraid.' I did not see myth, and I do not see myth, as a way to return to the past or as a way to project oneself in the future without bearing and confronting your present" (8). The metaphor of Aztlán continues to function as both an instrument for political struggle and a metaphysical "home." In the latter case, however, the figure is likely to lose its historical specificity and become susceptible to the kind of appropriation to which all free-floating signifiers succumb. Once Aztlán becomes a discursive construct without a political base, even Italians may be Chicanos and the term *Chicano* itself may be rewritten as an invention of European culture, deriving, it is suggested, from the Portuguese word for gypsy.[6]

The illusion of natural and transcendental identities must surely be undone in order to give way to an understanding that identities are not given but are constructed through intellectual and political praxis. In every case of dismantling origins, the configuration of categories such as class, religion, race, and gender in each specific context needs to be delineated carefully in order to avoid losing cultural studies to the kind of ahistorical idealisms that have dominated literary studies for centuries. Once local struggles are identified, what remains to be thought through is the extent to which writing or intellectual labor can contribute more directly to the transformation of society. At this point cultural studies draws upon the Marxist tradition, especially the work of Antonio Gramsci.

In an overview of cultural studies in Britain, the turn to Gramsci is referred to as one of the critical moments in the development of method (Turner 210–15; Brantlinger 68–107). Whereas many European Marxist writers made this turn only after a fascination throughout the 1960s with Althusserian thought, Gramsci's influence among some sectors of the Latin American left was fairly constant from the 1950s onward.[7] Specifically, the concept of hegemony as the articulation of diverse spheres of activity reintroduced religion, and culture in general, into the study of social domination and complemented antieconomistic theories that had been elaborated by thinkers such as the Peruvian José Carlos Mariátegui (1894–1930, see O'Connor's "The Emergence of Cultural Studies in Latin America").

My point is not that the importance of Gramsci was somehow anticipated earlier in Latin countries; rather, it is that a shared interest in the writings of Benedetto Croce, Georges Sorel, and Henri Bergson led Mariátegui to many of the same insights found in Gramsci's texts now worked out in a Latin American context. The more general point is that cultural studies will have to include a variety of different traditions and historical periods. Increasingly, the contributions of Raymond Williams, E. P. Thompson, and practitioners of the Birmingham School are being refunctioned for nonanglophone contexts as part of an international undertaking and a series of local interventions according to concrete political circumstances, for example, the place of Spanish studies in the rethinking of the humanities in the United States or the correspondence between the academic appropriation of Chicano culture in the 1980s and the increasing racism and redistribution of wealth in the Reagan-Bush years.

Whereas Gramsci's elaboration of the concept of hegemony has played a relatively abstract role in the U.S. academy, allowing for interesting ways of conceiving the social field but also leading to its appropriation by liberal-reformist and even conservative agendas, the Gramscian idea of "war of position" forces us back into the concrete world of collective action. In the war of position, counterhegemonic groups encroach upon and usurp the power of the elites, ultimately winning hearts and minds across a wide spectrum of interest groups. Marx's concern for the economic sphere and class struggle is not abandoned; it is linked to a complementary politics of culture designed to assist in the overthrow of established systems of privilege and exclusion. Marginalized groups enact alternative totalities, however contingent and open to ongoing debate these may be.

Writing and cultural criticism contribute to setting the stage for change insofar as they articulate emergent practices and prepare the ground for further praxis at strategic sites in the social field. According to Gramsci, "One can construct, on a specific practice, a theory which . . . can accelerate the historical process that is going on, rendering practice more homogeneous, more coherent, more efficient in all its elements" (365).[8] Within a context of heterogeneous social movements pursuing separate but related agendas, a cultural studies method may partially fulfill the need for mapping common ground upon which diverse groups can act together. The identification of potential points of contact might then produce a space in which a community based on mutual respect and a fair distribution of resources displaces appropriation and homogenization.[9]

Cultural Feedback and the Transformation of Common Sense

One must break down the historical barriers of collective psychology as well as the structures of power.

—Carlos Monsiváis (*Entrada libre* 32)

What is at stake in the 1990s for people in the Spanish-speaking world transcends any methodology interested in stopping its analysis at the so-called struggle for the sign. In most of Latin America, the 1980s was a decade lost to foreign debt, unemployment, and inflation. Central America continues to be the site of economic and state violence, while Latinos in the United States watch many of the meager gains of the late 1960s and early 1970s be rolled back or come under attack. The number of incoming Latino students at major universities is decreasing; undocumented workers are scapegoated for the economic crisis in the southwestern United States; neoconservatives put select minorities on display as examples of their commitment to diversity (from Richard Rodriguez, the MacNeil-Lehrer "expert" on Latino issues and a New Age romantic, to Linda Chavez, a former Reagan appointee and the author of the reactionary *Out of the Barrio*); and in San Diego County, Anglo teenagers assault and rob Mexican migrant workers as a form of entertainment.

Cultural studies workers will have to engage themselves with the production born of such unsettled circumstances and with the circumstances themselves. There continues to be a pressing need to reread canonical Latin American and Spanish texts and to trace the relations among national cultures and identities in the Hispanic world and also those between Latino and other traditions. But the engagement of cultural studies with larger social issues depends upon a deliberate transgression of institutional and ethnic boundaries and a broadening of my analysis. The "Chicano experience" cannot be adequately understood unless it is read next to and through the history of Mexico and Spain and also juxtaposed to the history of African Americans, Puerto Ricans, poor whites, and other disempowered groups in the United States. At certain critical junctures, the interconnectedness of such groups becomes particularly apparent: the Gold Rush period in California, World War II and Vietnam, and the economic hardship and competition for limited resources during the late twentieth century.

Contemporary forms of domination function best, it would seem, when the cultural production of these groups, and the groups themselves, are kept apart or reduced to simple dichotomies. The maintenance of a strict black-white opposition as the ground for U.S. social relations (an opposition reinforced by diverse works ranging from Michael Jackson's "Black or White" video to Spike Lee's movies) is conducive to the status quo, for it renders virtually invisible those groups that fall somewhere outside the dualism, thereby making a heterogeneous collective subject more difficult to imagine. This kind of segregation has not always been the case; Chicano and black coordinating committees (chaired by both women and men) in California's trade union movement during the late 1930s are only one suggestive example of collaborative work. If we are to understand and play some part in democratizing the present situation, these social circuits and past models will have to be laid bare and investigated.

Because any simple continuity within or autonomy of the Spanish-speaking tradition is illusory, cultural studies gains most from foregrounding the ever-changing function of cultural objects according to context. Writers who are actively intervening in the reproduction of those objects often display a better historical sense than do most critics. An example is Luis Valdez, a Chicano playwright who has adapted a Spanish medieval nativity play to the conditions of twentieth-century California. In *La Pastorela,* hell becomes a toxic waste site, and Christ the son of migrant workers.[10]

What a cultural studies project might undertake in response to such an adaptation would be an analysis of how the transmission of that play (from Spain to Mexico to California) involved a complex transformation of its political and cultural, that is, community-specific, functions. In doing so, the project would begin to delineate the limits of Chicano, Spanish, and Mexican identities and the historical relationships among them. What is included or excluded by these identities in terms of religious, class, and gender issues? How does one identity depend on the other for its own construction and reproduction? At the level of theory, what can this particular economy of relationships reveal about how systems of difference are produced and sustained?

The rather limited interpretive model of one-way transmission traditionally used to explain cultural and economic modes of imperialism—Europe to the New World or metropole to colony—might be replaced by a more complex mapping of what happens to social relations at the "center" once they are confronted with the inevitable return of what previously had been held at the margins. The importance of such a theoretical move is not to privilege one national (or continental) tradition over another, but rather to demonstrate the ways in which hegemonic (or dominant or colonizing) powers are always susceptible to changes introduced from the site of the nonhegemonic, thereby breaking through the deadend notion that power is homogeneous and always moves in only one direction. The model of "cultural feedback" would be a logical corollary to a theory of domination and might account for those members of a metropolitan culture who are temporarily removed from it and then return to play a significant role in its transformation. Two recent examples would be the participation of veterans of the Soviet-Afghanistan war in the blocking of the August 1991 coup attempt and that of Vietnam veterans in antiwar movements in the United States.

In Spanish history, the twin figures of the *indiano* and the *converso* are particularly interesting. In its most restricted sense, the term *indiano* referred to a native of Spain or Portugal, usually from a nonaristocratic class, who had traveled to the Indies, made a substantial fortune, and returned to Europe. (The term is usually translated into English as an "overseas Spaniard.") The earliest examples are well known: Hernán Cortés, Francisco Pizarro, and Pizarro's brother Fernando, who in 1535 returned to Spain with an Inca treasure of legendary proportions. In its widest definition, the term could include those born in America (more often referred to as *criollos*), or even the children of those who had made their fortune in the New World.

The term *converso* signified a Jew who had converted to Catholicism. It is a fact that many *indianos* were also *conversos*. What is especially revealing, however, is that in the writing of the period even *indianos* who were not *conversos* were represented as being so. The transference of qualities formerly associated with the Jewish *converso* to the *indiano* marks a curious detour in the history of Spanish capitalism. If the aristocratic imagination converted the *indiano* into a *converso,* it was because the dominant discursive formation was ill-equipped to construct figures that the New World situation produced. Thus, emergent figures such as the *indiano* were collapsed into residual ones like the *converso.* Although the construction of some figures (the merchant, for example) was refashioned throughout the early modern period in other national contexts, negative attitudes associated with money-making activities persisted well into the nineteenth century in Spain.

Once filtered through traditional ideologies, contact with America was reduced to contact with commerce and was represented as potentially destructive of aristocratic categories of quality and status. Those who had left subordinate positions in Spain, and, upon returning, actively sought to ascend within the peninsular hierarchy, carried the stigma of inferior origins and a recent fortune built on commercial enterprise. They were doubly marked as despicable. Even those who had gone to the Indies with their aristocratic status intact risked diminishing themselves. This is why Leonarda in Lope de Vega's play *El premio del bien hablar* (The gift of speaking well, 1624) declares, "Since my father's lineage is one of the noblest in the Basque country, how can it affect his honor if he comes and goes to the Indies? Even if the sea [i.e., commerce] has made him rich, it does not preclude his being a gentleman" (375).

One of the primary tropes with which the *indiano* was constructed was that of accumulated wealth. According to the writing of the period, the *indiano,* once his fortune was made and he returned to the peninsula, was prone to be particularly miserly (miserable). As one seventeenth-century writer, Fr. Benito de Peñalosa, put it, "When the *indianos* return to Spain, the more wealth they bring the more prudent and frugal they are; they fear being lost once again in dire straits, exposed to the dangers and trials of so many lands and seas" (Morínigo 195). In his novella *El celoso Extremeño* (The jealous Extremaduran), Miguel de Cervantes carries the figure of the greedy *indiano* into the realm of personal relationships. The transformation of Leonora, Carrizales' young wife, into an object to be hidden away in a vaultlike house confirms the trope of the *indiano* as avaricious and ultimately destroys her life and that of Carrizales.

What the structure of Cervantes' narrative makes visible is the trajectory of many Spaniards who used the Indies as a place to reorder their lives on both the moral and material planes, a process which, upon return to Spain, was represented by ostentatious wealth and increased social power. According to Cervantes, however, the American experience was available only to the most desperate of Spanish society, and it successfully transformed even fewer. Once the young Carrizales has wasted his inheritance, his thoughts turn to the New World, "So, seeing himself so short of money, and with few friends left, he had recourse to the solution to which many ruined people of that city are driven, namely that of going to the Indies, the refuge and shelter of all desperate folk in Spain, the sanctuary of bankrupts, the safe-conduct of murderers, the protection and cover of those gamblers known by the experts in the craft as sharpers, the general decoy for loose women, where many go to be deceived, and few find a way out of their difficulties" (147). We should not forget that Cervantes himself, a would-be *indiano,* had petitioned for and had been refused permission to go to the Indies in 1593.

Stinginess functioned as a general designation for the multiple defects of the Spanish returnee from America. However, contemporary discourse also produced an *indiano* who is generous (liberal) if not prodigal. In Lope de Vega's 1632 drama *La Dorotea,* the surprised Gerarda says to the *indiano* Don Bela, "Heaven grant you the long life your munificent hands deserve. I do not understand all the talk about stingy overseas Spaniards. Either you are an exception to the opinion generally held, or one single wretch gave all a bad name" (49). The possession of nonaristocratic wealth acquired outside of the patronage system by men of dubious ancestry problematized traditional categories of status. The generous *indiano* mimicks conventional aristocratic modes of consumption not only because luxury signifies both rank and privilege but also because religious discourse teaches that charity indicates nobility and, after all, the only true wealth is that of the next world. On the other hand, the thrifty *indiano,* always conscious of the hardships he had undergone in order to make his fortune, hoards his money and points toward a figure only barely visible at this moment of European history—the calculating and prudent bourgeois.

It is no surprise that in early modern Spanish writing the *indiano* took shape at the intersection of blood, money, and language. Before the initial stages of the Atlantic project, each of these discursive domains had struggled to control its boundaries; the ideology of blood purity (*limpieza*) worked to maintain what, in the critical language of our own time, are called essentialist categories based on the exclusion and domination of undesirable elements. But by the early sixteenth century, the new world situation dictated that each of these closed systems be reconfigured through a process of circulation and exchange. New forms of wealth contested the metaphysics of blood even as the myth of Castilian linguistic purity cracked under the strain of a previously unimagined empirical reality. At the center of these multiple exchanges stood the figure of the *indiano.* Because he could not be situated in any of the traditional categories, he problematized the entire field of social relations. The American experience transformed Spain and the internal hierarchies that held it together. Since the sixteenth century, returning "overseas Spaniards" have played a role in the ongoing invention of Spanish identity.

The movement of specific groups and cultural goods and the social effects generated by such movement—cultural feedback—is an equally important object of analysis for late twentieth-century studies. We may want to investigate, for example, the ways in which Chicano subcultural styles, produced out of the contact with other elements of urban culture in the United States, are returned to Mexico and take up different functions. The Mexican essayist Carlos Monsiváis has written about how, in the 1940s and later in the mid-1970s, what originated in the Southwest as counterhegemonic practices (the pachuco and cholo styles of dress, music, and language) are depoliticized and make the voyage south to be reenacted by middle-class youth in the large cities of northern Mexico (*Escenas* 291–95).[11] The children and grandchildren of immigrant families export to their "ancestral home" an uncanny and not always welcome cultural gift.

In his ethnographic survey of punk and cholo styles in Mexico and the United States, José Manuel Valenzuela outlines the political and economic relations as well as the transference of cultural products between the two countries. In the conjuncture of U.S.–Mexican unequal dependencies, popular culture on the southern side of the border is driven by international market forces and U.S. control of mass communication systems. Nevertheless, the contact between different subcultural communities can produce unexpected results, as in an anecdote recounted by a Mexican punk:

> [From Tijuana] I began to go to punk parties in San Diego.... Once a band was playing and they had a gringo [U.S.] flag so I went up between the instruments and pulled down the flag and said to my friend: Do you have any matches? Yeah, well light this and we burned the gringo flag in front of the gringo punks and some applauded and others got angry. A little of everything, no? There were some nationalist patriots, right? "We're Number One" and all the rest.... [Later, one of the band members objects to the flag burning] I asked him why he objected if they sang songs against the United States, and he said, "My brother died in Vietnam" and I told him, "Do you know who killed your brother? Your flag killed him. Your love for your country killed him, get it? And you should be against your flag because it killed your brother." (179)[12]

The discourse of patriotism is radically critiqued by an alternative voice from the so-called third world that at the level of style would seem to be part of the North American punk's cultural universe. The resultant contradiction likely did not lead to immediate politicization but may have unsettled the band member's uncritical acceptance of national myths of the United States long enough to view his own culture from the outside.

This kind of exchange, in which divergent perspectives are juxtaposed and problematized, is a relatively commonplace occurrence in all border communities; the relationships among various groups, however, continue to be complicated by nationalist and class biases. For example, one Mexican artist, Roberto Gil de Montes, who admits to incorporating graffiti in his work under the influence of Chicano street art, arrogantly insists on his own superior authenticity: "I certainly have nothing against Chicanos. After all, we gave birth to them. They come from what we are.... When they did try to be like me, it seemed ridiculous. So how could I identify with them? They were trying to become what I already was" (Benavidez 6). Such statements are driven by the will to cultural purity, a belief in transcendental art, and an inability to imagine complex identities and alliances.

Many of these exchanges might best be read as mechanisms of supplementarity. Social types, cultural forms, or styles enter a new environment and either transform it immediately or produce the conditions for future change. As with the *indiano* in Spain, who was symptomatic of an unsettled field of social relations and thus became a recurring figure in literature and a concretization of emergent subject positions, the cholo, *pícaro,* and other "characters" might be productively read as bearers of change (although not necessarily progressive change). Because each is related differently to hegemonic forces, it should not be assumed that the dynamic they produce constitutes either "subversion" or "resistance." The wealthy *indiano*'s economic status, for example, was markedly different from that of a contemporary working-class Chicano or an undocumented farm worker. In the final analysis, the *indiano*'s wealth invigorated a declining aristocracy even as it prepared a space for an emergent middle class whose political power in Spain was not solidified until the late nineteenth century.

In an institutional setting, the demystification of origins, the reimagining of communities, and the invention of new identities and a new consensus that cultural studies workers might undertake are directly linked to issues of pedagogy and activism. It is in the classroom that the status quo is either uncritically reproduced through the kinds of appropriations I have outlined or overturned in order to produce a new "common sense." But the desire to problematize accepted knowledge, which some poststructuralisms and cultural studies seem to share, is not easily realized by groups living within traditional cultural formations. I am thinking not only of Latino communities, where discourses of Catholicism and patriotism are strong, but also of the majority of the middle class in the United States, resigned to consumerism and civic inaction. The Brazilian educator Paulo Freire reminds us that "problematization does not come easily to silent, passively receptive masses, no matter where they are—in the 'countryside' of the world or in the classrooms or before the television sets of the 'cities'" (*Cultural Action* vii).

The neoconservative claim that U.S. universities are being taken over by "Marxist faculty" is absurd; most faculties and administration continue to be committed to maintaining the status quo through managerial practices and liberal rhetoric. But it is true that in many places an ideological struggle between progressive and reactionary forces is taking place for the content of the curriculum. It is no accident that cultural studies in the United States emerged at precisely the moment when racism and elitism reappeared in new and reinvigorated forms. In order to combat these familiar enemies in new garb, teachers and writers must engage students with democratic strategies designed to unsettle their common sense, our authority, and the disciplinary power of our institutions. If theses strategies are enacted, cultural studies may be able to produce, in the long run, a more inclusive project in which cultural exchanges take place not in an environment premised on authenticity or appropriation, hierarchy, or homogenization, but on the understanding that the subaltern can indeed speak for itself and, when it does, demand to be accepted on its own terms.

Notes

My thanks to Rosaura Sánchez, of the University of California at San Diego, for her comments on an earlier draft of this essay.

1. Personal correspondence quoted in Tyack, 197.
2. Schell seems to have little desire to contextualize the documents he cites and thus to understand the cultural work they accomplished in their original setting. This leads him to misrepresent completely modern Spanish society and to distort important terms (e.g., *hidalgo*).
3. See her "The Theoretical Subject(s) of *This Bridge Called My Back* and Anglo-American Feminism" in Calderón and Saldívar, 28–39.
4. As an uncanny site of heterogeneity and solidarity, the borderlands is also a place of ongoing struggle and praxis. In this sense, it is a historical and future-oriented "space" in ways Aztlán is not. For a moving account of border life, see Urrea.
5. The villains of Saldívar's piece are curiously named "postmodern homogenization" (255) and "patriarchal postmodernity" (263) instead of ethnocentrism, white supremacy, patriarchy, and exploitation.
6. Bondolfi expresses the hope that once Chicano literature is better-known in Italy, "quizá entonces la tierra mítica de Aztlán pueda llegar a ser también nuestra tierra prometida (perhaps then the mythic land of Aztlán may come to be our promised land as well)" (282).
7. On the European reception of Gramsci, see Mouffe (1–18); on Gramsci in Latin America, see Aricó.

8. Or, "Every revolution has been preceded by an intense work of criticism, of cultural penetration" (quoted in Germino 40).

9. For a similar proposal from a Latin Americanist's perspective, see Pratt.

10. The paternalistic and orientalist messages of Valdez' production and the fact that it was funded by PBS, British, and Spanish television make it an especially interesting and problematic case.

11. Much of Monsiváis' work already constitutes a cultural studies approach to Mexican society. In addition to *Escenas de pudor y liviandad,* see *Amor perdido.*

12. "Yo empecé a ir a San Diego a las fiestas de los punks.... una vez estaba tocando una banda, y entre ellos estaba una bandera gringa y yo me metí entre los instrumentos y jalé la bandera y a mi amigo le dije ¿traes cerillos?, simón, pues préndele aquí y quemamos la bandera gringa enfrente de los punks gringos y unos aplaudieron y otros pusieron cara de enojados y hubo de todo ¿no?, y que su país es el número uno y que no sé qué.... Le pregunté que por qué no le gustó, si ellos en su música cantaban en contra de Estados Unidos, me dijo: 'mi hermano murió en Vietnam' y yo le dije '¿sabes quien mató a tu hermano?, tu bandera lo mató, le dije, tu amor a tu patria eso mató a tu hermano, ¿me entiendes? y tú debes estar en contra de tu bandera porque ella fue la que mató a tu hermano.'"

☐ Passing as Pedagogy: Feminism in(to) Cultural Studies

Pamela L. Caughie

The "Degenerate Art" exhibition at the Art Institute of Chicago in May 1991 sparked my awareness of the pedagogical double bind that is the subject of this essay. In Gallery 6 of the exhibit, a video monitor displayed newsreel footage of the crowd at the original Munich exhibition of Entartete Kunst (Degenerate Art) in 1937. An exhibit of 650 works of art confiscated by the Nazis and displayed publicly in an effort to defame the avant-garde, Entartete Kunst was a product of and testament to Nazi censorship and oppression. The Chicago exhibition reassembled extant pieces from the original show, reinstating them in a "proper" exhibit context while documenting the "derisive intent" of the Nazi installation, reminding viewers, as the brochure says, of "the fragility of freedom."[1] The video exhibit in Gallery 6 allowed participants to watch throngs of earlier viewers passing by and pausing to regard many of the same paintings we were seeing here for the first time, but under conditions very different from the oppressive climate captured by the newsreel. Yet as I stared at the black and white images on the monitor, I wondered to what extent my situation as a viewer replicated theirs. Was not this show, like its predecessor, attempting to move its audience to share a particular attitude toward the art on display by means of its very *method* of display?

Although Entartete Kunst justified its excessive commentary (in the form of graffiti slogans surrounding the artworks) by passing as a means of saving German culture from degenerates and their art, Degenerate Art attempted to save art from politics by separating its historical and highly politicized introduction from its decontextualized exhibit of the artworks. Moreover, each audience was expected to come to share the organizers' opposition to a particular mode of cultural production. As I watched the newsreel, I became acutely aware of the double bind the spectator was in. You could not help accepting the moral and political position the show urged upon you; yet in accepting its truth, you succumbed to strategies of manipulation that you were moved to oppose. Clearly, the didactic messages of the two exhibitions could not have differed more, yet their pedagogy was much the same.

The relation between feminist criticism and women's studies programs on the one hand, and emerging cultural studies programs on the other, creates a similar double bind for feminist teachers. How can feminists not be "for" the paradigm shift from literary studies to cultural studies? After all, feminist criticism and women's studies programs have been employing a cultural studies model all along. Feminists have expanded the range of cultural phenomena that can be analyzed as "texts"; our criticism and pedagogy have been intrinsically interdisciplinary and even counterdisciplinary; we have worked to erode the distinction between high art and a popular culture often represented and devalued as "feminine"; and in our efforts to expose and change women's oppression under patriarchy, our work has been from the beginning cross-cultural in its analyses and arguments. Feminism has played a prominent role in the emergence of cultural studies.

But just when I am convinced that feminism is endemic to the cultural studies movement, I come up against defenses of a cultural studies model in which women's experiences are elided and feminism is co-opted in the name of a more inclusive paradigm. The potential threat to the momentum of feminism as a distinct force in the academy leads me to ask of the cultural studies movement, "What's in it for us?" I know only too well the risks I run in using the all-inclusive pronoun (as if I knew who "we" were) and the dangers of the "us-against-them" thinking that my question invokes. Indeed, the cultural studies model that feminism promotes works against such distinctions in its attention to the complex and contradictory subject positions available in various cultural practices. Still, when the question of co-optation comes up—as it inevitably does whenever those who historically have not been part of the power structure of the university are assured by those who have been that instituting a new program represents their best interests—I feel the pronoun is appropriate. I use it deliberately here to mark a gendered political division that in theory is culturally constructed and based on erroneous assumptions about gender identity but is there in practice nonetheless. So when I ask, "What's in it for us," I realize that in terms of institutional support (money) and prestige (power and visibility), the answer may be, "Not much." Cultural studies, especially to the extent that administrators see it as a stopgap to the increasing fragmentation of a politically problematic multiculturalism, threatens to drain resources from women's studies programs and to render women and feminists invisible once again. The threat a cultural studies paradigm poses to women's studies and feminism may be a measure of the recuperative strategies of male power. Cultural studies programs may occupy what Tania Modleski calls a "space of disavowal": Proponents can at once acknowledge feminism as one of the political and theoretical challenges of the past two decades that has led to a cultural studies model *and* "ward off the threat these struggles pose to the white male power structure" (122) by incorporating feminism and negating its difference in the name of difference itself.

And thus the double bind. My participation in the cultural studies movement within my university, like my attendance at the "Degenerate Art" exhibition, has forced me to question my moral position within a collective of like-minded people, the ways in which my adoption of a particular set of values or course of action may implicate me in the very attitudes and practices I set out to oppose. But I do not believe this double bind is specific to my experiences or to a feminist's position in a cultural studies program. Rather, this double bind is intrinsic to cultural studies, forcing teachers and cultural critics into the position of the "passer," the one who is actually positioned otherwise than where he or she professes to be.

Passing takes many forms, from the strategic adoption of a culturally empowered identity to the disempowering mimicry of a threatening difference. But all passing is marked by the double bind that opens a discrepancy between what one professes to be and how one is actually positioned in a society, institution, discourse, or classroom. The passer must always run the risk of self-betrayal in any particular performance. Thus, the double bind cannot be resolved only theoretically, but must be confronted performatively as well through a performative pedagogy that seeks to enact rather than endorse certain positions.[2]

In this essay, rather than trying to answer the question of whether cultural studies is good for feminism, or what the relation of feminism to cultural studies should be, I will consider the pedagogical implications of a cultural studies model.[3] However much cultural studies, like feminism, may radically reconceive pedagogy, proponents have not yet offered a pedagogy capable of confronting competing positions and unequal power relations in the university and the classroom. In this essay, Degenerate Art becomes an allegory of the cultural studies professor's potential blindness to the workings of his or her own pedagogy, allowing us to see how cultural studies passes as a pedagogy capable of serving the interests of many oppositional groups. Alternatively, a reading of Nella Larsen's *Passing* shows how the novel can serve as an allegory of the pedagogical situation in which we now find ourselves and offer a possible way of reconceiving passing for pedagogy. Passing has come to be thought of in one of two ways, either negatively as an appropriation of another's identity and experience or more positively as an expression of our culturally constructed and therefore changeable identities. But is it not possible that passing can be conceived of as a behavior especially suited to the double bind I am elaborating here, where the usual mode of resistance to dominant discourses and institutional structures is intellectually nonadaptive and morally untenable?

Unreliable Narrators

The exhibition at the Art Institute of Chicago is an example of this double bind to the extent that it created a discrepancy between what it said and what it did. What struck me most about Degenerate Art was the exhibition's excessive amount of introductory material. By the time one got through the four introductory galleries meant to incite moral outrage by documenting Nazi atrocities—burning books, persecuting artists, the purging of museum curators—one could hardly view the works from Entartete Kunst "on their own merits," as the brochure for the exhibition suggested. Despite the disclaimer by Frank O. Gehry, the architect who designed the original exhibition in Los Angeles, that "what you don't want to do is to make a work of art important simply because of its associations," the exhibition did precisely that. Indeed, the vast introduction to the main exhibit suggested that the organizers may have feared that without a great deal of interpretive assistance viewers might (as the original audience was encouraged to do) laugh at the milk cow by Emil Nolde, scoff at the crucifix by Max Beckmann, or protest the homosexuality of *Two Friends*. The excessive commentary sought to create in the audience not so much an esthetic appreciation as a shared moral sensibility.

I am not suggesting that art and politics can or should be separated, as if we could view artworks on their own merits. Clearly, this position is exposed as untenable by the very exhibition that professes to safeguard it. Nor am I suggesting that the members of the original audience, any more than the contemporary viewers, were "cultural dupes" (to borrow Stuart Hall's often-repeated phrase), easily manipulated by, and unselfconsciously buying into, the politics of the exhibition's organizers. What I am asking is, In opposing a dominant discourse or cultural policy, must we necessarily engage in related efforts to press upon others a moral and political consensus? For me, the Chicago exhibition raised the question of how one can oppose a political and cultural agenda without engaging in the kind of behavior one claims to resist. This is the double bind I am suggesting that is intrinsic to a cultural studies model.

The double bind calls out for a deconstructive approach. Indeed, that monitor in Gallery 6 marked for me the moment when the Chicago exhibit began unself-consciously to deconstruct itself. Without the video, Degenerate Art conveyed a straightforward lesson in the horrors of cultural oppression under fascism. With the video screen, however, the viewer potentially became aware of another kind of replication, not just the historical reconstruction of the content and context of the Nazi show, but the structural reproduction of its didactic strategies. My purpose is not to argue for deconstruction, but the video display made the case at least for a performative pedagogy, one that at once provides a safeguard against being manipulated even by the political discourse one endorses and, at the same time, acknowledges that no pedagogy can provide such a guarantee. That video display functioned as a deconstructive double gesture. A video camera and a second monitor placed next to the newsreel monitor, allowing us to see images of ourselves viewing others viewing the art, would have transformed the display into a performative pedagogy.

"Degenerate Art" presents an allegory of the double bind intrinsic to a cultural studies model and an allegory of the cultural studies professor's position in relation to the very oppositional discourses he or she attempts to bring together in the service of a new cultural politics. This double bind forces cultural critics into the position of passing. Following are two examples of how a cultural studies pedagogy may work against the very politics it endorses.

The first example is constituted by both the seminar on ethnography organized by James Clifford and George Marcus, leading figures in the cultural studies movement, and *Writing Culture,* the collection of essays that came out of the seminar, held in Santa Fe in April 1984. In "Partial Truths," his introduction to the collection, Clifford describes feminism as "an especially strong intellectual and moral influence in the university milieux" (19) that has been an impetus for the cultural studies movement, of which the collection is part of the growing literature. Such an admission raises the question of why women (with the exception of Mary Louise Pratt) and feminists were excluded from the seminar and the collection. Earlier, Clifford responds indirectly to this glaring absence by acknowledging that gender impinges upon the reading of cultural texts (17). (Notably, he does not say gender impinges on the *writing* of cultural texts.) He offers the example of the ethnographer Godfrey Lienhardt's use of "man" in the generic sense to refer to all members of a culture. As do many cultural critics, Clifford historicizes the text in order to explain this "discursive partiality": "The partiality of gender in question here was not an issue when the book was published in 1961. If it were, Lienhardt would have directly addressed the problem, as more recent ethnographers now feel obliged to" (18)—indeed, as Clifford now evidently feels obliged to address his own gender partiality.

Clifford's explanation is an example of the "historicizing impulse in cultural studies" (Nelson 33). However, a feminist critique does not stop at historical contextualization, as Clifford does, but goes on to analyze genealogically how that "discursive partiality" has informed cultural constructions of femininity and traditional notions of scholarship and how it continues to inform our assumptions about women and writing. Although Clifford explains the choice from a historical perspective, he leaves the systematic implications of such a choice largely unexplored. Feminist ethnography, in Clifford's view, simply is not "serious" scholarship, or at least it was not in the mid-1980s when the seminar took place. The collection, he explains, "was planned as the publication of a seminar . . . institutionally defined as an 'advanced seminar'" (20), and this designation of "advanced," apparently, mandated the exclusion of women writing from feminist perspectives.

By claiming that the scope and limits of the seminar were "institutionally defined," Clifford either ignores or elides his own position of power, suggesting that individuals (he and Marcus) had no choice in the matter. Yet institutions, as Barbara Herrnstein Smith says, "are, of course, all managed by *persons* (who, by definition, are those with cultural power and commonly other forms of power as well)" (51). Clifford's explanation of how participants were selected for the seminar is worth quoting:

> We [Marcus and Clifford] decided to invite people doing *"advanced" work* on our topic, by which we understood people who *had already contributed significantly* to the analysis of ethnographic textual form. . . . We invited participants *well known* for their recent contributions to the opening up of ethnographic writing possibilities, or *whom we knew* to be well along on research relevant to our focus. The seminar was small and its formation ad hoc, reflecting *our specific personal and intellectual networks, our limited knowledge of appropriate work in progress.* (my emphasis, 20)

The exclusion was not strictly a matter of personal bias, nor even a matter of "limited knowledge." The exclusion of feminists, Clifford explains, was due to an *absence* of writing. "Planning the seminar," he continues, "we were confronted by what seemed to us an obvious—important and regrettable—fact. Feminism had not contributed much to the theoretical analysis of ethnographies as texts" (20).

Although Clifford is cognizant of the facts that the very focus of the seminar may well have excluded scholarship by women and non-Western people, and that institutional politics have much to do with what and how people write, his defense of his exclusions reveals that he views feminism as defined by its concern with content while "advanced" work focuses on form. "Our fetishizing of form," Clifford admits, "is a bias that may well be implicit in modernist 'textualism'" (21). Yet he seems blithely unself-conscious of the fact that his form/content opposition becomes a hierarchy that is gendered and racialized. And it is this very "ignorance" as Shoshana Felman defines it—not simply a lack of information but a desire to ignore ("Psychoanalysis and Education" 29–31)—that allows Clifford to defend the decision not to redress the exclusion of feminists from the seminar by inviting them to contribute to the collection. To do so, Clifford says, would have been mere "tokenism" (21). But surely correcting an institutionalized exclusion can hardly be considered simply a symbolic gesture if it is directed at practices that have served historically and structurally to oppress and silence others. By excluding feminists from the collection and then representing their work in his introduction, Clifford unself-consciously engages in the very practices that *Writing Culture* seeks to expose: "silencing incongruent voices" (6) in the process of analyzing the politics and practices of representing those who have been silenced.[4]

Partiality—in the senses of both bias and incompleteness—is unavoidable in any writing or teaching, and partiality is, in my view as in Clifford's, preferable to falsely totalizing views and presumably objective perspectives. But an acknowledgment of partiality can become a way of defending against one's own biases and exclusions and a way of securing one's own authority. Clifford explains that a "banal" understanding of the claim that all ethnographies are fictions is that every truth or fact is constructed (6). So, too, a banal understanding of partiality is that all views are limited by historical and personal circumstances. Both views ignore that "cultural fictions" and critical paradigms "are based on systematic, and contestable, exclusions" (6). We need to act on those exclusions, to understand their *systematic* character and use them to refashion ourselves, our scholarship, and our teaching. Had Clifford included women writing from feminist perspectives in his seminar, they might not have simply "obscured" the focus of the seminar, as he feared. Rather, they might have resisted, challenged, and judged his limited definitions of feminism and textualism, exposing as a fiction what Clifford takes to be an obvious and regrettable fact, that feminism has not contributed to textual analysis. My point is not to argue that feminists *have* contributed to the kind of textual analysis Clifford endorses. My point is that by his very definition of textual analysis and his acceptance of institutional parameters, there is no way they could.

The discrepancy between what Clifford *says* about cultural criticism at the beginning of his essay and what he *does* in defending against charges of bias is an instance of passing. Clifford conceives culture "as composed of seriously contested codes and representations" and insists that "the authority to represent cultural realities is unequally shared and at times contested" (2, 6), and yet his pedagogy—the seminar he plans on writing culture—works to contain those very voices that would challenge his own representations and authority. This is what I mean by "passing as pedagogy," the way others are elided in the very process of claiming to include them, the way conflicts are not aired at the same time they are acknowledged as essential.

The second example of how a professor may pass in the classroom is Paul Smith's essay "A Course in 'Cultural Studies.'" The coincidence of its publication in the *Journal of the Midwest Modern Language Association* at the time of the Degenerate Art exhibition brought out the similarity between the pedagogical double binds that each, in its own way, creates. The spatial move from the introductory rooms of "Degenerate Art" to the exhibit of the artworks is structurally equivalent to the relation between the sections of Smith's essay: his description of the content, objectives, and pedagogy of his course "What Is Cultural Studies?" and his narrative of what actually transpired in the class.

The article begins with a series of disclaimers. Smith admits that no reportage is innocent, that any course is an intervention and any course description "an argument of a sort," and that his selections of readings are necessarily determined by his own "levels of knowledge, expertise, experience, and, indeed, willingness" (39, 41). This introductory material establishes his reliability as a narrator, as does the introductory material he provides his students. Smith's syllabus also opens with a disclaimer—"Inevitably, in the space of one semester we shan't be able to answer fully the question that the course's title poses" (40)—and then begins to answer the question by providing a definition of cultural studies, even "at the risk of prejudicing [class] discussion" in advance. Like the video monitor at the art exhibition, Smith's disclaimers undermine his conscious desires, placing him and his students in a double bind. The disclaimers reveal the impossibility of leaving students "more or less to their own devices" (43) while at the same time providing some direction that must inevitably bias the discussion. But also like the video monitor, Smith's disclaimers reveal an unconscious desire that is pedagogically far more interesting than his stated purpose.

What happens to Smith's course objectives and pedagogical values in the classroom? His narrative of the course suggests that despite his effort to allow texts and students to argue with one another, despite his insistence on cultural studies as "a resistant operation," the course evoked little dissent. For example, Patrick Brantlinger's *Crusoe's Footprints* was dropped after three weeks and only two chapters. "*We* decided," Smith writes, "that Brantlinger's book would not be particularly useful in this course" because of the author's "antipathy to the political project of 'cultural studies'" (my emphasis, 45). And at the end of the course, Dick Hebdige's *Hiding in the Light,* a central text, elicited mutual criticism as well, "students being somewhat less convinced of the 'positive potentialities' of postmodernism than [Hebdige]" (47). Resistance may be claimed as a value in the course content, but consensus structures the plot of Smith's narrative. If there were disagreements among the students, and between students and teacher, they were either unvoiced or unrecorded. Although Smith feels compelled to describe the racial and gender configurations of his class—two African-American students in a class of seventeen and "slightly more women than men" (43)—these make no significant difference in his narrative, as if all shared a common political and theoretical agenda with the professor.

Why might diverse students come to share resistance to a particular intellectual and political project? We should not be surprised to find that an answer lies in the professor's selections, emphases, and commitments. "I want to take some credit for the students' unwillingness in regard to the more optimistic views of the politics of 'postmodernism,'" Smith writes, "since we had spent a considerable amount of time discussing my own essay, 'Visiting the Banana Republic'—an essay which is by no manner of means a paean to 'postmodernism' or many of its theoretical discourses" (47). What *may* surprise us is that Smith takes credit for his students' unwillingness to entertain alternative "explanations of culture" (40). Moreover, he is not the least bit self-conscious about the ways in which his language here and his use of "we" discredit his reliability. For one so attuned to "the political functions of the academic" and to the ways in which subjects are "pulled into place" by cultural institutions and knowledges (44), Smith surprisingly ignores the ways in which institutional structures, and, indeed, his own disclaimers, shore up his authority and teach students to comply, even while theorizing a notion of resistance. Smith ignores "the dialectics of resistance and consent" (45) in his own classroom. Thus, his pedagogy puts him in the position of the passer and puts into question the reliability of the teacher (see also Easthope 116).

The unreliability of Clifford and Smith, like that of the curators of the art exhibition, emerges in the disjunction between the content of their work and their pedagogy. In all three cases, the introductory material makes all the right statements, but the pedagogical performance works against the stated objectives, paradoxically revealing an unconscious desire to do the right thing by putting authority in question. That is to say, the articles and the exhibition seem to say, "Question Authority," a command that places us in a double bind in that we cannot obey it without violating it. Yet the performance of the professors and the curators puts into question the very authority they claim, thereby playing out the double bind their stated objectives create. Lacking a performative pedagogy capable of dealing with their positions as passers, however, they are blind to their unconscious desires. All are ignorant of the possibilities that their unreliability holds for cultural studies.[5]

Positive Unreliability[6]

To explore the "positive potentialities" of passing, I want to discuss Nella Larsen's *Passing,* a novel I taught for the first time in the fall of 1991 in a course in African-American literature. *Passing* provides an allegory of the kind of pedagogy I am discussing. Teaching *Passing* in this course was like putting a video camera next to the monitor in Gallery 6; it provided the class with the opportunity to see their own "dialectics of resistance and consent" played out in the text.

First published in 1929, *Passing* is a story about the strained friendship between two mulatta women, Irene Redfield and Clare Kendry. Irene is married to a black doctor and lives in Harlem; Clare is married to a white racist and "passes" in white society. Having known each other in childhood, the women have not seen or heard from one another for more than ten years when the novel opens. They first meet by chance at the Drayton Hotel tea room, where Irene is herself passing temporarily. As the two friends catch up on their pasts, she tactfully avoids the issue of passing, for Clare's passing is more than a temporary convenience, as it is for Irene; its exposure is much more threatening. Irene thinks: "There were things that she wanted to ask Clare Kendry. She wished to find out about this hazardous business of 'passing,' this breaking away from all that was familiar and friendly to take one's chances in another environment. . . . What, for example, one did about background, how one accounted for oneself. . . . But she couldn't. She was unable to think of a single question that in its context or its phrasing was not too frankly curious, if not actually impertinent" (157).

Irene's reticence in this scene is similar to the response of many of my students when discussing black literature in a racially mixed classroom conducted by a white teacher. Indeed, the passage seemed to speak to our own positions within the class I was preparing to teach. For me, there was the question of background, both personal and scholarly, and the question of how to account for myself as a member of a different race—that is, questions of authority. For students, there may have been a frank curiosity about what it is like to live in "another environment," coupled with a discreet politeness. At times, they seemed reluctant to bring up issues that were potentially divisive and only too willing to assume the positions they felt were expected of them. Thus, we seemed to find ourselves in a double bind. If students asked about racial differences, they risked being impertinent; if they refrained from asking, they risked remaining, as Irene does, naive and ignorant. If I raised the issue of my race, I risked undermining my authority;[7] if I downplayed my race, I risked undermining my reliability.

But in its reticence on the narrative level (the word *passing*, for example, does not even appear until the fourteenth page of the novel), and in the extent to which communication between any two people in the novel is marked by reticence, resistance, mistrust, and misperceptions, the novel reveals more than a desire not to offend; it also reveals a desire not to know. In this sense, Irene's reticence in her conversation with Clare, like the reticence of students and teachers in a cultural studies classroom, may be less a matter of discretion than of self-protection. Our unasked questions may keep us "safe" by keeping us ignorant of knowledge that might displace us from familiar positions. Teaching *Passing,* then, can disclose the workings of what Gregory Jay calls the "pedagogical unconscious" ("Subject of Pedogogy" 789), what we resist knowing.

It is for these reasons that *Passing* goes some way toward answering the question raised by my opening discussion and by a cultural studies program: How do institutional and unconscious structures that govern exchange among students and between students and teacher—structures based historically and psychologically upon the assumption of a disinterested authority and a homogeneously receptive audience—foster unreliability and constrain oppositional discourse, which is essentially collective and inescapably ethical? Some scenes from the novel provide a better sense of how *Passing* functions pedagogically in this way.

Although in that initial meeting with Clare, talking with her "own kind," Irene feels impertinent asking about racial differences, later, talking with Hugh Wentworth, who is white, she is anything but reticent. During their conversation at the Negro Welfare League dance, the topic is interracial attraction. Hugh presents a common argument of the time, that white women are attracted to black men because they find them exotic, beautiful, and erotic. Irene objects to what Hugh means by the word *attraction:* "'I think that what they feel is—well, a kind of emotional excitement. You know, the sort of thing you feel in the presence of something strange, and even, perhaps, a bit repugnant to you; something so different that it's really at the opposite end of the pole from all your accustomed notions of beauty'" (205).

Why can Irene talk frankly with Hugh in a way that she cannot with Clare? One explanation is that they are discussing a common subject of debate among the Harlem intelligentsia. A safe topic puts them on familiar ground where the conventions are established so that neither interlocutor risks being impertinent.

However, Irene's relation to Hugh is not as open or friendly as it seems at first. Their relationship changes when racial difference becomes part of the dynamics of their exchange, not simply a topic of discussion. Irene and Hugh's conversation at the dance moves from the safe topic of interracial attraction to the issue of passing, the dangerous issue that Irene did not bring up in her earlier conversation with Clare. She points out the instinctual ability of her own people to detect the difference between the races, and the confirmed inability of whites to detect a passing Negro. Whites are so incompetent when it comes to detecting "passers," she says, because they look for tangible signs, such as physical features, when the telltale sign of race is something else. As Irene puts it, what marks the difference between the races is "[a] thing that couldn't be registered" (206). Although Hugh agrees that there may be something other than appearance, speech, or gesture that enables one to detect racial difference, he still denies that one can always tell. "Yet lots of people 'pass' all the time," he remarks. Irene responds, "Not on our side, Hugh" (206).

Irene shows Hugh that what he thinks he sees from one position, people passing, may not look the same from another. She exposes his own lack of awareness, his possible self-deception, and thereby helps him to see more clearly, although what she helps him see is "a thing that couldn't be registered"—racial difference. Yet Irene forces an even more threatening insight on Hugh:

> "It's easy for a Negro to 'pass' for white, but I don't think it would be so simple for a white person to 'pass' for coloured."
> "Never thought of that," he remarks.
> "No, you wouldn't. Why should you?" (206)

By making him see what he has never had to face—that, as a white man, he has no need to think about passing, whereas the issue is a matter of survival for blacks—Irene forces on Hugh an awareness of his own failure of imagination and of his own implicit racism.

Hugh senses in this exchange that Irene has exposed the racial difference that their friendship has supposedly covered over: "Slippin' me, Irene?" he asks, suspecting that, at the same time they have been talking frankly, she may have been talking ironically, even sarcastically, misleading him rather than leading him to see more clearly. As in the earlier passage from Irene and Clare's first meeting, it seems that to be frank is to be impertinent whenever racial difference is at issue. Once difference is asserted, the possibility of misunderstanding and even deception intensifies. If Hugh's question shows that he has detected his potential racism, it also suggests, in its very doubt and suspicion, his resistance to this knowledge, a knowledge at odds with his own self-concept as an intellectual and a friend of the black race.

In terms of the classroom dynamics, the exchange suggests that even if professors can overcome certain kinds of differences among students (racial, gender) by focusing on certain kinds of similarities (social, political), those differences may still intervene in ways of which the professors are unaware, and, once they make them conscious, suspicions and resistances may be aroused. Focusing on differences in the classroom can arouse mistrust; downplaying them can result in ignorance and self-deception. But we have also seen that focusing on a particular issue, such as racial politics or cultural studies, can be a way of ignoring other uncomfortable topics. Various strategies for safeguarding ignorance are acted out in the novel as well. Where Irene earlier opted for silence in order to protect herself from knowledge she resists knowing, Hugh protects his self-image by doubting the sincerity and distrusting the motives of the one who would teach him.

Passing continually places us, as readers and learners, in impossible positions. At the end of the novel, Irene must finally face the very real possibility of an affair between her husband, Brian, and Clare. Yet she resists this knowledge and regains her sense of security by convincing herself that the affair is her own fabrication. After all, she has no tangible evidence to support her "unfounded suspicion" so she can assure herself that "she has no real knowledge" (223) and remain secure in her own nonknowledge. If we accept, as Deborah McDowell suggests, that Irene has imagined this affair by projecting her repressed feelings for Clare onto Brian (ix–xxxv), then we risk acquiescing in her ignorance. But if we dismiss her rationalization and accept the affair she shrinks from knowing, we risk being misled by her own earlier suspicions and misperceptions. We seem to be caught again in an impasse between disbelieving in a real affair dismissed as a fabrication and misbelieving in a fabricated affair presented as real. In either case, we are uncomfortably aware that we may have been misled not only *by* Irene, the unreliable narrator, but also *like* Irene. Caught between denial and deception, we come to learn the lesson Irene would teach Hugh: We cannot always rely on tangible evidence or frank disclosures, and our desire for the certainty and security associated with knowledge may cause us to miss the very thing we want to know, a thing that cannot be registered.

However, if this is the lesson *Passing* would teach, we can learn it only by acknowledging Irene's own resistance to knowing, by recognizing her insights as partial and her authority as vulnerable. We can only learn the lesson of *Passing* to the extent that we are willing to learn from an unreliable narrator.

Ironically, Clifford describes precisely this kind of unreliability and the double bind it creates for learners when he discusses Richard Price's ethnographic study of an Afro-American people and the "strategies of ellipsis, concealment, and partial disclosure [that] determine ethnographic relations" (7), and that determine relations between students and teachers in cultural studies classrooms. During his fieldwork with a Maroon society of Suriname, Price learned that the stories told by way of passing on knowledge from one generation to the next were always partial, incomplete, the knower deliberately withholding information. Thus Price's own ethnographic study is fragmentary, "full of holes," as a way of presenting "an inherently imperfect mode of knowledge" (7–8). Far from leading to the despairing conclusion that we can never truly understand other people, an understanding promised by the liberal humanism underlying the traditional literary studies paradigm (see, for example, Easthope 9), Clifford says (quoting Price) that this unreliability "teaches that 'knowledge is power, and that one must never reveal all of what one knows'" (7). I am arguing here that, as cultural studies professors, we need to do more than describe these structures of exchange; we must find ways of putting them into practice in our classrooms.

Passing as Pedagogy

In my course, *Passing* became more than another novel of the Harlem Renaissance; it became a performative pedagogy. In our discussions of this novel, the desire to speak as or for the other was "conspicuously self-enacted" (Herrnstein Smith 117), no longer seen as another's desire or demonstrated through the course content alone. Passing became more than a thematic expression of the racial tensions explored in the novel; it became a metaphor for our positions in the classroom.

To understand the relation of passing to pedagogy—as feminists must in order to participate in a cultural studies program—is to understand the ways in which we are always already passing in the classroom in that the roles we assume are structured by academic conventions, intersubjective exchanges, unconscious desires, and are constantly at risk of being displaced by encounters with others. Easthope makes a similar point in his discussion of a cultural studies pedagogy. In asking "what form of identification and positioning" does a cultural studies model "inscribe for its pedagogic subject" (166), he argues that cultural studies offers a "more dispersed identification" (167) where one's identity is problematized as provisional, not natural. The subject is an effect, not a source, of knowledge, a position, not a presence (ch. 9). All of this sounds familiar to feminists who have promoted a concept of identity in process and analyzed identity as a discursive construction, and what Easthope describes is precisely what passing as pedagogy would act out in the classroom. Simply to affirm this theoretical position in a cultural studies classroom while proceeding to teach as usual, however, is yet another form of passing. A performative pedagogy would do something more, or other, than restating arguments about socially constructed identities. A performative pedagogy would make provisional and vulnerable subject positions part of the dynamics of the classroom exchange, not simply a topic of discussion. Theorizing about positionality is not the same as taking responsibility for the positions that instructors assume and put into play in the classroom, just as passing is not the same for Hugh, no matter how adept he is at talking about it, as it is for Clare and Irene, who actually do it.

Passing as a performative pedagogy, one that brings into play within the classroom the very structures of authority that form the subject of critique, is especially suited to a feminist's position in a cultural studies program. It can enable us to act on, and act out, the very different positionings that are both acknowledged and obviated in cultural studies agendas. Passing in this sense can keep us from confusing the structural position of authority, which historically has been white and male, with the production of knowledge about others. A performative pedagogy seeks to confront the structural silencing of incongruent voices, which is inevitably reproduced whenever we attempt to speak as, or for, the other and to unite various groups in the service of a new cultural politics.

The metaphor of passing figures the condition in which we all find ourselves as members of a classroom and an institution profoundly changed over the past few decades, in part because of efforts to acknowledge diversity, to critique the politics of representing others, and to theorize notions of difference and resistance. If we are all passing in the cultural studies classroom, then we cannot assume in advance that we will come to share certain values or viewpoints, not only because we are all different, but also because the very differences among us are part of the classroom dynamics and have their own performative role to play. Put another way, to the extent that passing informs the resistance, ignorance, and differences that structure classroom dynamics, it puts into question any expectation that teaching will end in a shared understanding or reach some kind of consensus. A performative pedagogy would confront both the ethical appeal and the potential injustice of any effort to establish a collective opposition. Such a pedagogy would discredit any effort to establish a moral and political consensus that did not at the same time provide a mechanism for self-consciously displacing the authority of that position.

But passing entails risks, not the least of which is the risk of being misidentified. When I gave a version of this essay at the President's Forum of the M/MLA Convention in 1991, Gerald Graff, also a member of that panel, quoted my sentence about providing a mechanism for displacing the authority of one's position in support of his teach-the-conflicts model. Yet earlier Graff had angered many feminists when he told us that the way to enact his pedagogy would be to invite feminist-bashers into our classrooms. When Graff quoted me, I felt that he had appropriated my passing metaphor to endorse his own form of passing. My point is not to accuse Graff of passing; my argument throughout has been that passing necessarily figures a professor's position in a cultural studies paradigm. Nor do I mean to criticize Graff for mistaking my position on passing, for passing depends upon the possibility of misidentification. Rather, my use of this incident is performative. My point is to problematize once again any apparent consensus between feminism and cultural studies by reintroducing the very feminist difference that Graff's assumption of my position passes over. Like many men endorsing a cultural studies pedagogy, Graff had ignored the power differential within the university. As a white male and a national spokesman for Teachers for a Democratic Culture, Graff is in a position to invite those who disagree with him into his classroom for open debate. But a feminist and a woman in a university and a society where incidents of racism, sexism, and violence against women are on the increase may be in no position to risk *in the same way* an authority that many of her students and colleagues have never attributed to women or feminism to begin with.

Modleski could be writing about Graff and Clifford when she refers to anthologies (and seminars) that "assume and promote a liberal notion of the formal equality of men and women, whose viewpoints are structurally accorded equal weight . . . [thereby] eliding the question of power asymmetry" (6). A performative pedagogy, such as Modleski endorses, would not simply stage the conflicts; it would empower women and others to represent positions that have always been represented for them. If the shift from literary to cultural studies seeks to rectify "the dominant culture's misrepresentations of workers, women, Afro-Americans, and other 'subaltern' groups," as Brantlinger argues (112), then members of those groups teaching and writing in an institution that has historically marginalized, trivialized, and "conspired to silence" them can more readily bring about a new order than those "already authorized to speak by virtue of their gender" (Modleski 53).

Modleski's argument brings out an important aspect of the performative for feminist teachers in cultural studies programs. A performative act, as Derrida defines it, "produces its own subject, which gives the person the right to do what he [or she] is doing" ("Women in the Beehive" 200). A performative pedagogy would not only self-consciously reproduce the structures of authority it seeks to undermine, but it would also authorize new subject positions. In this way the performative act responds to the double bind that feminists face in cultural studies programs, the fact that our teaching of the power relations inherent in the practices of representing others has not significantly altered the power relations and representation of others in higher education.[8] Given that feminist scholarship and cultural studies both critique the politics of representation and the construction of subjectivity within the dominant culture, it is all the more imperative that feminists force cultural studies to confront directly the disparity in representation within the university itself, from curriculum to personnel. If a cultural studies paradigm replaces hermeneutics ("What does it mean?") with poetics ("How does it work?") (Easthope 43), feminism adds a performative dimension ("What does it do?").

I am not suggesting that feminism is the conscience of cultural studies. I am suggesting that a performative pedagogy can help us to use the double bind to raise questions about how we might proceed in the absence of collective consent and in the face of "genuine evaluative conflict" (Herrnstein Smith 27). By its very definition, a performative pedagogy must be continually reenacted and reinscribed, for each pedagogic situation creates its own dynamics. There is no general performative device, no way for feminists to be sure that appropriation will not occur, no way to guarantee that oppressive structures have been successfully subverted, no way to ensure the audience will (or will not) laugh at the milk cow by Emil Nolde. If this realization leads us to despair of ever fulfilling a cultural studies agenda, it may be because we have not yet learned to face the ways in which cultural studies forces us all into the position of passing. By acting on this insight, feminists can realize the positive potentialities of our own vulnerable positions in a cultural studies program. As Herrnstein Smith writes, "It might be thought there was some communal value to ensuring that all authority was *always* subject to interrogation and *always* at risk" (161). The resistance we feel to giving up the reliability we have long associated with pedagogical authority may well be the measure of the fear of our own displacement.

Notes

I would like to thank Anne Callahan (Loyola University Chicago), Isaiah Smithson, and Nancy Ruff for their help on this essay; portions are excerpted from "Not Entirely Strange . . . Not Entirely Friendly: *Passing* and Pedagogy," *College English,* November 1992. Copyright 1992 by the National Council of Teachers of English. Used with permission.

1. Quotations are from the brochure for "'Degenerate Art': The Fate of the Avant-Garde in Nazi Germany."

2. The term *performative* comes from J. L. Austin's work. In *How to Do Things with Words,* Austin initially distinguishes between two kinds of utterances: "constatives," statements of fact that can be evaluated as true or false, and "performatives," statements in which "the uttering of the sentence is, or is a part of, the doing of an action" (4). The performative cannot be evaluated in terms of its truth or falsity, for the performative is not *about* something but *does* something. It does not refer to some set of circumstances existing prior to or apart from it; rather, it *produces* what it is supposedly about, brings some set of circumstances into existence. The concept of the performative has been borrowed and elaborated by deconstructionists and feminists. See, for example, Butler, Derrida's *Limited Inc.,* Felman's *The Literary Speech Act,* and Modleski.

3. Balsamo cites the collection *Women Take Issue,* by the Women's Studies Group of the Birmingham Centre for Contemporary Cultural Studies, as one of the first books to confront the relationship between feminism and cultural studies. The essays address the absence of women from the Centre's early publications and, more important, "the absence of feminist work and 'woman' from the theoretical frameworks and problematics which animated scholars at the Centre" (52). Balsamo provides an overview of several strands of feminist cultural studies.

4. For a similar critique of *Writing Culture* that focuses on its exclusion of black voices, see bell hooks's *Yearning* (126–31). While others, including Clifford, have noted the exclusion of feminist voices in *Writing Culture,* the "absent presence" of blacks, hooks argues, has not been acknowledged.

5. By suggesting how Clifford's, Smith's, and the curators' methods of presentation fail them as pedagogy, I do not mean to imply that each is doing the same thing. All may be unreliable, but each is unreliable in different ways. Passing takes many forms.

6. The heading plays upon Johnson's title "Rigorous Unreliability" (*A World of Difference,* ch. 2).

7. Fuss and Collins argue that the knowledge acquired by experience is always more convincing than the knowledge derived from reading when teaching African-American literature.

8. See Wallace's "Negative Images: Towards a Black Feminist Cultural Criticism" for an analysis similar to my own and Modleski's but focusing on the exclusion of black women's voices in the academy. Wallace offers a critique of passing (although she does not use the term) in the work of Henry Louis Gates, Jr. Gates writes of the need for men to learn "to speak in the voice of the black mother," thereby appropriating her voice, Wallace says, although she "is powerless to appropriate his 'voice'" (251).

☐ Elder Wisdom: Native American Culture Studies

Lee Francis

Let us begin then with a story. And so, it is said, in the time before, all the People came together for a Great Powwow.[1] There was one sacred drum, and the People sang and danced for a long time. After a while, everyone had heard the thousand thousand songs of the one great drum so often they had memorized them. After a while, some of the People became tired of singing the same songs and decided to do something different. They began to build a great tower so they could see and talk with Grandfather Sky. As the tower got taller and taller and the People climbed higher and higher, they were not able to hear the great drum or the People still singing far below. The People at the bottom of the tower, who had agreed to hold the base and keep it steady for those who were climbing up to see and talk with Grandfather Sky, lost interest and, one by one, began to drift away. Finally, there was no one to hold the tower steady, and it came crashing down.

All the People who had been climbing the tower were dazed and disoriented from their long fall to the ground. The People who had not climbed the tower rushed to help their fallen relatives. They asked them, "Are you hurt?" but the relatives who had fallen could not understand the words. They listened to the great drum and the singers on the ground, but they were able to understand only one or two of the songs. And that is how it came to be that the People were no longer able to understand one another.

The Great Powwow ended with the People leaving and the circle of unity fragmented. Some went east, some south, others west, and the remainder went north. Although they parted to the four directions, they all still carried in their hearts the beat of the great drum, which reminded them of their common link to Mother/Grandmother Earth. After a while, the People of the four directions began to make their own drums, and soon a thousand thousand drums began to beat. As the thousand thousand drums continued to beat, the People remembered themselves and their duties. They remembered that it is important to continue holding onto the tower for the relatives. They remembered, as we do today, that it is important to sing our songs clearly so our relatives who are climbing the tower will not forget their harmonious place in the order of things.[2]

Although the voice of Native People has been glaringly absent from the discourse on culture studies, nonetheless, as the foregoing story points out, it is important for the People to continue singing our songs clearly. For centuries, scholars among the People have addressed the concepts that inhere in culture studies and the institutionalizing of such programs within the academy. Yet, it would seem that non-Natives are woefully ignorant of the scholarly contributions of the People.

Mainstream scholars are able to cite a dozen or more feminist, African-American, and European "authorities" whose thoughts are important to the discussion, and yet there seems to be an intellectual inability to connect the subject of culture studies with the work of Canasatego (Onondaga), Ward E. Churchill (Creek/Cherokee Métis), Vine Deloria, Jr. (Hunkpapa Lakota), Linda Hogan (Chickasaw), Joy Harjo (Creek), N. Scott Momaday (Kiowa), Ohiyesa [Charles A. Eastman] (Santee Dakota), Leslie Marmon Silko (Laguna Pueblo), Tekahionwake [E. Pauline Johnson] (Mohawk), Henrietta V. Whiteman (Cheyenne), and James Welch (Blackfeet/Gros Ventre). These and other Native Americans have been writing in English for more than two centuries. That the editors of this volume have taken particular care in extending an invitation to a scholar of the People to participate in the conversation is noteworthy because it is the essence of what distinguishes culture studies from the ethnic studies programs of the 1970s and early 1980s. But will non-Native relatives hear and understand what the scholars and elders of the People have been saying for centuries?

Here There Be Indians

Native People of the sovereign nations have long practice at the art of institutionalized culture studies.[3] The most succinct response promoting culture studies came from Canasatego, an Onondaga elder of the sovereign Six Nations.[4] He responded June 18, 1744, on behalf of the elders whom the commissioners from Maryland and Virginia invited to send their boys to William and Mary College.

> We know that you highly esteem the kind of learning taught in those Colleges; and that the Maintenance of our young Men, while

with you, would be very expensive to you. We are convinced, that you mean to do us Good by your Proposal; and we thank you heartily. But you, who are wise must know that different Nations have different Conceptions of things and you will therefore not take it amiss, if our Ideas of this kind of Education happen not to be the same as yours. We have had some Experience of it. Several of our young People were formerly brought up at the Colleges of the Northern Provinces: they were instructed in all your Sciences; but, when they came back to us, they were bad Runners, ignorant of every means of living in the wood . . . neither fit for Hunters, Warriors, nor Counsellors, they were totally good for nothing.

We are, however, not the less oblig'd by your kind Offer, tho' we decline accepting it; and, to show our grateful Sense of it, if the Gentlemen of Virginia will send us a Dozen of their Sons, we will take Care of their Education, instruct them in all we know, and make Men of them. (Drake 270)[5]

Some two hundred years later, in 1978, Patricia Locke (Mississippi Band Chippewa/Hunkpapa Lakota), the former president of the National Indian Education Association, strongly restates the sentiments of the Haudenausaunee elders: "It is important that the child learns dual cultures and multi-cultures from the fourth grade onward. . . . But great care should be taken so that the student does not walk a path that will cause him to fall over the brink into complete acculturation and assimilation" (105). Although the People have strongly advocated culture studies for centuries, our non-Native colleagues in academe have only latterly begun to address the concepts put forth by Native thinkers.

One scholar at the forefront of the debate is Patrick Brantlinger, who discloses that "more than anyone else's, [Raymond] Williams's influence is evident" (ix). While for Williams the notion of cultural analysis as the vehicle for investigating "our common life together" was somehow new (ix), the People have long contemplated and debated the social and cultural significance of ideas and practices that impinged on the People and all our relations. The following is a small sample of the thoughtful cultural commentaries expressed by the People across the North American continent over many decades.

> Cultural values vary from group to group and there is no way under the sun that these variations can be swept away in the interests of administrative neatness. Let us accept that diversity exists and let each group capitalize on its own cultural heritage as it sees fit. (Dillon Platero, Navajo, 49)

I believe there are no people of any colour on this earth who do not believe in the Great Spirit—in rewards, and in punishments. We worship him, but we worship him not as you do. We differ from you in appearance and manners as well as in our customs, and we differ from you in our religion. (Petalseharo, Skidi Pawnee, 81)

We ... bear a responsibility to that place, to the community of earth and language that has formed us. When we write we inadvertently tell who we are and where we come from. We also know our histories and tell even the most painful but true parts, because after all, these are a part of us too. (Joy Harjo, 44)

Civilized people depend too much on man-made printed pages. ... the Great Spirit has provided you and me with an opportunity for study in nature's university, the forests, the rivers, the mountains, and the animals which include us. (Tatanga Mani [Walking Buffalo], Stoney, 106)

Contrary to popular belief, education—the transmission and acquisition of knowledge and skills—did not come to the North American continent on the Nina, Pinta and Santa Maria. Education is as native to this continent as its Native people. We Native Americans have educated our youth through a rich oral tradition, which was—and is yet today—transmitted by the elder of the tribe. (Henrietta V. Whiteman, 105)

Native American literature, like the life and culture of which it is a part, is immeasurable centuries old—perhaps 30,000 years or more ... and its roots are deep in the land—too deep, I would venture to say, for a mere five centuries of European influence to upturn in any lasting, complete and irrevocable way. (Geary Hobson, Cherokee/Chickasaw, 2)

Admittedly, these commentaries are only brief glimpses into the ongoing conversation concerning culture studies among the People. However, I would posit that if "intellectual work cannot and should not stop at the borders of single texts, single historical problems or controversies, or single disciplines," and, further, that if it is true that "the connections of texts and histories with our own lives and experiences must be recognized and become part of what we analyze" (Brantlinger ix), then it follows that no serious advocate of culture studies can legitimately ignore, discount, or dismiss the People's collective and individual experiences and analyses.[6] As Churchill says, "No American theory can write the Indian off as irrelevant; the Indian's is the first vision in this hemisphere, not only as a matter of chronological fact, but because the Indian experience was and remains formative to this society's psychological character" (11). Brantlinger cites the following as the "main" lesson: "In order to understand ourselves, the discourses of 'the Other'—of all the others—is that which we most urgently need to hear" (3). He then quotes from or refers to the works and thoughts of Europeans, African Americans, and feminists; out of two hundred and twelve pages, Brantlinger devotes a single passage to Native Americans. Evidently, for Brantlinger, "all of the others" does not include the contributions of the People. Of course, his indifference to the reality of "Here There Be Indians" is an attitude with which the People of the Sovereign American Indian Nations and Tribes are very familiar after five hundred years. The cliché "white man speak with forked tongue" is as relevant in the 1990s as it was in the 1490s.

What culture studies offers, from the perspective of the People, is a format for hearing the voices of *all* the others, including Brantlinger's, in order to understand ourselves as individuals and in "our common life" (Brantlinger ix). Moreover, it is also critically important for scholars among the People to sing our songs, admonish, and specifically point out what occurs when we accept the "Not in My Back Yard" (NIMBY) canon[7] which, by my definition, is welded to the politics of exclusion.

NIMBY: The Politics of Exclusion

Culture studies in the United States has been a way to address a perceived crisis in the humanities; much of it originated out of the Marxist paradigm that developed out of the Anglo response to the racist, classist British society of the 1960s. Our difficulty in the United States lies in taking this Anglo-Marxist-flavored concept and, like Cinderella's shoe, making it fit the ugly stepson's foot. Vine Deloria, Jr., a scholar and humorist, discusses Marxism and its relationship to a Native worldview and points out that "American Indians and other tribal peoples ... reject a universal concept of brotherhood in favor of respectful treatment of human beings with whom they have contact. It is not necessary, they argue, that crows should be eagles. Both Marxists and Christians should heed that insight since in attempting to transform the world into eagles they have merely produced vultures" (136).

One such vulture was the ill-fated ethnic studies programs and departments produced in the 1960s in universities throughout the United States. Their history offers an important caution to modern culture studies. Ethnic studies flourished in a grand spirit of intellectual unity among disempowered Native People, African Americans, Asian Americans, and Chicano Americans. It flourished in a time when we were filled with the idealism of youth. We were certain that our elders' values, attitudes, and beliefs were wrong. We wanted a better world. We wanted peace and harmony. We wanted to transform the world into eagles.

The first confrontation occurred at the University of California at Berkeley following the passage of the landmark Civil Rights Act of 1964. Activist students began signing up other students to go to Selma, Alabama, to register black people to vote. The chancellor of the university, with the complete concurrence of then-Governor Ronald Reagan, autocratically informed the students that the university would not tolerate their actions on state property (i.e., the campus). In what was to become known as the free speech movement, the struggle of good against evil found its home at an entrance to the Berkeley campus, Sather Gate. It was the dawning of the Age of Aquarius, and we knew what was wrong with this nation. It was racism. It was the hypocrisy of "do as I say, not as I do." It was lack of economic power for the deserving poor underclass. Our rallying cry became "power to the people."

The movement was initially led by student members of the Black Student Union on campuses across the United States who exhorted the rest of us to join in the battle. Coalitions and collectives became the order of the day. Chicano and Chicana students and allied faculty linked arms with their black brothers and sisters. In addition to the Black Student Union and Black Panthers, we had La Raza Unida (the Race United), Brown Berets, and the American Indian Movement (AIM). Our heroes and leaders were Abbie Hoffman and Mario Savio, Martin Luther King and Angela Davis, Dennis Banks (Chippewa) and Russell Means (Lakota), Corky Gonzales and Ries Lopez Tijerina, Chairman Mao and Al Wong. Black power, brown power, yellow power, and red power joined together.

United in purpose, we jubilantly opened Pandora's box. We proceeded to riot for educational opportunity, economic equality, peace, and justice at San Francisco State University, Berkeley, and Kent State. We protested and demonstrated at Oberlin, Yale, Princeton, and Dartmouth. We demanded open admission policies at universities so that anyone who chose—not just privileged, elite white Americans—could go to college and get a piece of the proverbial American pie. In the name of equality, we demanded that no one be rejected simply because of poor academic preparation or lack of money for tuition and books. We demanded special programs, and university after university across the country acceded.

In the wake of our unified protests, demonstrations, and riots came the Educational Opportunity Program and ethnic studies in 1968. Here was proof, so we thought at the time, that we could, indeed, transform the world into eagles. The Marxist paradigm, as we understood it, served as the basis around which we built our new Camelot. All power and authority was vested in the people of the community. Activists from the particular ethnocultural communities were hired to teach the smorgasbord of courses offered by their respective programs. Only activist leaders who had been approved by their community outside the university and students within the university were appointed as chairs of the respective programs. Faculty meetings held without students and members of the community present were denounced, and faculty attending such meetings were vilified and shunned.

Within five years, however, the internecine wars began, as activists qua administrators were faced with budgetary cutbacks. We began to fight among ourselves about who deserved more or less of the reduced resources. I recall too many meetings where competition and exclusion rather than collaboration ruled. The Marxist paradigm was crumbling, but we were enamored with our vision of turning the world into eagles. We failed to notice that the crow had become a vulture.

As internal unity began to fragment, the united front presented to the world outside ethnic studies also came under assault with the legitimate call of the women's movement for women's studies programs.[8] Within the university community, women students and faculty rightly demanded that their contributions in the sciences, arts, and literature be incorporated within the curriculum. In the interests of administrative neatness, their demands were met by the creation of women's studies programs on campuses throughout the country. Initially, all women, regardless of ethnocultural background, were included in the movement, and all women were said to be equal. Sadly, like their colleagues in ethnic studies, it soon became apparent that white women had become more equal than their sisters who were not white. Same song, second verse; instead of an eagle, another vulture was produced.

Concurrently, there were "serious scholars" suspicious of the massive social upheaval.[9] Like their ethnic studies colleagues, they looked to Mother England for a solution and found it in Marx. The solution was imported and named "American studies." American studies, it was hoped, would solve the problems of both turf and academic "rigor." In response to the perceived floundering of ethnocultural and gender-specific programs, with their community-based, untrained (i.e., nondegreed) instructors, the "serious scholars" envisioned American studies as the embodiment of universal brother-and-sisterhood within the walls of the academy. Junior instructors, under stringent supervision by senior professors from the "real" disciplines, would teach Americans about America. The idea was to create an academically "rigorous" discipline that incorporated the ideals of Marxism without bowing to the will of the community and student activists. Another vulture.

Scholars of color (tenure-track and tenured) in the late 1970s and early 1980s understood full well that "real scholars" viewed those teaching in ethnic, women's, and American studies as intellectual lightweights with questionable academic credentials; this brought an escalation to the fragmentation. Overtly "personing" the barricades, scholars of color hotly defended the legitimacy of their respective programs within the institution. African-American scholars reasonably argued that their special scholarship required that the (then) black studies programs become departments in their own right. (Their most convincing argument was full-time equivalent.) A number of universities bowed to "reason" and raised (now) African-American studies to departmental rank. Covertly, these same articulate scholars of color set about negotiating appointments in the "real disciplines" of English, history, sociology, anthropology, and psychology. Each had his or her own special intellectual agenda centered on gender, ethnocultural politics, or both. Any who opposed were shouted down because of their obvious racist values, attitudes, and beliefs. More fragmentation. More vultures.

In the 1990s, the rhetoric implicit in the NIMBY canon continues in the academy. For example, in a 1992 article in the *Chronicle of Higher Education,* Patricia Mainardi, a professor of art history, "[supports] the new scholarship, which focuses on politics and gender rather than the formal properties of a work of art," while, in the same piece, Samuel Y. Edgerton, Jr., also a professor of art history, declares that "we've become an advocacy group for marginals who want to be part of the power structure" ("College Art Association" A9). To enter this debate, one need only substitute "English" or "literature" for "art history" and carve out a slice of intellectual territory to defend against all challengers. Also important is the ability to hurl such epithets as "sloppy scholarship," "marginals," "intellectual fraud," and "racist polemics" at those who would question or cast aspersions on one's vaunted scholarship.

What is distinctive about this decades-long academic debate is that elder wisdom has been ignored, dismissed, discounted, marginalized, or—as to be expected from scholars—footnoted. Perhaps the unwillingness to apply the elder wisdom of the People stems from the fact that when the original premise—an assertion of superiority and exclusion—is false, all that proceeds from it is false. As Deloria points out,

> Although the Christian church has long since abandoned its role as educator in favor of the state, the underlying assumptions by which the Western state now engages in universal education at the primary and secondary levels are identical to both ancient ecclesiastical goals and more modern desires to create a responsible citizenship.

> ... American Indians have continually rejected the Western educational format all the while insisting that their children receive an education which enables them to understand whites and compete successfully with them in the social, political and economic realms.... Unfortunately, but predictably, American society has responded to Indian educational demands by attempting to change Indian social and cultural patterns—revealing that American education is a socializing process, not one that imparts insights and information about the world. (129–30)

The elders among the People have long considered this issue. For example, in 1785 Corn Tassel (Cherokee) declared,

> much has been advanced on the want of what you term civilization among the Indians; and many proposals have been made to us to adopt your laws, your religion, your manners and your customs. But, we confess that we do not yet see the propriety, or practicability of such a reformation, and should be better pleased with beholding the good effect of these doctrines in your own practices than with hearing you talk about them, or reading your papers to us upon such subjects.
>
> You say: Why do not the Indians till the ground and live as we do? May we not, with equal propriety ask, Why the white people do not hunt and live as we do? (154–55)

In 1828, in a speech delivered to the U.S. Senate, Sagoyewatha (Seneca)[10] pointed out:

> You say that you are sent to instruct us how to worship the Great Spirit agreeably to his mind; and if we do not take hold of the religion which you white people teach, we shall be unhappy hereafter.... We understand that your religion is written in a book. If it was intended for us as well as for you, why has not the Great Spirit given it to us; and not only to us, but why did he not give to our forefathers the knowledge of that book, with the means of understanding it rightly?...
>
> We are told that your religion was given to your forefathers, and has been handed down from father to son. We also have a religion which was given to our forefathers, and has been handed down to us their children. We worship that way. It teacheth us to be thankful for all the favors we receive, to love each other, and to be united. (69–70)

The foregoing passages emphasizing mutual cultural respect are only a brief sample of the efforts by the elders of the People over a period spanning several centuries to advise their intellectually younger non-Native relatives concerning the erroneous premises that right-thinking originated with Europeans and that education should be exclusionary.

In the 1990s, we again exhort. All theories and practices predicated on the politics of exclusion implicit in the NIMBY canon—regardless of one's gender, ethnocultural background, or sociopolitical perspective—inevitably bring fragmentation and vultures. Accept the fact that everything, both seen and unseen, is connected. Celebrate and honor diversity of thought instead of excluding that which does not fit the model of reason. Remove the cultural blinders and walk in another's moccasins as the People have done (and continue to do). Take that experience and analyze it within the context of our common life together, including all that is seen and unseen. That is the culture studies which the elders of the People have long advocated. Culture studies must transcend the ocean of confusion—reject the NIMBY canon's politics of exclusion in which it has become engulfed—if it is to avoid becoming simply another, albeit noble, vulture. Annette Arkeketa West (Otoe/Creek), referring to her "daughter's confusion," addresses the issue of cultural education:

> she flees the books
> laid before her
> the telling of words
> a teacher takes for
> granted at the jr. high
>
> and she will fail
> because in our home
> we speak
> the color
> of the
> heart.
>
> (275)

From the time before time, the People continue to "speak the color of the heart," and the heart is the last place our non-Native relatives look to find understanding. How is it possible not to hear the heart of our mother the Earth? Is there a place for the heart, the Good Red Road, in culture studies?

Singing Our Songs

The 1.8 million sovereign people of the more than five hundred distinct nations and tribes that survive into the twenty-first century and live on what we call Turtle Island (i.e., the North American continent) continue to be actively engaged in the conversation related to culture studies. The oral (pre-1490 to the present) and written (post-1500 to the present) literature of the People on the subject of culture studies is extensive. Much of it revolves around hearing and understanding the voices of all as a method for gaining a clearer understanding of our harmonious place in the order of creation.

Among the People, both cultural similarities and differences continue to be examined in the process of actively seeking to understand the voices of the Others among the diverse nations and tribes. This endeavor to gain a clearer understanding of ourselves in our common life and of our harmonious place in the order of creation—which I would like to identify as culture studies—began among the People more than five centuries ago. In identifying similarities, the People found that they held (and continue to hold) in common a number of values, attitudes, and beliefs, including inextricable linking of theory and praxis, respect for elders, reverence for the Earth our Mother, and observation of the sacred directions. These similarities are honored and celebrated. The People of the respective nations and tribes know their treaties, their traditional friends, and their enemies. Above all, the People respect one another's language, customs, and social structures. For the People, a crow is not required to become an eagle.

Among the People, understanding our respective place within the interconnecting web of creation is a fundamentally important experience. Including non-Native relatives within this framework is equally important. We must, as we have for centuries, continue to explore, think about, and discuss the interwoven web of ideas and actions of both our non-Native relatives and the People to gain a clearer understanding of our common life and collective harmonious place in the order of creation. Although there is much in non-Native culture to honor and celebrate, a fundamental question is why our non-Native relatives refuse to learn about the mind-heart ways of the People, or of any other people for that matter. The concept of intellectual reciprocity seems to be alien to a majority of our non-Native relatives. It would seem that, in their view, the only view is their view. The only important thoughts are their thoughts. The only important conversations are the ones they have with each another. The only profound philosophy is the philosophy they invented to explain their view of reality. This goes beyond insensitivity. It is the bedrock of a dangerous intellectual myopia embodied in the NIMBY politics of exclusion. Out of this myopia can come only such social chaos that the recent South Central Los Angeles devastation and horror will be prosaic by comparison.

Understanding our interconnectedness emerges, partially, through critically thinking about others and experiencing the world through their eyes. This entails, at the very least, reading the extensive literature written by the People. In our conversation and teaching, we must be as comfortable with the works of Deloria, Silko, Gloria Anzaldua (Chicana American), Mario Barrera (Chicano American), Langston Hughes (African American), Zora Hurston (African American), Betty Bao Lord (Chinese American), and Ronald T. Takaki (Japanese American), as with those of Jacques Derrida, Michel Foucault, Paulo Freire, Karl Marx, and Williams. We must each sing our songs and sing the songs of our relatives. Continuing to divide and conquer the world of ideas into small, disconnected slices without experiencing the world through the eyes of relatives who do not share our ethnocultural perspective or gender will prevent us from gaining the necessary understanding of the interrelatedness of all that is seen and unseen.

Conversely, discovering the intricate patterns, the weavings, the interrelationships that connect all human beings, will enable us to move beyond our current cultural and color-blind groping. To do this, culture studies must be about celebrating and honoring differences as well as similarities. The People have always attempted to respect and honor the mind-ways of our non-Native relatives. Culture studies can be a viable dynamic within the university; it will, I hope, enable our non-Native relatives to hear, understand, respect, celebrate, and honor the mind-ways of the People.

Of importance to the People are issues such as how culture studies is to be implemented and integrated into the university curricula and which departments will oversee it. Also of concern is who and what criteria will determine the pedagogy. Who will teach? Will the sciences incorporate Native sciences? Will mathematics courses base their paradigms on the mathematical paradigms of Native People? Critically important is whether all cultures will be under the microscope, or only the cultures of people of color. The manner in which these and a host of other theoretical and practical issues are addressed will be discussed among the People at length. However, given the paucity of Native People who are academic deans and vice presidents within the current university structure nationwide, it is doubtful that the voice of the People will be heard, much less acted upon, with anything more than lip-service. Once again, an elder of the People has addressed the issue. T'du-u-eh-t'sah, a Laguna Pueblo/Chippewa woman elder tells us, "There is a sense of something missing in the world today . . . at least in my world . . . and it is very hard to understand exactly what it is. So what to do about it? Try and find as many souls as one can that see through the blinders with which we are all being equipped free for nothing."[11]

Thus, I sing the songs of the People in the hope that my voice will add to the conversation. It is my duty and responsibility to sing, to remind my relatives that all is connected, woven together. And I speak the "color of the heart" because reason informs the People that, without the heart, the mind cannot survive.

Notes

1. The use of "And so . . . ," "the People," and "powwow" requires comment. All stories in the Laguna Pueblo tradition begin with "Hu-em-eh ha-ah" (And so). Not to follow the form would be much like failing to follow the rules for writing a classical Italian or Shakespearian sonnet. Throughout this essay, I will use the word *People* whenever I refer to the Native American people of the sovereign nations, tribes, bands, villages, pueblos, rancherias, and communities. People with a capital *P* is how we refer to ourselves in our respective languages. For example, in my "Keresian" (dominator culture's term) language, we call ourselves "Hano," which loosely translated means "the People." A powwow is a recent phenomenon that has its origins in the soldier-warrior societies of the People before the 1800s. With the advent of the so-called Ghost Dance religion and the horror of the Chief Big Foot Massacre (known among non-Native Americans as "Wounded Knee"), the outward form changed to avoid non-Native reprisal.

2. Storytelling has always been one of the ways among the People respectfully to point out universal truths that the hearer as well as the speaker would be wise to apply to their thinking on a particular matter. For myself, then, I apply the story by entering the conversation concerning culture studies although it is not a conversation in which I am eager to engage. However, I am fully cognizant of the importance of the task.

3. Jerome Buckanaga (Minnesota Chippewa) points out that "several hundred years of history and a substantial body of law (5,000 statutes, 2,200 regulations, 389 treaties, 2000 federal court decisions, and 500 opinions of the Attorney General) have defined the unique [sovereign] status of Indians and Indian tribes in this society" (65).

4. The Six Nations (the Haudenausaunee or Iroquois Confederacy) first came to the notice of Europeans around the fifteenth century. Oral tradition among the People places the founding around 950 B.C. The Haudenausaunee is comprised of the Elder Relations (the Onondaga [Many Hill Nation], the Mohawk/Ka-nin-ke-a-ka [People of the Flint], and the Seneca) and the Younger Relations (the Oneida [People of the Standing Stone], the Cayuga [People of the Pipe], and the Tuscarora, who were adopted in the eighteenth century).

5. Cheeshatemauck (Massachuset) was the first from a sovereign nation to attend and graduate from Harvard. He graduated in 1666 (Hodge 240).

6. For the People, everything is connected. The relationships of all that is seen and unseen are extensively discussed by Vine Deloria, Jr., in "Circling the Same Old Rock," *Marxism and Native Americans,* 113–36.

7. NIMBY, an appropriate acronym in current usage outside the walls of the academy, captures the essence of the politics of polarization currently taking place within those walls.

8. Many in the women's movement consider "Women, Culture, and Society: A Theoretical Overview," by Michelle Rosaldo to be the match that ignited the torch.

9. Those of the dominator culture are always "serious scholars" by virtue of their ethnocultural status. Everyone else must "earn" his or her way into the "real" disciplines of English, history, and the "hard" sciences.

10. Known among the Europeans as "Red Jacket," Sagoyewatha was born around 1752 and died January 20, 1830. A respected leader of the Seneca, he was a superb orator.

11. T'du-u-eh-t'sah, who died at the age of seventy-five, was my mother, and her wisdom and strength is missed. Of her five children, two hold Ph.D. degrees (one in American studies, the other in higher education and social change), one a diplomate (M.F.A.) in piano and voice, one a B.A. in arts administration, and one a B.A. in business.

☐ Griots, Bluesicians, Dues-Payers, and Pedagogues: An African-American, Autobiographical, 1960s' View of Culture Studies

Eugene B. Redmond

> We have elevated struggle to the level of fine art.
> —Harold Washington, Chicago, 1986

The scroll unfolding before you documents the first institutionalized study of black culture in higher education in the 1960s and offers some observations on the institutionalized study of black culture during the 1990s. Herein is a narrative of creativity, spirit, and struggle in collaboration with, and sometimes in spite of, the institution. Establishing the institutional mother-bases from which to launch social change via literary arts, scholarly research, and cultural activism has been the main concern of many black community organizers and academicians since the 1960s. These leaders have maintained a balance between their residential and their institutional communities. To paraphrase our nineteenth-century ancestors, "We got one mind for ourselves and one for the overseer."

We in the multifarious struggle have always had our "work cut out for us," as the elders used to say of themselves and of the children who grew up during the 1940s and 1950s. This was true whether we peered down long rows of okra, strawberries, or corn; encountered books, lists to be memorized, or freedom marchers; or dealt with trees awaiting protective whitewash, uncut firewood, piles of coal, railroad ties, dirty clothes, unploughed fields, unpainted outhouses, uncleaned fish, hostile rednecks, picket lines, or church chores.

We have also had our work cut out for us during these long decades of cultural, literary, institutional, and community activism—cut out for us whether we were poets, novelists, essayists, rappers, playwrights, orators, professors, pamphleteers, administrators, cultural architects, coaches, unionists, agitprops, activists, students, preachers, soothsayers, counselors, soul doctors, therapists, healers, readers, ideologues, or simply anonymous nurturers. When one is committed to creating theories, strategies, battle plans, programs, centers, literatures, curricula, identities, or rationales for redirecting targeted institutions, there is always struggle.[1]

Black Culture during the 1960s—In the Streets

A Change Is Gonna Come.
—Sam Cooke, 1960

Now the largest black municipality in the United States, East St. Louis, Illinois, was—during my childhood years of the 1940s and 1950s—a teeming river town of about eighty-five thousand African Americans, Poles, Jews, Armenians, Greeks, Italians, and Irish (with a Mexican "minority"). Separated from St. Louis, Missouri, by the Mississippi River, East St. Louis's cacophonous mosaic included heavily trafficked bridges, as well as railroad yards (the second largest after Chicago), packinghouses, blues, steel mills, night clubs, glass factories, hustlers, chemical plants, jazz, lumber yards, numbers racketeers, fundamentalist churches, gospel, a red-light district called the "Valley," the rattle of slot-machines, ominous convoys of underworld limousines, and sporadic bursts of gunfire at night.

During the mid-1950s, I attended East St. Louis's Lincoln Senior High School, whose distinguished alumni include Miles Davis; Donald McHenry, who became ambassador to the United Nations; Barbara Ann Teer, an actress, dancer, and, later, founder and director of the National Black Theater of Harlem; Leon Thomas, an actor and singer who toured with the Count Basie Band in the early 1960s; Harry Edwards, a champion athlete, leader of the 1968 black Olympic boycott, pioneer of the new discipline of the sociology of sports, and a professor of sociology at the University of California at Berkeley; and James Rosser, president of California State University at Los Angeles. The East St. Louis jazz and blues sound was already known around the world through such artists as Miles Davis and Josephine Baker. Ike and Tina Turner, who played several talent shows during my senior year at Lincoln High, were woodshedding at the Manhattan Club in East St. Louis before ascending the national stage. (The Olympian Jackie Joyner-Kersee would not emerge from this river-town cultural matrix until the 1980s.)

When I finished three years of service in the Marine Corps in the early 1960s, I returned to East St. Louis to get a degree in English at Southern Illinois University, join comrades in the civil rights crusade, undergo my apprenticeship as a "great American novelist," and—from 1963 to 1969—report on and editorialize about new cultural, political, and racial revolutions—including East St. Louis's violent rebellions of 1967—from my post as executive editor of the *East St. Louis Monitor*, a "Movement"-born community newspaper.

The 1960s was not a monolithic decade. There were several 1960s in which many meaningful skirmishes occurred on many different levels. At the forward point of this protracted war were the cultural-activist units of the National Association for the Advancement of Colored People (NAACP), Congress of Racial Equality (CORE), Urban League, Southern Christian Leadership Conference, public schools, community colleges, universities, unions, churches, community associations (including new nationalist groups such as the Black Muslims, Black Panthers, and US) and, later, reformed street gangs. There were also scores of new white revolutionary groups operating both above and below ground: Weathermen, White Panthers, and Students for a Democratic Society (SDS), as well as socialists, communists, and the plethora of splinter groups of both the left and the right. By the mid-1960s, cultural and political activism—the Movement—was integral to everyday life in East St. Louis and throughout other U.S. metropolitan areas.

The Movement's most famous success of the period was the March on Washington for Jobs and Freedom in August 1963. We community and college editors and reporters who attended the march filed stories on the event when we returned to our newspapers. Special emphases were often placed on southern black folk culture and its enormous influence upon the civil rights orators and spokespersons, as well as on the entertainers and organizers who participated in the march. We also strung stories and anecdotes to numerous Negro weeklies and alternative presses that could not afford to send writers to Washington or purchase wire services. Such ventures, undertaken by hundreds of small presses and underground publishers and editors, laid the groundwork for later campus-residential collaboratives that became central (indispensable, really) to the Movement.

Locally, we (students, teachers, street activists, leaders, budding poets, novelists, and playwrights) plunged into the struggle, fighting racism, discrimination, sexism, war, poverty, illiteracy, voter apathy, school segregation, racial red-lining of black neighborhoods (i.e., coding them for steeper prices on foods, gas, credit, and homes), and insidious race-baiting by unscrupulous realtors. This latter practice led to the now-famous "flight of the whites," a phenomenon that ultimately created a predominantly black inner city in East St. Louis and in urban areas throughout the United States. We "integrated" public facilities, especially the "public" Jones Park Swimming Pool; downtown department store lunch counters; the Majestic Theater; and restaurants and bars near the university's East St. Louis and Alton campuses. Through picketing and sit-ins, we helped secure jobs for blacks in banks and city government, and at Bell Telephone and the utility companies. In the early sixties, East St. Louis was a simmering—not melting—pot of races, students, veterans, poets, actors, activists, and social philosophers.

In the black community, we read and performed required European, biblical, and mainstream American texts. But during Negro History Week—and from street historians and race philosophers—we learned of such African Americans as Frederick Douglass, Sojourner Truth, Carter G. Woodson (the father of Negro History Week and Black History Month), W. E. B. Du Bois, Langston Hughes, Richard Wright, Zora Neale Hurston, Paul Robeson, Mary McLeod Bethune, and James Weldon Johnson. Popular figures like Duke Ellington, Billie Holiday, Cab Calloway, Lena Horne, Sidney Portier, Louis Armstrong, Ella Fitzgerald, and Billy Eckstine were flashed to us via *Ebony, Jet,* the Negro weeklies, radio, television, and movie shorts.

Pursuing these means and media, we were unknowingly performing at least four tasks. We were arming ourselves with cultural and intellectual weapons historically needed for defense against suspicion, doubt, and often venomous allegations and falsifications regarding black humanity. We were establishing contact points for the cultural and intellectual integration of African-American and European-American thought and expression. We were preparing for the race- and gender-baiting responses to the civil rights movement, the black consciousness movement (including the demand for black studies), the women's liberation movement, and the multicultural revolution. And, finally, we were simultaneously recovering, creating, recording, and living black culture.

Black Culture during the 1960s—In College Classrooms

Say It Loud: I'm Black and I'm Proud!
—James Brown, 1968

Until the mid-1960s, U.S. colleges and universities had only patronizingly absorbed aspects of the Movement, primarily in the form of ad hoc or extracurricular appendages: teach-ins, festivals, concerts, visiting lecturers, begrudging honorary degrees, and often questionable studies of poverty, racism, and oppression. Black cultural forms, or "race arts"— blues, gospel, jazz, speech, and folklore—inundated white culture directly through Duke Ellington, Moms Mabley, Willie Mae Ford, Chubby Checker, Sam Cooke, Big Mama Thornton, Fats Domino, Ella Fitzgerald, Ray Charles, Miles Davis, James Brown, and rhythm and blues; or indirectly by way of imitators like Stan Kenton, Frank Sinatra, Julie London, Benny Goodman, Elvis Presley, and rock and roll. But liberal-to-radical professors, administrators, writers, and students spoke almost always in the tone of Big Brother or Big Sister. It was, after all, thought best that blacks and other disenfranchised citizens should ape the ways of the Establishment—get a piece of the rock by integrating into the mainstream and becoming oblivious, by becoming invisible, and, hence, "no problem." Except for a few instances in which a course or unit in black culture was offered at a historically black college, too little systematic thought was given to the teaching of black studies.[2] But another civil rights storm was brewing, and it blew us from integration to black power.

During the early stages of the black studies movement, an offshoot of the black power movement, students, faculty, and other people as well occupied buildings on various campuses; issued demands (such as establishing black studies programs, admitting more black students and faculty, developing stronger black presences in campus cultural life, and setting up comprehensive plans to help students complete degrees); and then hunkered down for the tense vigil preceding the negotiations. The storms of occupations, demands, and negotiations left few institutions of higher learning untouched. Like the women's and multiethnic movements it spawned, black studies was conceived as an intergenerational, campus-community cooperative, often dependent on friends or kindred spirits already safely positioned within the institution. (Someone had to be an intermediary between the old bureaucracies and the new ones when the dust cleared and the din quieted.) At the same time, no two black or women's studies programs, centers, projects, or courses were the same. The black studies movement, like the decade that helped shape it, was not a simple, mass-produced, replicated phenomena (see Karenga).

Notable among the events of the late 1960s and early 1970s were the twin thrusts of black power and black arts. Black studies actually started in the streets, with cultural and political activists boning up on their culture and history in newly developing cells of the Movement. Many activists during the 1960s were also theoreticians, scholars, poets, novelists, and playwrights who had been trained by such race men and women as Sterling Brown, John Henrik Clarke, Melvin Tolson, J. Saunders Redding, Margaret Burroughs, Du Bois, Hughes, and Bethune. At the same time, several new books, including Arna Bontemp's *American Negro Poetry,* LeRoi Jones's *Blues People,* Kenneth Clarke's *Dark Ghetto,* Ralph Ellison's *Shadow and Act,* Harold Cruse's *The Crisis of the Negro Intellectual,* James Baldwin's *Nobody Knows My Name* and *The Fire Next Time,* Lorraine Hansberry's *A Raisin in the Sun,* and LeRoi Jones and Larry Neal's *Black Fire* placed the issues of black freedom and struggle in cultural, literary, and ideological contexts.

The backbone of the civil rights movement, which included the prison population, student activists, and unemployed black youth, was quickly being politicized, "blackened," and polarized by white racism, Malcolm X, the Black Panthers, CORE, the Black Muslims, any number of grassroots or campus black collectives, and the Student Non-Violent Coordinating Committee (SNCC), with its cry, attributed to Stokley Carmichael, of "Umgowah! Black Power!" Many high school and college campuses had Black Panther, SNCC, CORE, or NAACP youth chapters and regularly received *Muhammad Speaks,* the Black Panther paper, and any of the endless new underground, "revolutionary" publications. African history, African leaders, African place names, African literature, African clothing, African jewelry, and African dreams were dominant themes in this new saga of return to the black self. Hence, black studies rode into college and university campuses on the back of a separatist movement that rebelled against racism, patronizing liberalism, cultural arrogance, and white hegemony.

As the civil rights movement got "blacker," intellectuals, artists, cultural workers, and organizers began looking to black and third world indigenous sources for explanations and justifications of black power, black art, and black studies. Malcolm X, of course, was on the ideological cutting edge of the new movement, along with such people as Frantz Fanon (*Black Skin, White Masks*), Carmichael (now Kwame Touré), H. Rap Brown, Huey Newton, Angela Davis, Che Guevera, Nathan Hare (who founded black studies at San Francisco State College), LeRoi Jones (now Amiri Baraka), and, of course, Martin Luther King, Jr.

Unlike the Harlem Renaissance of the 1920s and 1930s, which was centered in New York City, artists and activists of the 1960s operated throughout the country. Also unlike the intellectual, artistic, and social movements of the 1920s, the new black arts renaissance of the 1960s had stronger, more tangible international connections through its back-to-Africa components.[3] Indeed, black power—thanks to Malcolm X's life and death, the fiery messages of Brown and Carmichael and their regional surrogates, and the grief and rage following the assassinations of King and many lesser-known leaders—had captured the imagination of a broad spectrum of the black (and nonblack) population throughout the world.

Among those at the forefront of black power were the Black Panthers and US. The Panthers, in addition to conducting free breakfast programs for children, staging political education clinics, and marketing the *Black Panther Newspaper,* often appeared in public bearing arms. They also engaged in highly publicized shoot-outs with the police. US, on the other hand, assumed a stealthier posture, usually concealing weapons and operating under a shield of martial arts training for black youths, who were called "Simbas" ("young lions" in Swahili). Much of the potentially deadly force of US was hidden behind a screen of cultural work known as "Kawaida," an umbrella concept of ancient African values and practices.[4]

Although both groups were inspired by the example of Malcolm X, significant differences allowed only uneasy truces between them; the

Panthers and US often engaged in violent clashes over culture, ideology, and methodology.[5] While the Panthers were influenced by third world struggles and Marxism-Leninism, the chief influences on US were slavery-era black freedom fighters and African philosophy, culture, language, and self-defense techniques. Within Black Panther and US cells, and in hundreds of activist and arts gatherings, these versions of black power were refined and articulated. From such laboratories came the shape and direction of black nationalism, black arts, and black studies. At numerous universities, colleges, public schools, parks, street academies, and rallies throughout the United States, the labors of cultural workers and militant activists generated new black-based community centers and institutionalized black studies programs.

The black power-black arts movement was launched in cities throughout the nation. The NAACP, Urban League, CORE, SNCC, Black Panthers, US, Black United Front, Republic of New Africa, and Black Muslims held daily demonstrations, workshops, and forums on the streets and inside institutions. The entire country was ablaze with change, dialogue, negotiations, "relevance," dissent, and direct action. Differing positions led to numerous debates and cultural skirmishes: Blackness and African things were not universally embraced in the United States, not even by blacks.

In East St. Louis and St. Louis, facing each other across the Mississippi River, we were alternately staggered and exalted by the new shift in the black revolution. Local theater activity gives some idea of the intense intellectual, artistic, political dialogue that swept the cities. Hansberry's *A Raisin in the Sun,* Baldwin's *Blues for Mr. Charlie,* and Douglass Turner Ward's *Happy Ending* and *Day of Absence* were among the most popular of the plays that had civil rights themes. Under Clifford Harper's direction, *Happy Ending* and *Day of Absence* were presented in 1966 at Lincoln High School; the productions were "revolutionary" because Lincoln's exclusively black student body customarily presented nonblack class plays. Lena Weathers directed one of my plays, *Shadows Before the Mirror,* at East St. Louis's Southend Neighborhood Center in 1966. Clifford Odets's socially relevant *Waiting for Lefty* was performed in 1962 with an all-black cast at Southern Illinois University's East St. Louis campus, a significant breakthrough in the diet of Shakespeare, Williams, Albee, and Pirandello.

Local Black Panther chapters were set up; a Black United Front unit was formed; the Black Artists Group (BAG) was established in St. Louis; for the first time, radical black political and cultural activists were elected to the East St. Louis school board; former street gangs such as the Black Egyptians and the Imperial War Lords were converted into

African-centered, community-oriented cultural organizations; and wholly new cultural units like the Black Liberators of St. Louis, Black Culture, Inc., Impact House, and Black River Writers Press of East St. Louis were created. Almost without exception, each of these organizations included elements of the community's religious, educational, cultural, economic, and gender tapestry. Within institutionalized education, none of the movements was more significant than the Experiment in Higher Education, which joined with Katherine Dunham's Performing Arts Training Center at Southern Illinois University-East St. Louis.

The First African-Centered College Curriculum

My black mothers I hear them singing
    Sons, my sons,
dip into this river with your ebony cups
A vessel of knowledge sails under power.
Study stars as well as currents.
Dip into this river with your ebony cups.
My black fathers I hear them chanting.
—Henry Dumas, "Black Star Line"

The Experiment in Higher Education (EHE) and Katherine Dunham's Performing Arts Training Center (PATC) originated between the Watts Rebellion of August 1965 and the nationwide urban upheavals in the later 1960s. Both EHE and PATC were culture-based, mission-oriented, revolutionary, and unequivocally tied to the Movement. EHE was funded by the state of Illinois and the Office of Economic Opportunity as part of the War on Poverty; PATC's funds also came from the state of Illinois, as well as from Rockefeller and Danforth Foundation grants. Both EHE and PATC were operated under the aegis of Southern Illinois University; EHE was housed in Southern Illinois University's East St. Louis Center, and PATC was established in quarters across the street. I filled a joint appointment at both as teacher-counselor and senior consultant, thereby beginning my career in formal multicultural education and a long, valuable, and treasured apprenticeship to Katherine Dunham.[6]

EHE was designed to augment the university's general studies program by preparing its student body, most of which was black, for upper-level entry at Southern Illinois University's Edwardsville campus or at a comparable university. Its two-year curriculum was arranged to give students a "relevant," pre-major preparation without the soul-splintering that usually results from unmonitored Eurocentric training. The EHE curriculum reflected the needs of what by the late 1960s had become a predominantly black East St. Louis of about seventy thousand people. The curriculum took traditional basic studies courses and stood them on their heads. European texts either received refreshingly new interpretations or were filtered through African-oriented courses of study. The inclusive approach embraced different cultures—black, white, urban, rural, street, drug, prison, youth, African, women's, and Native American—and encouraged a reassessment of traditional college curricula. The unique university was student-centered, culture-focused, community-oriented, and international in the reach of both its faculty and curriculum. Courses in continental African philosophy, literature, and folklore were interspersed with studies in European-American and African-American culture.

The EHE curriculum was not only, as its name implied, experimental, but it was also experiential. Its brochure, published in 1967–68, stated boldly that "curriculum is a misnomer in EHE, for it is not the usual collection of courses taught at other universities. Course content focuses on knowledge and information which helps the student understand his environment. The community, then, is his 'classroom.' . . . the discussions allow the student to relate course content to his own experiences." Academic demands at EHE were strenuous. Students had to master an emerging black-centered curriculum, as well as the traditional Eurocentric one, in addition to special-focus units on third world cultures and indigenous American "minorities." Nevertheless, as the brochure noted, "In providing a different approach, EHE has never 'geared down' standard educational materials."

Central to the EHE concept were its teacher-counselors, men and women who anchored the teaching and work experience segments of the program. The brochure noted that "Teacher-Counselors differ from traditional educators in that their backgrounds allow them to lead seminars, effectively communicate with ghetto youngsters, and make optimum use of the skills the youth bring with them to college." The brochure went on to observe that "we have attempted to merge teaching and counseling." Augmenting EHE's program were the curriculum planners (pedagogical theorists who worked with teacher-counselors), an African-centered, multicultural team battle-readied by the beatnik movement, civil rights, work with social action agencies, volunteerism via Peace Corps and VISTA, the reading of works such as Michael Harrington's *The Other America,* and the wave of black power and black consciousness sweeping the nation.

The majority of EHE students would not normally have sought or gained admission to an institution of higher learning. Recruited through East St. Louis area high schools, special education programs, churches, welfare agencies, and antipoverty data banks, the cultural matrix from which the students came was communal (extended family), ritualistic (folkloric, choreographic, and stylistic), oral (acoustical, songified, rap-oriented, and sermonical), messianic (belief-centered, priest-prone, passionate, and compassionate), and proud (ethnocentric). When it came to screening and selecting students for EHE, Deputy Director Donald Henderson noted, "One rule of thumb in selection is . . . if the candidate displays a degree of 'hip-ness' that would 'get-him-over' on the street then . . . he is very likely to be potentially skilled enough to 'make it' in college" ("Higher Education for the Disadvantaged: A Commentary," 53, n.1).

The EHE courses emphasized material and assignments that were culturally relevant to the present as well as the past. Much translating and transliterating of experiences and expression occurred in profoundly reconceived classes. For example, as a parallel to what was called "Introduction to Sociology" on the Edwardsville campus, Joyce Ladner and I team taught "The Socialization of the Black Child" for EHE students. (At age twenty-four, she was then the youngest black Ph.D. in the United States; she is now vice president for academic affairs at Howard University.) We used both sociological texts (*The Mark of Oppression* and *The Souls of Black Folks*) and literary works (*Invisible Man, For My People,* and Gwendolyn Brooks's *Selected Poems*), and we included materials on black children's African background. A parallel course in Western civilization became "African/World Civilizations." Philosophy, ethics, and consummate survival skills were taught using John S. M'Biti's *African Religions and Philosophies,* Robert DeCoy's *The Nigger Bible,* African and African-American folk wit (*The Negro Caravan* was a staple), and the writings of Ptahhotep, Aesop, Aeschylus, Shakespeare, Katherine Dunham, Mark Van Doren, Immanuel Kant, Black Elk, Sitting Bull, and Alfred North Whitehead. We interspersed multicultural creativity and thought, sifting it carefully through a filter of blackness, cultural activism, and socially relevant issues.

In introductory writing courses (called "freshman English" at white universities), expository and creative writing were merged, as were written forms and oral traditions; emphasis was on understanding how the English language worked through translating its different "brands." For example, our students wrote down passages from the Bible, Shakespeare, folklore, Baldwin, and Hurston. They collected samples of speech from their communities, recorded their own voices on tape, and did contrastive listenings, critiques, and re-presentations of these brands of English. The "sermonical" writings of Baldwin were paired and compared with actual sermons that students heard in local churches and on street corners. Students wrote their own sermons, later delivering them to classmates, teachers, and members of the community. People at EHE were simultaneously involved in "Afrocentric" education, "writing across the curriculum," "interdisciplinarity," "culture studies," and "street teaching" long before such concepts became fashionable elsewhere.

This experimental, interdisciplinary, and team-taught education occurred both on campus and in the community. There were field trips, where students' neighborhoods were reexplored in tandem with trips to culturally different locations. There were the aptly named student newspaper, *Soul Script;* the special creative writing and speaking workshops I developed, "Rap/Write Now"; and our annual theatrical programs, called "Psyche-Out Productions." Additional experimentation, cross-pollination, improvisation, and risk-taking occurred in partnership with Upward Bound at the experimental high school housed in EHE's East St. Louis quarters. The local staff of Upward Bound (a component of the nationwide War on Poverty) had direct access to the resources of EHE, which oversaw the Upward Bound program administratively and pedagogically. Within this intergenerational, educational continuum, EHE students served as tutors for the experimental high school. Upward Bounders, in turn, tutored elementary students and conducted literacy workshops for elders in the community, who, in turn, informally taught the tutors.[7]

Complementing EHE's more academic curriculum was Katherine Dunham's Performing Arts Training Center, which was inaugurated in 1967. A renowned choreographer, anthropologist, and former prima ballerina, Dunham had resettled in Illinois. During the thirty years preceding her arrival in East St. Louis, Dunham had performed, taught, written, and directed in fifty countries. She had also appeared in and choreographed such films as *Stormy Weather, Cabin in the Sky,* and *Casbah.*[8] Under Dunham's direction, PATC offered courses at its own facilities in Beaulah House (a former women's residence across the street from EHE's quarters) and in community centers, churches, senior citizens' complexes, parks, restaurants, homes, and schools.

Like EHE, PATC was a two-year school. Unlike EHE, however, PATC's emphasis was not on a general studies equivalency for students seeking four-year degrees. Instead, PATC aimed to provide its young charges with self-esteem, direct contact with African and third world cultures, a Kush combined with Greek-derived sense of mind-body balance, and a two-year associate's degree in cultural and performing arts. Course offerings were clustered into three areas: (1) performing arts (dance, drama, music, and martial arts); (2) applied skills (African hair braiding, African wood carving, visual arts, visual design, commercial design, pattern making, and theater crafts); and (3) humanities (conversational Wolof, Yoruba, Swahili, Haitian Creole, Spanish, and French, as well as esthetics, the social sciences, "African Nations Today," African government, and various theater courses).

In addition to the course work, special lectures, seminars, workshops, and master classes were taught by Dunham herself and an array of distinguished visiting scholars, entertainers, and artists such as Harry Belafonte, William Strickland, John Henrik Clarke, Eartha Kitt, Lucille Ellis, Eugene Haynes, Paul Osaghi Osifu (a Nigerian sculptor), Topper Carew (an architect), Michael Babatunde Olatunji (a Nigerian folklorist, drummer, and recording artist), and Erich Fromm.[9] Drummers, dancers, singers, actors, stilt walkers, honkers, guitar players, blues bands, storytellers, griots, sitarists, multilingual poets, and revolutionary speechifiers could be experienced on almost any day in East St. Louis.

EHE and PATC worked together, cross-listing courses, exchanging faculty, team teaching, coauthoring research reports, coproducing cultural events, and jointly conducting regional, national, and international field trips to France, Haiti, and Nigeria. While EHE faculty and students provided the theoretical, ideological, academic, and intellectual basis for "blackness" and activism, PATC balanced those offerings with its mobile units that emphasized the cultural, artistic, cross-gender, and spiritual features of the new black revolution. The EHE-PATC approach was cultural, consciously African-centered, and Pan-African (a favorite phrase of ours). We started with the cosmologies and ancient thought of Africa and the black diaspora—for example, the Olmec deities found in Jalapa, Veracruz, and near Tres Zapotes, Mexico—and included Kwame Nkrumah, Sekou Touré, [James] N'Gugi Wa Thiongo (*The River Between*), Chinua Achebe (*Things Fall Apart*), Ezekiel Mphaphele, Credo Mutwa (*Indaba, My Children*), M'Biti (*African Religions and Philosophies*), and Amos Tutuola (*The Palm-Wine Drinkard*) along with Du Bois, Hurston, Ellison, Margaret Walker, Hughes, Wright, and Hansberry. Admittedly, pretty heavy stuff, but it was the basis of the cultural, pedagogical, theoretical, and practical approach we took to black studies in East St. Louis during the 1960s.

As a teacher, performer, mentor, friend, and confidant, Katherine Dunham introduced me to multicultural education. Her life defined the concept of multiculturalism; she was a cultural arts pioneer and the first black woman to develop and sustain an independent black professional theater company. Dunham was also a social activist; for example, she protested segregated hotels and included scenes of U.S. lynchings in her choreography. She invented interdisciplinary, mixed-arts education: dance-anthropology, music-chorus, ritual-drama, and dance-theater. The "Dunham technique" was a cross-fertilization of African, Caribbean, Asian, and European forms, and it was embodied in an interracial company and staff. Dunham's dynamic model of education—crossing dance, language, cultural arts, anthropology, and human development—was realized in schools in Chicago, New York, and Haiti, as well as in East St. Louis.[10]

The Experiment in Higher Education-Performing Arts Training Center consortium became a fulcrum of intellectual and creative energy; a magnetizing force for a worldwide cadre of scholars, theoreticians, activists, and artists; and a base from which to launch black studies nationally and internationally. During the heyday of black studies, the late 1960s, the consortium consulted, collectively or individually, with hundreds of colleges and universities, from San Francisco State College to Howard University to Oberlin College to Harvard University.

Most universities and colleges did not have the luxuries that EHE-PATC enjoyed: time, resources, and a think tank to develop theoretical bases and actual courses. In the mid-1960s, the cry had been "Freedom now!" Later in the decade, the cry was "Black studies now!" The cultural rush was on. Never mind choice of department or program, the major or minor, lower or upper division, required or elective, African-based or slavery-derived, lecture or discussion, ad hoc or permanent, humanities or social sciences. Hurried movement, installment, and visibility were what were important. Because black studies demands and curricula were usually hammered out in the late hours—between picket lines, rallies, armed confrontations, and negotiations—conceptualizing, staffing, and designing courses often happened quickly. Ubiquitous forces pressed us to put our money where our mouths were, sometimes before we were ready to open them.

The 1960s provided battle training for persons engaged in the movements for civil rights, black power, black arts, and black studies. In the 1970s, evangelical in our fervor, we learned by leading. EHE-PATC helped launch careers for many of us. As we worked out structures and pedagogies for black and ethnic studies programs, a new breed of scholars, poets, critics, theoreticians, administrators, and architects of consciousness arose to fan out across this country and others (the Movement was international via Canada, the West Indies, Latin America, Europe, and Africa). Everything was new, unrehearsed, experimental, complex, and multiplicitous.

Initially, the black cultural experience was the best known, and many of us never gave a great deal of thought to the need to master any other "colored" culture. And for most of us, the gender question was not so central as it should have been. After all, it was black—mostly male—studies that had taken center stage. Were we not the ones on television and the front pages of daily newspapers? However, concern with what had been labeled "interracial" during the 1960s coincided with the "multicultural" and the "cross-gendered" during the 1970s and 1980s. In the 1970s, my base became California State University at Sacramento. I remember the shock and dismay I felt at being told for the first time by a Chicana, or a Native American, that I knew nothing about her or his culture. In addition, female colleagues and students began to hyphenate their surnames, assert their own, Other identities, and offer cogent critiques of patriarchal society. The word *pride* started to appear in tandem with words like *gay, women, elder, lesbian,* and, yes, even *white.* Again, the words of the black elders bounced off the din-filled walls of the Movement: "You got your work cut out for you, but it ain't easy."

Black Studies/Culture Studies in the 1990s

... let me blues ya fo' I lose ya.
—Southend saying,
   East St. Louis, Illinois

The consortium formed by the Experiment in Higher Education and the Performing Arts Training Center came to an end in the late 1970s. Although changed substantially, Dunham's PATC still exists. It is now subdivided into the Katherine Dunham Center for the Performing Arts (administered by Southern Illinois University at Edwardsville) and a private, foundation-run complex including the Katherine Dunham's Children's Workshop, the Katherine Dunham Dynamic Museum, and the Dunham Fund for Cultural Arts. In 1992, a pared-down PATC celebrated its twenty-fifth anniversary in an East St. Louis whose population had dwindled to forty-five thousand. The subsequent careers of many of EHE's students, teachers, and administrators indicate that EHE was a successful educational venture. However, EHE and PATC never really became institutionalized within the larger university structure. The university continued but EHE did not, and PATC does not function as an integral part of the university. Conversely, one could say the consortium became *too* institutionalized. EHE and PATC survived only by being fragmented into pockets of arts and services, unable to continue the process of mutual energization, disconnected from the philosophic whole that once held them together, and without the sure identity that had generated so much planning, activity, and hope. Of course, black studies, which drew heavily on the East St. Louis experiment in the 1960s, survives into the 1990s.

But black, ethnic, and gender studies of the 1980s and 1990s face the possibility of being eclipsed by culture studies. We are experiencing another shift in the see-saw syndrome common to all oppressed "minority" cultures: now blessed/now cursed, now valued/now devalued, now lionized/now ignored, now funded/now reallocated. Trapped in the mocking throes of this syndrome, "real" institutional advancement or security for black studies seems to be out of the question, at least until the next crisis in the streets or until university administrators or state legislators need more minority visibility. By turns, it seems, the most important cultural, ethnic, gender, and class struggles of our time have moved front and center; occupied their day in the sun; fizzled or been consumed by the next one; and reemerged later, as if to say, "I told you so."

As a child of the black power-black arts movement, black studies has undeniable roots in ancient African cultural traditions and modern African-American nonacademic communities. It is also wedded to black cultures in the broader Americas through a legacy of pre-Columbian African explorations and discoveries, mercantilist and capitalist exploitation, slavery, resistance and rebellion, creolization, oppression, Jim Crowism, lynching, discrimination, second-class citizenship, and highly stylized systems of survival. Prefacing the word *culture* with terms like *African* or *black* conjures up a familiar catalog: folklore, language, spirituals, blues, jazz, cuisine, dance, art, life-styles, extended families, religiosity, slave narratives, polyrhythmic structures, sermonical oratory, impassioned speeches, and mask-draped writings.

The best of the early, archetypal black studies programs observed an international approach that used the paired principles of the African "continuum" (diachronic) and the African "extension" (synchronic). The African continuum holds that ancient African things and thoughts predominate wherever cultures of African extraction exist. Complementing the continuum, the African extension states that black or African things, when removed from their mother-bases, undergo transmutations and cross-pollinations in multicultural contexts. That is, they become African Brazilian, African Canadian, African Asian, African Caribbean, and African American. Understandably, then, it is not possible to comprehend one black diasporan culture without comparing or contrasting it with another.

Afrocentric educators, in insisting that the conceptualization of black studies be grounded in pre-European, African-centered curricula and pedagogies and New World cross-pollinations, are assuming a position taken by some of our most distinguished scholars: Du Bois, Hurston, Woodson, Dunham, and others. Such scholars have held that the scars resulting from the trauma of being uprooted, made homeless ("motherless child"), enslaved, and dehumanized can never be confronted, let alone healed, unless traumatized neo-Africans reclaim or reassemble their ancient selves. A process of cultural and self-reclamation rather than an immersion into a shore-to-shore mentality (i.e., that of the U.S. borders) should be the literal backbone of black or African-American studies.

As I contemplate the growing popularity of what is now called "cultural studies" or "culture studies," I am conscious of the distinctiveness and integrity of black New World cultures, aware of the continuum and the extension of African cultures, and mindful of the trauma at the heart

An Autobiographical View of Culture Studies 123

of African-American experience. My experience at EHE-PATC and elsewhere leaves me concerned. Black studies was born in the streets out of violent rebellions, temporal urgency, racial oppression, social change, political necessity, and cultural activism. Given that birthright, black studies should remain on the cutting edge, never becoming too comfortable to accommodate new movements and expressions—such as rap and Afrocentricity—but slow to embrace superficiality. When I consider culture studies, part of me wants to respond, "It's already been done. We were there. We have been doing it. Where were you?" But I know that relations between black studies and culture studies are more complex than that.

I think of the decades between 1960 and 1990 as the Period of the Four Cultural Revolutions, each encompassing both street heat and institutional responses. First came the civil rights, free speech, antiwar, Great Society, and black power movements of the sixties that empowered black studies and a host of new cultural, community, and institutional systems. American mainstream speech was enriched by such terms and phrases as "we shall overcome," "hell no, I won't go," "flower power," "blackness," "great society," "war on poverty," "black culture," "rock," "burn, baby, burn," "black is beautiful," "Motown," "black experience," "soul," "pan-Africanism," "Africanity," "black caucus," and "Afro-American." Then we witnessed the heyday of the women's liberation struggle during the mid-seventies (bringing women's studies, new "sheroes," recovered and revalued literature, and more inclusive histories); environmental activism; affirmative action; and "minority" studies (Asian, black, Native American, Latino, gay, and lesbian). We started hearing "ms," "sisterhood," "minority caucus," "Chicano," "La Raza," "gay pride," "bloods," "yellow power," "Indian pride," "barrio," "Earth, Wind and Fire," "feminist press," "Shameless Hussy Press," "AIM," "Fleetwood Mac," "Attica," "Gray Panthers," "God is a woman," and "minority literature."

Third came the literacy revolution of the late seventies—"Why high school graduates can't read!"—that questioned English studies and sent "specialists" to sentence-combining seminars. Behold, the literature versus theory standoff and the drug-crime-poverty crisis: "deconstructionism," "hermeneutics," "intertextuality," "subtext," "texto y contexto," "black English," "interlinear," "interface," and new MLA commissions. Finally, in the fourth phase, that of the late eighties and early nineties, all of the previous phases combined (although in some cases unwillingly) under the aegis of multiculturalism, new pluralism, ethnic diversity, cultural studies, culture studies, curriculum of inclusion, and a continuation of the drug-crime-poverty crisis. "Black power" rides again in the guise of Afrocentrism, rap, and increased representation in Congress and the Senate.

This temporal frame of roughly thirty years does not include other revolutions in this century or the last. But each one has simultaneously been characterized by major cultural offensives and then by serious retrenchments and setbacks. The struggle keeps getting strangled by those who control the image making/breaking and myth making/breaking power. I am not sure that the culture or cultural studies now threatening to subsume, deconstruct, or recreate black, ethnic, women's, and multicultural studies is anything new. Along the span of modern American cultural history, there have been numerous literary upheavals, artistic revolutions, academic rebellions, and social explosions. Each has, in the end, been mainstreamed into a white event or phenomena. Wherever "bohemia" surfaces, real people are hurting underneath its exotic expressions and creating brilliant things out of their hurt (check out the blues). The invisible, silent Other is invariably purged from official texts chronicling important moments in literature, history, culture, or genius in general. Time and time again, criticism, literature, fashions, food, music, language, folklore, and survival modes become co-opted by institutions and lifted from the cultures and people that created them.

Although it is possible that culture studies is a necessary fifth revolution, it may also be another descent in the see-saw syndrome. If this latest culture studies offensive is going to embrace "multiculturalism"—ethnic diversity, cultural pluralism, cross-gender studies, inclusive anthologies, nonconformist sexual and religious expression, a mix of canonical and noncanonical texts, experimental and experiential studies—then it is welcomed to the round table of the new cultural world order. I want to join that struggle. But if the current culture studies seek to slide along the surface of the real thing, dipping down here and there to anoint and appoint its token representatives while it muffles dissent, co-opts struggle, and retrenches white male hegemony, then it is "an enemy of the people."

Notes

1. This essay is indebted to Maya Angelou's evocative paradigm of "Passion, Compassion and Style," an oracular flourish in her vast archive of dramatic one-liners that I hear while accompanying her on lecture tours.

2. Malcolm X regularly chided Africa's descendants for not knowing their history and culture; similar tongue-lashings came from Du Bois, Marcus Garvey, Melvin B. Tolson, Hurston, E. Franklin Frazier (who foresightedly called for studies of black urban culture as a way of heading off drugs, crime, and the breakdown of the family), Woodson, Bethune, Leo Hansberry, and Queen Mother Moore.

3. Marcus Mosiah Garvey, however, who up until the Malcolm-King era had

been the most successful black nationalist leader in America, attracted tens of thousands of blacks in a back-to-Africa call during the 1920s.

4. In 1965, Maulana Karenga and US founded Kwanzaa, an African-American holiday celebrating black cultural roots, self-determination, and creativity. "Kwanzaa," meaning "first fruits" in Swahili, is practiced by millions of blacks in the United States and the West Indies. It is an example of a brilliant cultural creation of the 1960s that survived into the 1990s. Few, if any, black campus and community organizations fail to observe Kwanzaa, which is celebrated December 26 through January 1.

5. Unbeknown to either US or the Panthers, J. Edgar Hoover's FBI instituted Cointelpro, a covert surveillance disruption operation aimed at triggering internecine warfare among various militant groups and neutralizing any black activist leadership deemed a threat to the internal security of the United States. Hoover's definitions of "threat" were spun primarily from racist fantasies and paranoia. A documentary film, *FBI's War on Black America* by Denis Mueller and Deb Ellis, describes this government-led vendetta and is available on home video.

6. EHE was led by a cross-cultural team of activist-educators, including Director Hymen Frankel, Deputy Director Donald Henderson, and Education Director Edward Crosby.

7. Upward Bound's most famous alumnus is filmmaker Warrington Hudlin, who later graduated from Yale University, founded the Black Filmmaker Institute, and, with his brother, filmmaker Reginald Hudlin, produced such films as *House Party, Boomerang,* and *Bebe's Kids.*

8. Dunham's widely publicized, forty-seven-day, "conscience and compassion" fast in 1992 in support of Haitian refugees is typical of the activist fervor that has characterized her entire career.

9. Included among EHE-PATC's faculty, staff, administrators, and consultants were Joyce Ladner, the author of *Tomorrow's Tomorrow;* Hyman Frankel, formerly of the World Planning Organization; Pearl Reynolds, Lucille Ellis, Archie Savage and Ural Wilson, former members of the Dunham Company; Henry Dumas, the author of *Goodbye, Sweetwater;* Donald Henderson, now provost at the University of Pittsburgh and a member of the editorial board of *Black Lines;* the master drummer Mor Thiam, loaned by the Senegalese Royal Ballet; Hale Chatfield, a poet and the editor of *Hiram Poetry Review;* Raymond Mbala and Philip Anala, African studies scholars from the continent; Jeanelle Stovall, the administrative assistant to Katherine Dunham; Suzanne Diop, formerly a member of the Senegalese supreme court; the Haitian drummer Rene Calvin; Charles White, a painter; Julius Hemphill, a composer, one of the founders of Black Artists Group (BAG), and now a member of the World Saxophone Quartet; Eusebio DaSilva, a Brazilian dancer and capoeira expert; Clifford Fears, a master dancer; Shelby Steele, who is now teaching at California State University at San Jose and is the author of *The Content of Our Character;* Edward Crosby, now director of Pan-African studies at Kent State University; Christiane de Rougemont, a French dancer-choreographer who supervised a Dunham School in Paris; Oliver Jackson, a painter who is now at California State University at Sacramento;

William Davis, formerly the assistant dean of students at Oberlin College; Oscar Brown, Jr., a composer, actor, and singer; Fela Sowande, from Howard University via Nigeria and the author of *The Africanization of Black Studies: From the Circumference to the Center;* and Camille Yarbrough, an actress, singer, and activist.

10. In the mid-seventies, I wrote about the work I had done with Katherine Dunham, PATC, and EHE during the late 1960s (see Clark).

☐ Asian Immigrant: Confessions of a "Yellow Man"

Sheng-mei Ma

What I Learned in Graduate School, and How I Make a Living Now

I came to the United States for graduate study in 1982 and spent the next eight years in the English program of a midwestern university learning when and how to use the definite article THE. In my native tongue, there is no equivalent for such a word, so I had tremendous difficulty. Even today, I continue to be haunted by THE, for in this definite article—traditionally considered an adjective—lies a noun, a phantom that flashes across the classroom and embarrasses me in front of my students and colleagues. I can almost hear the snickering in the corner whenever I misuse THE or other elfish words like it. In it I find crystalized all the shame and frustration I have felt for the past decade in this country, learning the master's language—first as a graduate student, then as an assistant professor.

True, I studied other subjects as well at this university. I took quite a few classes, passed the qualifying examination in nineteenth- and twentieth-century British literature, and wrote a dissertation on Holocaust literature. But that training is becoming increasingly irrelevant to how I make a living now. What I was force-fed in graduate school simply failed to prepare me for the kind of teaching expected of me as an Asian professor. While discrepancy between what one learns and how one makes a living may be the unhappy experience for many of my colleagues, I believe my case as an international graduate student from non-English-speaking Asia presents a unique means of revealing latent discrimination and hypocrisy in my profession.

My role as marginalized graduate student has now given way to the title of assistant professor, and the fashion in academe has packaged me into a marketable commodity. My exotic existence serves the politically correct purpose of questioning the long-accepted price tags of the Euro-American canon, a function for which I am suited less by virtue of my expertise than by virtue of my skin color. For instance, the courses in which I currently have an overflow of students are world literature and Asian literature, areas in which I received minimal academic training, but which, somehow, my background qualifies me to teach. Due to the limited choices in curriculum at my alma mater, I was trained to be a traditional modern Anglo-American literature specialist, but no school was willing to hire me as one. Instead, all the universities interested in me saw me as an addition to their multicultural programs. It is a happy coincidence that I enjoy my teaching assignments tremendously. But for Asian immigrants, the lack of connection between Ph.D. program and job market remains glaring.

In the job market, the assumption of multicultural expertise based on my ethnic origin is an ironic footnote to my humiliating experience in graduate school. When I first applied for an associate instructorship ("AI-ship," or teaching assistantship), the only viable way for graduate students to support themselves and their families, I was turned down. At a subsequent private conference, after giving the official line that there had been too many applicants for too few jobs, the chair of the committee mentioned two things "in passing." One was that I did not come from the most prestigious university in my home country. I should have responded right away that students from that "prestigious" school would not have come to this university. But even if his explanation were legitimate, quite a few European students from second- or third-rate universities in Germany, France, Belgium, and elsewhere were given AI-ships the first time they applied. The natural corollary would be that a second-rate European university was superior to its Asian counterpart. Again in a casual manner, the professor made what must have been a calculated move to further justify the rejection; he corrected a grammatical error in my application. "I served as a military 'policeman,' not 'police,'" he said with a grin. Surely, he seemed to imply, a person who could be so ignorant as to make this slip did not deserve to be an AI. I have never forgotten that smug smile, the same smile I encountered the following year when I applied again.

At the conference a year later, he began by commending me for the way I had worked him into the cover letter of my application, in which I had argued that the reasons offered for my earlier rejection, including my inferior alma mater and the error of "policeman," were utterly inadequate. I was given partial financial support—not as a regular associate instructor, but as the "movie man," that is, the "media assistant" responsible for pushing and operating the seven-foot, fully enclosed black metal rack installed with a television monitor and reel-to-reel projector. I have always suspected that it was reserved for international students, particularly those from Asia, because my successors were first a Hong Kong student and then two Koreans, who were deemed diligent but "not quite there" (the committee chair's exact words) for teaching.

I remained in this stressful and degrading job for years, while the majority of graduate students, American and European alike, moved on to better teaching positions in the department. During those years, I identified with Sisyphus. One year I wrote a short protest poem and submitted it with my AI application. The opening went like this: "Tied to a big black box / Rolling it up, only to roll it down again. . . ." At last, the department half-heartedly allowed me to teach just one section of freshman composition for international students, in addition to continuing my duties as the movie man. Subsequently, I was entrusted with freshman composition for American students and, at long last, with literature courses.

I firmly believe that a full associate instructorship eluded me for years because I am Asian. Many, if not all, European students in the program got regular three- or four-year AI contracts the first time they applied, whereas I had to apply every year, only to be repeatedly given the post of media assistant. I do not believe that they were more qualified to teach than I.

It is ironic that the department's concern over my qualifications, such as my use of "policeman" and "THE," made my life miserable in graduate school, for as a Ph.D. I received several job offers, in part as a result of my non-Western background. Although I was not a permanent resident of the United States and thus not a minority scholar, I was an attractive buy anyway to a number of institutions because of my ethnic identity. I was encouraged in various job interviews to take on courses such as third world and minority literature immediately, even though I was not trained in those fields.

This experience is not uniquely mine. I met an Indian professor from New England who teaches third world literature despite the fact that his specialty is contemporary American literature. I know a Japanese-American professor who has always concentrated on American poetry but was asked to teach Chinese and Japanese literature as a second area of expertise. Nevertheless, we certainly do not see ourselves as charlatans, selling our ethnicity to unwitting students; indeed, I feel better prepared than most of my colleagues in the department to teach these courses. Yet it remains mind-boggling that while we had to contort our bodies and souls to fit into traditionalist graduate programs in English, we are now bestowed with the sacred mission of revamping those very programs. Does it not make more sense to take advantage of our background at the outset and train us as critics in, for instance, multiculturalism and culture studies?

The reality of graduate school, however, jars against this rhetorical question. My dissertation proposal for a comparative study between Holocaust literature and the literature of the Chinese Cultural Revolution was summarily rejected by the director of the graduate program in English without any committee or departmental discussion. The director commented that such a study, with the bulk of works in translation, should be conducted in the comparative literature department. This occurred in spite of the fact that I had published an article contrasting the two bodies of works in *Holocaust and Genocide Studies,* a prestigious journal in the field. When I inquired further about the decision, the director's facial muscles began to twitch, her voice tinged with contempt. I felt that I was made into a heretic, profaning the English studies fiercely defended by her and other purists.

Such faculty, with their unspoken but prevailing set of priorities regarding graduate students of different nationalities, were directly responsible for the lack of recognition and support I experienced in graduate school. I did receive generous assistance from three professors, two of whom were viewed as marginal figures themselves in the department.

I attended no literary conferences as a graduate student. Which conference, professors' corrections in red appeared to intimate, would accept *my* paper? But in the time since my employment as an assistant professor, I presented papers at numerous regional, national, and international conferences. I won no award from the department and the graduate school at that midwestern state university; I was literally discouraged by the director of the graduate program from applying for scholarships. However, I have been awarded several grants from my present university and one NEH Summer Institute Fellowship. What accounts for my sudden outburst of vitality since 1990? Why did I come alive and reach a new level of intensity once I left graduate school?

In spite of my recent success, those eight years in graduate school are a layer of skin very hard to shed. I still have little confidence in scanning verse. Awkward moments still erupt in the departmental party when I miss a joke and just laugh along, nor would my sensitive colleagues venture to ask me—over a glass of wine—about, say, the three greatest American novelists of this century. I continue to suffer from this inferiority complex irrevocably internalized in graduate school and at times reinforced now.

Confessions of a Postcolonial Yellow Man

Am I being embarrassingly personal, especially when intertextualized with such distinguished scholars as the ones in this collection? Unlike most of these critics, whose works all relate to culture studies in one way or another and analyze facets of postcolonialism, I lived and still live it. Most of them can afford to be theoretical, whereas I continue to wrestle with the basic tool of domination and rebellion—the English language. Poststructuralism, deconstructionism, New Historicism, and any number of high-flown jargons with which academics have been conducting an incestuous exchange in books, journals, and conferences have very little to do with my experience. I have yet to learn how one can become abstract and philosophical about personal humiliation and injustice. I have no intention of criticizing these critics, but my writing is evidently concerned with equity on a more fundamental, factual plane. Moreover, since I have already chosen to be personal rather than theoretical, I might as well take it to the extreme. In order to understand why I am where I am, and what I am, one must also examine my past—the source of a typical, hidden self-hatred for postcolonial "Yellow Man" (to borrow the protagonist's name from D. W. Griffith's 1919 silent film *Broken Blossoms*).

To begin with the immediate past, English studies, as I suffered it in graduate school, proved to be an extension of the postcolonial mentality that sought to exclude the Other by creating and upholding a canon. Many canonical writers have indeed reflected and encouraged the anti-Other sentiment. The "savage woman" who "shall rear my dusky race" in Tennyson's "Locksley Hall," a statement of Victorian patriarchal sexism and racism; Conrad's dark continent and barbarians in *Heart of Darkness;* the blatant anti-Semitism in T. S. Eliot's "Burbank with a Baedeker: Bleistein with a Cigar," showcasing a subhuman "Chicago Semite Viennese"; the notorious Chinese caricatures created by American writers such as Bret Harte, Jack London, Frank Norris, and John Steinbeck (Kim 3)—all of these contribute to the canon.

The problem is that the conservative English program did not provide an atmosphere in which I could freely explore the implications of such hegemony, nor was I independent and mature enough to break loose from the Confucian respect for authority (in this case, white) as well as from my postcolonial upbringing in a cold war Asia that privileged the ways of the West. The postcolonial approach that the English department adopted is a microcosm of Western treatment of the East; it is an expression of the phenomenon Edward Said defines as "Orientalism": "a *distribution* of geopolitical awareness into aesthetic, scholarly, economic, sociological, historical, and philological texts; . . . it *is,* rather than expresses, a certain *will* or *intention* to understand, in some cases to control, manipulate, even to incorporate, what is a manifestly different (or alternative and novel) world" (*Orientalism* 12). Orientalism, as Said conceives it, "has less to do with the Orient than it does with 'our' [Western] world" (12). But this commendable self-reflection ignores the impact of Orientalism on the Orient. Because Orientalism veils a power relation of legitimizing the domination of the Other, it follows that Asia would begin to see itself as an inferior race to be patronized and as one that needs to emulate the West. That is exactly the looming shadow under which I grew up.

My immediate past, however degrading it might seem, was, in fact, the fruition of the romantic dreams (Occidentalism?) of my more distant past. When I was growing up during the sixties and seventies in Taiwan, the whole island was inundated with American pop culture; Taiwan was, and perhaps still is, virtually an American colony. Television had just been introduced, and we children gathered every evening in the living room of a well-to-do neighbor who bought the very first set in the compound to watch westerns and other Hollywood shows. Newspaper censorship of "pornography" did not seem to include the degenerate Americans, and I secretly clipped pictures of half-nude blondes. I prided myself on my ability to "sing" in English before I actually learned the language in junior high school. Called upon, I was glad to comply and often performed in front of my classmates, their mouths agape. I picked up the sound and the tune from my elder brothers, who, like all young men, sported long hair and played guitar. The first song that I memorized was "Cotton Fields," recorded by Harry Belafonte in the early 1960s. I like to think that it is a song about slavery in the South; I have never wished to find out what the mangled lyrics actually meant.

Postcolonialism ran deeper than just imitating the master's language. Its most sinister manifestation took the form of self-hatred among the colonized. As a child, adults showered praises on me for my relatively fair skin, commenting how much I resembled "a little *mei-kuo-ren*" (American, but, literally, "beautiful country person"). The transference from a genetic cause to a cultural identification reveals the idolization of the West by the colonized. However, I recall one neighbor adding that my only flaws were my flat nose and my large, round nostrils. He suggested that I should sleep with my nose tightly clipped with a metal clamp, the heavier the better. Although I could tell this was a malicious joke, I spent hours in front of the mirror inhaling and shaping my nostrils into the long, slender kind seen on television, the kind I and other kids adored.

Thus, the facts that I have been highly motivated in the study of English throughout my school life, that I gained a Ph.D. in English literature, and that I am a professor of English are not accidental.

My college education in Taiwan aggravated my idolatry of the West. The English program I attended in the late seventies followed New Criticism closely and was traditionalist in the narrowest sense, requiring the study of all the canonical writers in English and, to a lesser extent, American literature. This training severely constricted my vision. Instead of contextualizing poets like Keats and Byron in the British and Chinese culture, I was to appreciate these romanticists on what was taken to be the intrinsic merit of their works.

I majored in English literature, as did so many other college students, because English seemed the thing, the road leading to the West. In reality, however, Asian students are often barred from entering English studies in the United States—perhaps with the exception of students from India, Pakistan, the Philippines, and other countries where English is the official language. In the United States, university faculty in comparative literature, history, foreign languages, and other humanities departments include many Asian professors who were educated as English majors in their home countries. In Asia, English departments have historically been stepping stones that allowed aspiring young men and women to prepare themselves linguistically and culturally to go abroad for graduate school. If culture studies were institutionalized in English departments here and could, indirectly, influence English departments abroad, graduate programs in the United States could admit international students with not only a linguistic readiness but also with a deeper understanding of where they come from, where they are, and where they wish to go.

How much a captive of postcolonialism I still am! In reflecting on my past, I have championed the cause of culture studies so that the Other, which is really myself, could be reshaped in the Western image and then, in turn, serve more efficiently in this "beautiful country." A sense of déjà vu—my life all over again.

An Asian Immigrant in Asian-American Studies

"The colonized man who writes for his people," asserts Frantz Fanon, "ought to use the past with the intention of opening the future, as an invitation to action and a basis for hope. But to ensure that hope and to give it form, he must take part in action and throw himself body and soul into the national struggle" (*Wretched* 232). I believe that Fanon's insistence on action to change the present reality still holds true for a great number of intellectuals. Therefore, to rephrase Fanon, I recall the past for the explicit purpose of changing the present institution—Asian-American studies in particular—in the United States. The agent of change is culture studies, whose bridging of text and culture and whose natural alliance with multiculturalism lend credence to, in the context of Asian-American studies, the raising of issues most urgent to Asian immigrants.

Constructed and constricted by my Taiwanese and graduate school experiences, I see myself as an Asian immigrant caught rather awkwardly in the fabric of Asian-American studies. Despite my deep interest in this flourishing field, I have found it difficult to identify fully with the agenda of Asian Americans. I have encountered, at literary conferences, cool receptions from Asian Americans, a gesture implying that I belonged in the East Asian literature section across the hall. Many people in Asian-American studies do not consider immigrants like myself genuine Asian Americans; immigrants do not have the authority to speak to these people's issues.

The same academic stereotyping exists among my white colleagues. Ruth Yu Hsiao, who currently teaches Asian-American literature, among other subjects, at Tufts University, offers a succinct example. She once tried to explain to a white colleague that she was in English, not Chinese. But her colleague, who eventually became the dean of freshman, simply did not believe her and kept insisting that she must teach Chinese. I wonder to what extent this dean-to-be was misinterpreting a plain English sentence because she assumed that this Chinese woman with a negligible accent must have misspoken.

It is perhaps unavoidable, although regrettable, that—in addition to the gap between Asian immigrants and whites—there is a gap between Asian immigrants and native-born Asian Americans. Telephone interviews and follow-up questionnaires confirmed this disparity among Asian-American professors in English in the Northeast Modern Language Association (NEMLA). In my attempt to understand how other Asian Americans fare in our discipline—to determine whether some of their experiences were similar to mine—I opened my telephone conversation with inquiries about ethnic background and experiences as graduate students and faculty members, asking specifically about how respondents' ethnicity affected their careers. The follow-up questionnaire allowed them to elaborate on the points they had made over the telephone and decide whether they wished to be named and quoted.

I must admit a certain amount of guilt over the fact that, among the professors I interviewed, I felt rather closer to the Asian immigrants, slightly more formal toward those who had emigrated at an early age, and somewhat distant from those who are American-born. A third-generation Asian-American professor, for example, put up with my long questions despite her reservations and feeling "slightly forced." The feeling might, of course, be due to the fact that we were strangers, but such problems did not arise during my conversations with immigrant professors. The atmosphere was warm and even passionate as we shared our similar experiences of being discriminated against.

Consider how close the following experience is to my own. In 1981, while still a graduate student, Professor Hsiao, who came to the United

States in her late teens, was perturbed when her teaching assignment was switched from a course on the "Modern Mind" to one on "Methods of Tutorial Instruction" (a remedial writing course). The reasons for this change were, she says, "fallacious, degrading, and inconsiderate." The most preposterous reason given by the chair of the teaching assignment committee was that it would be to her advantage to have more experience in pedagogy in order to find a job teaching English to native or non-native speakers. She vehemently rebutted this in a 1981 letter: "Should I choose to teach English as a second language in the future, that choice should be mine alone, and I would prepare myself by going to an institution where proper training is offered. It seems inappropriate for the English Department . . . to make that decision for me now." She did not respond to the most racist and sexist remark made by the chair, a remark she recalls with a great deal of anger. She had, after all, to work within the department. Her gracious but revealing letter to the same professor in 1984 tells the rest of the story.

> You may recall, two [three?] years ago you expressed the concern that my "Oriental reserve" would put me at a disadvantage with American teenagers in the classroom. This concern seemed to me an unfair prejudgment at the time, but it challenged me to overcome any barrier my cultural and racial background could create in the classroom. I am happy to send to you the enclosed student evaluations from the past semester, for they seem to indicate that I was able to reach most of the students. I hope these evaluations will put your concern to rest.
> I note with regret your resignation . . . as I have profited greatly from your teaching of Shakespeare and the high standards you set for teaching in general.[1]

Hsiao had told the professor during the 1981 conference that she was bringing up two American teenagers of her own. But raising teenagers was clearly not as good as having been one in this country, and the decision to change her assignment was final. She brought up the Shakespearean's phrase "Oriental reserve" only after the professor had resigned and relinquished power. I understand her timing perfectly; I would never have written the first part of this essay while still in graduate school. Nevertheless, these scars, untold for years, stay with us all our lives.

Despite the understandable identification among the immigrant generation, I cannot allow myself to be defined and, in turn, define myself in an essentialist manner. One of the major tasks of Asian-American studies ought to be reaching out to all possible constituents rather than splintering Asian Americans further on the grounds of shared and unshared experiences. The difficulty in achieving this ideal is that although a major premise of culture studies is to refuse to see text and individual as essences, the academy—through its practices of hiring, teaching assignments, and publication—encourages a narrow, reductionist interpretation of minorities. Henry Louis Gates, Jr., has on many occasions spoken of and written about one of his brilliant Ph.D. students who was not able to find a job in African-American studies because he is white.[2] Gates was shocked by his colleagues' insistence that a white man was, by nature, unable to penetrate black discourse. But one's identity is much more complicated than that.

In my telephone interviews, the first response to my opening question of ethnicity was invariably, "How do you define Asian American?" I have interviewed professors, such as Roxanne V. Lin, who came to the United States at five or six but who insist they are Chinese. I have also met with an Asian professor who had chosen not to be naturalized after having lived here for thirty years but who also claimed that she had often forgotten that she was Asian. Paradoxically, she was unhappy with her present position and was about to return to Asia.

To fail to negotiate these blending identities and conflicting interests of various groups within Asian-American studies gives rise to even sharper confrontations. One peculiar manifestation of this intraracial strife is what I have come to call the phenomenon of "imagining immigrants"—creating and manipulating voiceless immigrants to serve Asian-American writers' purpose of defining themselves. Imagining immigrants not for what they are, but for what they can be made into in the interest of another group bespeaks a rift between FOBs (immigrants *f*resh-*o*ff-the-*b*oat) and ABCs (*A*merican-*b*orn *C*hinese). By simply replacing the last letter of ABC with a capitalized *J* or with other letters, the term can be applied to American-born Japanese or other groups. People use these derogatory terms to belittle one another.

In the present stage of the evolution of Asian-American literature and art, imagining immigrants is especially problematic, for the immigrant generation remains silent or silenced, its stories told by second- or third-generation Asian Americans. These immigrants have usually devoted their lives to hard work; most are without the means—language and cultural immersion—to express their travail. Thus, Maxine Hong Kingston recounts her mother's "talk story" in *The Woman Warrior;* the voice of another superstitious and strong-willed mother is preserved through the radio play *Mei Mei: A Daughter's Song,* composed and produced by her daughter, D. Roberts; and the hardships in Mary Paik Lee's *Quiet Odyssey: A Pioneer Korean Woman in America* have become public because of the editing of an Asian-American historian, Sucheng Chan. This filtering of an older generation's experience through the lenses of native-born Asian Americans in itself merits research.

The muteness of the immigrant generation grows out of a present divided by an American job and an Asian home. Despite the fact that a large number of these immigrants were well educated in their home country, they are often separated from American society at large by their cultural background, language, and, in some cases, economic status. Most lead a dual existence: They work in an American setting, usually under American supervisors, but their home lives are led in enclaves of Oriental grocery stores, Oriental restaurants, and Asian newspapers (even cable television) that report primarily on news back home or within the Asian community. The four mothers in Amy Tan's *The Joy Luck Club,* for example, form a mah-jong club, in part to insulate themselves from the alien world, if only for the duration of the absorbing game.

In fact, this division of a single day into work for Americans and home life as an Asian reflects the traumatic severing of past and present. Crossing the Pacific Ocean literally rends their life and self in two, the halves at times left quite incongruous. The culture they leave behind becomes more and more vague despite attempts to cling to it, yet the culture in which they find themselves remains aloof due to their inability to assimilate and the reluctance of society to assimilate them.

Exasperated by this dilemma, immigrants develop various coping strategies. Some, as the work ethic of Confucianism encourages them to do, abandon themselves to their jobs. Others escape into the mirage of a Chinatown or other metropolitan Asian centers. A great number of immigrants, however, cope by investing hope in their American-born or U.S.-educated children, who symbolize the American dream of success, freedom, and individuality that has eluded a number of the immigrants themselves. Simultaneously, these immigrants, influenced by the Eastern tradition of filial piety, hold out ancient models of stringent familial and social obligation to evaluate their children's behavior. Such an expectation is dualistic and self-contradictory, and most youngsters choose to react with indifference, scorn, or, in the worst scenario, violence.

Indeed, in Asian-American literature and art, particularly in works reflecting the friction between generations, a parricidal complex against immigrant parents seems to lurk beneath the text. In Roberts's radio play, the Asian-American narrator at one point considers stabbing her mother, who is berating her mercilessly. The narrator checks this subconscious urge immediately and feels ashamed of herself. This unseemly contention surfaces as well in David Henry Hwang's plays *FOB* and *Family Devotions.* In the former, the second-generation Chinese American's deep resentment against the FOB, the Chinese newcomer who symbolizes a shared ethnic root, highlights the problematics of Asian-American identity. In John Okada's *No-No Boy,* such a problematic culminates in the son Ichiro's repressed and terrifying parricidal complex against his Japanese parents. More often, this subconscious drive is manifested not as literal murder or an explicit death-wish against parents, but as a metaphorical extirpation of the writer's Asian origin. The writers try, often instinctively, to write their ancestors—and, by implication, part of themselves—out of existence. The older generation, seen as antagonists or clowns, is depicted as fading away, its control over the young vanishing until the Asian-American protagonists are reborn as emancipated individuals.

The most subtle externalization of the parricidal complex is the hidden racist discourse in the Asian-American texts mentioned earlier. While outwardly affirming their ethnic background, as it is stylish to do in this era of multiculturalism, the writers paradoxically distance themselves from their ancestry by projecting white society's stereotypical perception of Asians onto a group more Eastern than themselves—Asians and Asian immigrants. The fear of being viewed as the alien Outsider drives them to portray Asians, the Real Other, in terms of all the white racist and sexist notions associated with the group. This identification with the mainstream results in the caricaturing and distorting of the portrayal of Asians, evidenced by pidgin English, exotic mannerisms, and alien ideas. Such a misrepresentation cannot be due entirely to a lack of exposure to and understanding of the East; part of its source has to come from a will to submerge the self in the American society, even at the expense of Asians and Asian immigrants, a circle most intimately known to the writers as their immigrant parents.

Hwang's plays may represent a working out of his ambivalent identity, but they offer an ill-advised approach for Asian-American studies. As a discipline against traditional disciplines, Asian-American studies should challenge the fabric of English departments, raising rather than "terminating" different, however frail, voices of the marginalized and disenfranchised. In addition, it should intensify the establishment of interdisciplinary links with other departments, not only English but also Asian.

The great divide between Asian and Asian-American studies betrays insecurity on both sides. In its embryonic stage, Asian-American studies might feel threatened if compared to and mistaken for Asian studies, which has a long academic history. On the other hand, Asian experts must stop viewing Asian-American studies as some sort of mongrel whose hybridized existence would "contaminate the purity" of Asian studies. Gay Wilentz's *Binding Cultures,* a recent collaboration of two interrelated disciplines, explores the cultural lineage between African and African-American women writers. There is much to be learned from Wilentz's pan-African approach. Although I do not suggest a pan-Asian methodology for every researcher, I do think that to continue to study Asian-American experience merely within the confines of American culture precludes many possibilities. Asian and Asian-American writers and scholars must engage in a dialogue to search for a better understanding of their separate and intermingled existences.

Asian . . . Asian-American . . . American

Any seemingly objective research in fact stems from a number of personal causes determined more by social forces than by individual will. I hope that I have demonstrated both how my postcolonial past in Taiwan and in the Midwest led to this essay and how Asian-American literature and studies address some of the identity problems that I and other Asian Americans have experienced. I, an Asian immigrant in academia, have remained quiet and self-effacing for too long, allowing myself to be defined by others. Collectively, the image of Asian immigrants is being constructed, more so now than ever before, by Asian-American writers and artists.

To redress the misconception about Asian immigrants, I propose that Asian-American studies embrace the experience of "Asian . . . Asian-American . . . American" as a totality, as a cultural continuum in which dissonant components are shaped by one another, whether an immigrant or an American-born Asian, whether Wu Ch'eng-en's sixteenth-century *Monkey,* Timothy Mo's *The Monkey King,* Gerald Vizenor's *Griever: An American Monkey King in China,* or Kingston's *Tripmaster Monkey: His Fake Book.* Although it is critical that we recognize the inherent dissent among and within minority groups, it is suicidal to polarize them. Asian-American studies in particular, like culture studies in general, must integrate and use varying perspectives rather than exclude any one of them lest it become the hegemony it tries to subvert.

Notes

I am greatly indebted to Ruth Yu Hsiao (Tufts University), Roxanne V. Lin (University of Vermont), Leverne Nishihara (Trinity College, Connecticut), Ranu Samantrai (Smith College), Ramchandran Sethuraman (University of New Hampshire), Nobuko Tsukui (George Mason University), and two others who wish to remain anonymous for sharing their experiences with me. I also wish to thank the English department and the School of Letters and Sciences at James Madison University for their generous financial support of this essay.

1. As means of further explaining her situation, the 1981 and 1984 letters were generously enclosed with Professor Hsiao's response to my questionnaire.

2. Gates made this reference to his Ph.D. student in a talk titled "On Transforming the American Mind" at the conference "Cultural Diversity and Liberal Education: Negotiating Difference in the Academy," held in Chicago on November 5–8, 1989. He has made the same point on many other occasions, indicating his concern with the academic trend toward essentialism.

PART 2: *The Impact of Culture Studies on the Institutions of English Studies*

☐ Rhetoric Returns to Syracuse: Curricular Reform in English Studies

Steven Mailloux

Let me begin with two stories about the invention of rhetoric in ancient Sicily around 467 B.C. The first story tells us that, after the deaths of the Syracusan tyrants Gelon and Hieron, a man named Corax invented rhetorical theory as a way of teaching citizens how to argue in the courts to regain their confiscated property (Cicero, 49). In this account, rhetoric is an enabling device for changing the economic and political order. But a second narrative about rhetoric's birth describes Corax as a powerful figure in the retinue of Hieron, and it is said that he invented rhetoric only as a way of maintaining his power in the new republic. By his rhetorical skills, Corax was able to influence the democratic assembly and guide the direction of the newly organized state ("Prolegomena" 24–25).[1] According to these two conflicting narratives, then, rhetoric at its legendary origin appears as a theoretical practice *either* for instituting radical change *or* for maintaining traditional power relations.

These contradictory accounts of rhetoric in ancient Syracuse can stand as an equivocal prologue to the following story of rhetoric and reform in a modern Syracuse. My institutional history of curricular change at Syracuse University turns out to be rhetorical three times over: first, this history is partial, interested, strategic, attempting to persuade others to accept my view of events and positions; second, it discusses the rhetorical politics of the curriculum debates and theoretical perspectives vying for institutional prominence in the profession of English studies; and, finally, it focuses on how rhetoric itself was (or was not) a topic of the debates in the Syracuse English department.

The Magic Triangle

I was chair of this thirty-five-member department from August 1986 through July 1989, and I will limit the time frame of my chronicle to this three-year term. During my first semester, I proposed rhetorical study as a framework for bringing together the distinct segments of the department: creative writing, traditional literary history and criticism, linguistics, English as a second language, critical theory, composition, and cultural studies. There were radical disagreements within and among these different groups of faculty. My proposal of rhetoric and cultural rhetoric was intended not to resolve these differences, but to explain and organize them in a new and productive way.

Understanding "rhetoric" as the effects of texts, of their production and reception, I came to define "cultural rhetoric" as the study of the political effectivity of trope and argument in culture.[2] But it was not my primary goal to persuade my colleagues to accept any particular definition. Rather, I urged them to work with the vocabulary of rhetoric, to rethink their own theories and practices in its terms, and to propose their own definitions. That is, I presented "rhetoric" as a framework for reinterpreting our disciplinary activities.

I came late to the history of rhetorical conflict in the Syracuse English department. Two recent events in that history turned out to be particularly significant for the outcome of my curriculum proposals. The first was the institutional separation of the composition program from the English department. The semester before my arrival, a decision had been made to transform freshman English into a new, college-based, universitywide Writing Program, which eventually became budgetarily and administratively independent from the Department of English. The new director, Louise Wetherbee Phelps, hired at the same time I was, reported directly to the dean of arts and sciences, and the Writing Program eventually became a separate curricular unit, with the old freshman writing courses receiving a "WRT" rather than an "ENG" designation. Writing Program faculty were given joint appointments (technically 60 percent Writing Program, 40 percent English department), but had their offices in a different building from the rest of the English faculty. These institutional rearrangements evolved over several semesters, but early on I failed to realize how significantly my plans would be affected by such changes in the material circumstances of the curricular debate.

The second important event before my arrival was the establishment of a specific rhetorical practice within the department. Long before I appeared on the scene, my new colleagues, primarily those interested in poststructuralist theory, had developed the practice of writing memos to argue for curricular change. I had never seen anything like it. After I accepted the offer to become chair, three different people sent me packets of past memos, a testimony to the archive that had already been created and a concrete foreshadowing of what was to come. These memos were

Rhetoric Returns to Syracuse 145

remarkable examples of polemical critique, theoretically sophisticated and intellectually challenging.

During my first semester, fall 1986, I proposed replacing the traditional coverage model for organizing the undergraduate English major. Instead of conceptualizing our object of study in terms of literary historical periods, I suggested we rethink our shared enterprise in terms of a new set of categories. My first suggestion was that we begin working with *rhetoric, theory,* and *culture* as our primary terms, and that such a trio of categories could be spatially represented by a triangle:

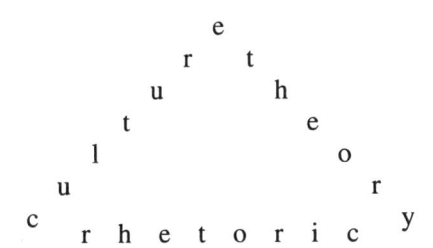

```
                    e
                r       t
            u               h
        t                       e
    l                               o
 u                                     r
c       r   h   e   t   o   r   i   c     y
```

At one of the year's first department meetings, I tried to foster discussion of this model by roughly glossing its terms, equating culture with history, rhetoric with politics, and theory with philosophy. This triangular proposal and its simplistic interpretive glosses were then taken up in various memos by department faculty.

Some of the theorists attempted to work with my suggested terms, whereas others rejected the proposals completely. Of the former, Stephen Melville provided the most important addition: filling the middle of the triangle with the term *reading*. Although he accepted the triangle as "a useful way to think about the department," he disagreed with the preliminary glosses I had given it. Instead, he proposed an alternative interpretation of its terms: "'Culture' picks out the specificity of any linguistic act—that it is performed in a particular language and in a particular world and history. 'Theory' points toward the explicitly communicative dimensions of any such act, that such an act means to convey a meaning. 'Rhetoric'—perhaps the most difficult term in the current constitution of the department—points to the fact that anything said is said in a certain way that exerts effects both upon its receiver and upon the message itself (effects traditionally recognized as persuasive and tropological)" ("Toward a Re-Imagining of Our Object," October 1986, 2).[3] Melville's comment about the "most difficult term" in our debates turned out, at least for my own rhetorical plans, to be especially prescient. But for the eventual outcome of our departmental discussions, it was his proposal for filling the

146 Steven Mailloux

center of the triangle that became most important. There he placed "our common object—linguistic practices in general, the reading of texts in particular" (3).

One of the most powerful critiques of my triangular proposal came from the department's political left, the position with which I most often identified. Jean Howard and Felicity Nussbaum, two materialist feminists, wrote of "the Mailloux triangle as modified by various hands" that "a possible danger of this schematization is that it will enable us to rename what we do without changing anything. If rhetoric = writing, culture = period courses, and theory = theory then we are effectively held right where we are" (October 1986 [1]). While granting the "widely accepted view that we want to be a department of reading and writing (although these terms are also contested)," Howard and Nussbaum argued for "a department of Text Critique which focuses precisely on the role of textual production and reception in the circulation of ideology and the construction of particular modes of subjectivity, and which aims to produce students who actively occupy positions from which to critique and intervene in the discourses by which the real is established and power relations secured" (2).[4] The memo also suggested one way in which the department was being remapped, a fact that became increasingly important as the curricular discussions continued: "For us, the greatest value of the discussion of the rhetoric-culture-theory triangle to date has been to reveal that any reading of the department based on a binary opposition between theory and non-theory is at best reductive. There are differences of more importance" (1). Indeed there were.

Not all the objections to the curricular triangle took the form of serious critique. There were also responses in a quite different rhetorical vein. One such memo began:

To: Members of the English department, soon to be given a more Advanced Name
From: the She-Ra, Princess of Power Space
    Retrogradation has once again hegemonically privileged itself in antinominiacal contestatory opposition to the non-essentialized astral projections of the Divine Will. Triangles printed on flat pieces of paper? Prima facie outmoded, kids. What we need is a Departmental plan revolving first around an irregular, open, eleven-sided polygon. These sides will be labelled:
Recrudesence
Effervescence
Irridescence
Antidisestablishmentarianism

Neo-hegelian theosophy
Metapsychosis
Quarks
Quirks
The Royal Road to Geometry
The Royal Nonesuch
Telekinesis

The memo concluded triumphantly: "Excelsior! Today the department, tomorrow the solar system!"

In response to both serious and humorous criticisms, I attempted once more to clarify my position by addressing my own memo to "the Chairman's argument" (November 10, 1986). Taking up the triangle as modified by Melville:

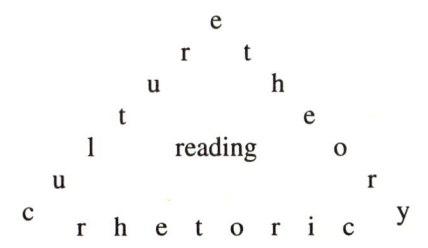

```
               e
            r     t
          u         h
        t             e
      l    reading     o
    u                   r
  c    r h e t o r i c    y
```

I claimed that "the Chairman . . . had failed to exploit the heuristic power of the term 'rhetoric' as strategically, as imaginatively as he might have" (1) and proposed rewriting the triangle still again:

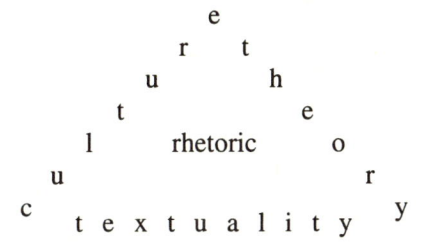

```
               e
            r     t
          u         h
        t             e
      l    rhetoric    o
    u                   r
  c    t e x t u a l i t y
```

I went on to argue that each side of the triangle named a potential set of courses—on textuality, culture, and theory—and that these categories of courses could be understood in relation to various definitions of rhetoric.

What did my proposal imply about relevant definitions of rhetoric? This question could be answered by taking each side of the triangle as a domain for defining *rhetoric*. From the perspective of textuality, rhetoric is simply tropes and arguments in texts. (This mundane definition borrows from two long rhetorical traditions—rhetoric as figurative language and rhetoric as persuasion—two traditions currently represented, for example, by deconstruction and reader-response criticism, respectively.) From the perspective of culture, rhetoric is the materiality of cultural politics in discourse. (This definition needs more justification, which would begin with a Foucauldian thesis that relations of power/knowledge permeate rhetorical practices and a Burkean thesis that rhetorical practices—the employment of tropes and arguments—constitute cultural discourse.) And from the perspective of theory, rhetoric is the emphasis on local practices and historical beliefs, in contrast to philosophy's concern over general foundations and universal Truth. (This definition participates in the rhetorical line from the Greek Sophists and Isocrates through Chaim Perelman and contemporary neopragmatists.)

Textuality, culture, and theory do more, however, than simply function as perspectives for defining (and arguing over) rhetoric. Rhetoric itself also provides a frame for defining and arguing over textuality, culture, and theory. "Rhetoric is a subject matter *and* a mode of inquiry" (2). A major organized around rhetoric would emphasize the dialectical relation between what would become three categories of courses and the rhetorical framework.

The English and Textual Studies Major

Many other topics were covered in the memo exchanges—arguments about classroom pedagogy, statements by the Student Marxist Collective, debates over creative writing, and much, much more. I am thus leaving out an enormous chunk of what I sometimes call "the return of rhetoric to Syracuse." In any case, by the end of my first year, that return had become somewhat sidetracked, at least from my perspective. True, the new Writing Program had successfully replaced freshman English courses with freshman and sophomore writing studios, which were putting rhetoric and composition on a stronger theoretical base and giving instruction in writing an unprecedented visibility at Syracuse. But this return of rhetoric was happening outside the English department. (On the Syracuse Writing Program, see Zebroski; see also Phelps, "Developmental Challenges," "Institutional Logic," and "Practical Wisdom.")

My failure in arguing for "rhetoric" was most evident at the end of the first year, when a new triad of terms was adopted to organize the major. Although the form of the triangle had been preserved, its sides were now labeled "history," "theory," and "politics," and we moved into the 1987–

88 school year focussing on "textual studies" not "cultural rhetoric" as the organizing term for the continuing discussion of the new major.

Although the flurry of memos slowed in the second year, one interesting exchange relevant to rhetoric's return did take place. In the fall, two department members, Mas'ud Zavarzadeh and Donald Morton, who had been active in the previous year's "memo wars," published a critique of the not-yet passed Syracuse curriculum as part of a larger attack on reformist curricular changes taking place at universities such as Carnegie Mellon and Duke. In "War of the Words: The Battle of (and for) English," these postmodern Marxists claimed that Syracuse's "'new' curriculum reintroduces a politically oppressive form of eclectic pluralism by simply providing three levels of study: the political, the historical, and the theoretical. Once again (as in the traditional curriculum), the notion [is] that a liberal education should produce a well-rounded individual" (18). In contrast, they argued, a truly radical pedagogy attempts to empower the student, making him or her into "a critical subject who knows that knowledge is a social product with political consequences and is therefore willing to 'intervene' in the way knowledge is produced not only in the classroom, but in all other sites of culture" (19).

My memo in reply to Zavarzadeh and Morton quoted from a document being written by the department's Theory Group: the "new curriculum in textual studies . . . attempts to distinguish between a traditional pluralism, in which there are many separate viewpoints and each exists without locating itself in relation to opposing viewpoints, and a plurality of interested yet interlocking positions, in which each position acknowledges its allied or contestatory relation to other positions." The Theory Group argued further that the "pedagogical goal of such a curriculum is to make students aware of how knowledge is produced and how reading takes place and thus make them capable of playing an active and critical role in their society, enabling them to intervene in the dominant discourses of their culture" (November 11, 1987, 1–2).[5] I asked Morton and Zavarzadeh whether the pedagogical goals stated here were really all that different from those advocated in "War of the Words."[6]

An additional claim in "War of the Words" struck less at the department's future major than at my rhetorical version of it, a version that by fall 1987 was no longer a viable candidate for adoption as an overarching framework. Zavarzadeh and Morton claimed that "Syracuse's 'new' curriculum is similar to many other 'new' curricula in that it is part of a concerted effort by conservatives to contain change by recycling traditional educational ideas and practices by up-dating 'literary studies' as the study of 'rhetoric.' By reviving the concept of 'rhetoric' that is basically 'formalist': its main concern is 'how' discourses are produced and received without any concern with 'why' they are there to begin with" (18).

In my reply, I found it noteworthy that in a previously published essay the authors had equated rhetorical reading with a caricature of deconstruction. In "The Nostalgia for Law and Order and the Policing of Knowledge: The Politics of Contemporary Literary Theory," Zavarzadeh gave rhetoric over entirely to a form of de Manean deconstruction that he then characterized as a(nti)political formalism.[7] Indeed, "Nostalgia" dismissed any political definition of rhetoric and, instead, reduced contemporary rhetorical study to some kind of apolitical tropology. "War of the Words" made a similar move by again ignoring political definitions of rhetoric and reducing rhetorical inquiry to formalist analysis or, at best, a version of legitimation study that focused on "'moral' (but not political) questions" (19).

But why should rhetorical study be so limited? Who else insists that rhetorical analysis never asks "why" but only "how"? Why should rhetoric and politics be so absolutely separated? Among other things, this separation hinders inquiry into one of the most important contemporary topics in critical theory and cultural studies: the relation of rhetoric to ideology. Such an inquiry would ask a number of pressing questions:

> How does ideology consist of beliefs and practices constituting interested positions within a cultural conversation at specific historical moments? How does an ideology attempt through trope and argument to convince individuals of the objectivity and universality of its interpretation of the real? How does a crucial part of an ideology's interpretive rhetoric involve producing subjects within socio-political positions consistent with the ideology's world view? How does an ideology function agonistically to represent its adversaries' positions as the exact opposite of how they represent themselves? Is this rhetorical process the only way to salvage the notion of ideology as a false consciousness representing the real in camera obscura? Is ideology always and only constituted in a rhetorical contest that is historically specific and politically situated? (November 11, 1987, 4; see also Burke, Wess, and Cooper)

All of these questions, I argued, were excluded by Zavarzadeh and Morton's depoliticized definition of rhetoric.

This exchange over rhetoric was provocative and useful for my own rhetorical purposes, but unfortunately for those purposes it was very much a sideshow to the main event. By the time of "War of the Words" and my response, rhetoric was no longer the center of departmental discussion. In fact, by the following semester, in the proposal voted on by the department, the term *cultural rhetoric* made only a very minor appearance. Instead, the "problematics of reading" and "modes of inquiry" were the prominent concepts, and the major was officially designated as "English and Textual Studies." In April 1988, the department voted 20-7-1 to replace the old English major with the new major in English and textual studies: a curriculum dividing courses according to whether their mode of inquiry is historical, theoretical, or political and requiring students to take courses from each of these groups.[8]

Although my specific rhetorical proposals were not adopted, I participated in the rhetorical process of invention and negotiation that created this new major, and I am proud of what my colleagues established. The new curriculum is a collective accomplishment, with all the strengths and weaknesses that implies. A result of innovative thinking and difficult compromises, the new curriculum presents one of the first detailed alternatives to the traditional coverage model for English studies. Across all three categories of courses, the English and textual studies major provides one example of how recent developments in critical theory and cultural analysis can be institutionalized.

The Misfortunes of Rhetoric

But one troublesome issue remains, Why did rhetoric lose out as an organizing term? My answer may seem simplistic: A rhetorical framework proposed by a rhetorician beginning with politics did not convince an audience whose conceptions of rhetoric began with either language or composition. My original proposal to use the study of rhetoric as a redefinition of our enterprise was initially an attempt to convince my colleagues to work with the term *rhetoric* as a focus of curricular discussion. My political definition of "cultural rhetoric" was an illustration of how one might enter the debate over what rhetoric could mean and how it could be studied.

For several reasons, this strategy did not work. First, those colleagues most amenable to accepting "rhetoric" as a useful piece of vocabulary were located in a new composition program that became institutionally separate from the English department. Although they remained officially within the department (with their dual appointments), their daily practices, their own conversations, their own institutional interests were now centered in the Writing Program. The challenge of creating a university-wide, four-year composition curriculum almost from scratch gave these potential allies little time to participate in the debates over the English department's undergraduate major.

Not realizing that I was already at a rhetorical disadvantage, I focused my attention on the Theory Group, an informal collective consisting of eleven to thirteen faculty who were the strongest advocates for curricular change. Early in the fall semester of my first year, I discovered an important fact about the rhetorical context for curricular debate in the department: the most significant difference was not, as I had thought, between antitheory traditionalists and the Theory Group, but between two kinds of poststructural theorists in and outside the group. Crudely put, the rhetorical divide was between the theorists who emphasized language and the play of signification and those who emphasized politics and the materiality of discourse. On one side were the so-called language theorists—especially deconstructionists and semioticians; the other side included the so-called political theorists—postmodern Marxists, materialist feminists, and one Foucauldian rhetorician. In arguing for rhetoric as an organizing term, I tried to convince my theory colleagues to view their positions as different stances on rhetoric: One side began with language and was oriented to rhetoric as trope; the other began with power and was oriented to rhetoric as argument. Unfortunately, I could not persuade the theorists at least to try working with these (admittedly reductive) labels for their positions.

In a sense, I rhetorically failed precisely because of the very definitions of rhetoric I was attempting to thematize. That is, I wanted arguments over the definition of rhetoric to serve as a way for articulating positions within the curricular debates, but it was the dominant definitions of rhetoric currently in place that helped defeat my attempt. Specifically, I lost out in the institutional politics of naming partly because many people in the department viewed rhetoric through a narrow understanding of composition study. Unfamiliar with the rich theorizing and sophisticated research in this emergent discipline, some did not take rhetoric seriously as disciplinary knowledge and viewed composition simply as the intuitive art of teaching writing, something "they" did over there in the Writing Program.

Another, more debilitating, definition of rhetoric circulated in the Theory Group: the equation of rhetoric with the formalist dynamics of the text, including the kind of dynamics often associated with American deconstruction and its view of textual tropes working to subvert textual arguments. Both the political theorists and the language theorists agreed about this nonpolitical definition of rhetoric. I convinced neither side of the viability of my more political definition of cultural rhetoric, and, most important, I did not convince even my closest allies, the politically oriented theorists, to accept the definition of rhetoric as a useful area to stage our debates. Rhetoric oriented toward language (and not power) seemed the only rhetoric they could accept as such.

Rhetoric and the Future of English Studies

A few years after the end of my term as department chair, I look back at the rhetorical politics of our curriculum effort, not claiming to have some transcendental distance from the institutional events but instead realizing how much I speak from a position very much within their rhetorical history.[9] I wonder about the development of the graduate curricula in the Writing Program and the English department at Syracuse University and about curricular reform elsewhere. The Syracuse Writing Program, not surprisingly, was the only place where something from my original rhetorical proposal explicitly stuck. The new Ph.D. to be developed there will probably be called a degree in composition and cultural rhetoric. The fact that the Writing Program understands "cultural rhetoric" differently than my more political definition does not bother me. "Cultural rhetoric" might after all help to open up a space at Syracuse where issues of culture, politics, pedagogy, and rhetoric can be negotiated and theorized.

As for the English department, my predictions are equally speculative. On the one hand, several members of the original group pushing for curriculum reform have left the university. On the other hand, the great advantage of institutionalizing new disciplinary movements is that a program like English and textual studies is less dependent for its survival on specific individual professors and, in the short run, can rely upon institutional inertia to prevent an immediate abandonment of progressive reforms, the same inertia, ironically, that in other departments helps traditionalists defend outworn curricula. The first full year of English and textual studies course offerings (1990–91) resulted in positive evaluations from students, and the number of department majors, which had grown dramatically during the previous five years, remains relatively stable despite a sudden drop in total university enrollment.

As for the English department's graduate program and other graduate programs throughout the country, I would like to make the following recommendation. English departments and composition programs have much to gain politically and intellectually by working as institutional allies within American universities. However, to accomplish this alliance in the 1990s, these two changing disciplines must work out their agendas with respect to each other. The best, perhaps only, way for such cooperation to proceed successfully is through the development of local institutional agreements among groups in literary studies, composition, cultural studies, critical theory, linguistics, creative writing, and other fractions of traditional English departments. No national, disciplinarywide solution seems possible at the present time. But some more or less general rhetorical suggestions might still be in order.

Local agreements and alliances should be negotiated in full awareness of the controversial history of the relation between traditional English departments and their composition programs. English faculty throughout the country should not reconceptualize their curricula in their own terms (cultural studies, literary theory, or whatever) and then ask their understandably suspicious composition colleagues to join up. Rather, they should adopt a term traditionally associated with composition study and use that concept as a way of rethinking their own theories, practices, and structures. Of course, the term I suggest is *rhetoric*. More specifically, the notion of *cultural rhetoric* could be used as a means to renegotiate the relationship between English departments and composition programs, as well as their joint relation to other disciplines throughout the university. This has not yet happened at Syracuse, and may never take place there, but changes in the Writing Program and future discussions of its relation to the English department could provide opportunities for moving in the direction I am advocating.

Indeed, some self-representations of the Syracuse English and textual studies major suggest interesting possibilities for its future reinterpretation in terms of rhetoric. In one sense, rhetoric makes an appearance only as a subcategory under theoretical inquiries; in another sense, it is everywhere in the new major. Unnamed as such, rhetoric nevertheless provides a way to understand the framework in which differences are marked in the new curriculum. What is it but "rhetorical contestation" that is being referred to in this passage from a collectively written document explaining the new major:

> In literature departments at the moment, arguments about the formulation of [disciplinary] questions are as intense as arguments about their answers. The traditional curriculum, however, does not call attention to these issues or to the different positions from which textual study proceeds. Faculty may disagree profoundly; and even though students may find out about those disagreements by chance as they move from course to course, the curricular structure implies that it is more important to master certain predesignated works organized by genres, periods, and authors, than to inquire into the grounds of such categories or into the ends and means of reading. Ideally, a new curriculum would shift this emphasis without simply reifying a fashionable methodology or settling for a vapid pluralism as a way of defusing disagreement. At Syracuse, we have tried to construct such a curriculum, one that foregrounds differences among modes of critical practice, acknowledges its own provisionality, and looks to its own further transformation. ("Not a Good Idea")

This passage seems fully involved in a rhetorical perspective. A curriculum that aims to foreground "differences among modes of critical practices" appears to have made rhetoric its framework even while tending to ignore it explicitly.

I could end this essay here and be like the general who, after losing a battle, simply declares victory and leaves the field. But other accounts are too powerful to ignore. There are the competing narratives with which I began, the conflicting stories from ancient Syracuse that remind me of the unpredictability of rhetoric's political consequences. And then there is this final little exchange from modern Syracuse, which makes me even more nervous about my obsessive rhetoricizing of all activities within my ken. While visiting a friend's house, my daughter, then nine, pretended to be the Good Witch of the North. She waived her wand and confidently declared, "Everything turn into everything else." Looking around the room, the friend observed, "Gee, it worked."[10]

Notes

My thanks to Peter Carafiol, Michael Clark, Michael Sprinker, and the late Alvin Sullivan for comments on an earlier version of this essay. I would also like to express my gratitude to those people who invited me to present pieces of this narrative to audiences at several universities and conferences during the last few years. Finally, I would once again like to thank Vice Chancellor Gershon Vincow and, especially, my faculty colleagues for the opportunity to serve as chair of the Syracuse English department. This essay is dedicated to members of the English department at Syracuse University from 1986 to 1991.

1. I am grateful to Karen Bassi and Jeffrey Carnes for help in translating this Greek text by an anonymous Christian author of the fourth or fifth century. (See also Hinks, Wilcox, and Farenga.)

2. This definition of "cultural rhetoric" was not the first one presented to the department but, rather, the result of a series of responses to requests that I clarify my theoretical terms. For more discussion and illustration of this political notion of rhetoric, see Mailloux, *Rhetorical Power* and "Misreading."

3. For Melville's deconstructive take on rhetoric, see *Philosophy Beside Itself.*

4. For more on materialist feminism, see Newton and Rosenfelt; Nussbaum, especially 131–38 and works cited on 245n14; and Wayne, which includes Howard's "Scripts and/versus Playhouses: Ideological Production and the Renaissance Public Stage" (221–36).

5. The circulating document from which I quoted was written by members of the Theory Group; it was later revised and eventually became "Not a Good Idea: A New Curriculum at Syracuse" by Steven Cohan, John W. Crowley, Jean E. Howard, Veronica Kelly, Steven Mailloux, Stephen Melville, Felicity Nussbaum, Bill Readings, Bennet Schaber, Linda Shires, and Thomas Yingling. Unpublished essay, December 1987. Copy available on request.

6. There was, however, at least one important difference between the two statements, a difference in what might be called the "logic" of these pedagogies, which I tried to articulate: "My only problem with [your pedagogical] statement is the 'therefore.' I still don't understand why you think it logically follows that once you get students to see how the Real is not naturally given but socially constructed, once you get them to recognize how their interpretations of texts result from their 'situatedness in a complex network of gender, class, and race relations' ("War" 19), how it necessarily follows that they will 'therefore' intervene in the rhetorical/ideological process they now understand, and intervene in such a way that changes their class's patterns of political oppression. Maybe they will, maybe they won't. This is not an argument against your project, just a less assured prediction of its success" (November 11, 1987, 5). For a response to "War of the Words" from faculty at Carnegie Mellon University, see Shumway and Smith.

7. An opening footnote states that this section of the essay was written by Zavarzadeh. The article has been revised and incorporated into Zavarzadeh and Morton, *Theory, (Post)Modernity, Opposition*.

8. Historical inquiries "assume that texts bear meaning as they are produced and read in specific historical formations." Theoretical inquiries "investigate the conditions under which texts can be said to bear meaning, as well as the questions of whether and how such meaning can become available to a reader." Political inquiries "assume that texts are bearers of political meaning: that is, they mediate power relations." Classes in the category of historical inquiries focus on, for example, "periods and the problem of periodization, reception aesthetics, modes of historical inquiry, and specific histories of genres"; theoretical inquiries "include courses in psychoanalysis, deconstruction, hermeneutics, rhetoric, and poetics"; and political inquiries include "courses in modes of ideology critique, Marxism, cultural rhetoric, and materialist feminism" (*The English Newsletter: Undergraduate News from the English Department, Syracuse University* 1 [March 1990]: 3–4).

9. My position within and relation to that history has changed significantly over the last few years. One important change occurred when, having achieved my goal of helping to establish a new curriculum, I decided not to accept a second three-year term as department chair. Another took place when I left Syracuse to teach rhetorical theory and cultural studies at the University of California, Irvine, where I became an advisor to the composition program and, not incidentally, returned home to Southern California.

10. I am grateful to Peter Mortensen for this anecdote.

☐ Institutional Identity at the State University of New York at Albany: The New Ph.D. in English

Warren Ginsberg

To a large extent, the new program in "Writing, Teaching, and Criticism" at the State University of New York at Albany is the product of the Department of English's attempt to read its history since the mid-seventies as a cultural text. That is to say, the curriculum we have developed has grown out of a particular set of interests at a particular moment. The interests concern the discourse and practice of creative writers, literary critics, and theorists of rhetoric and composition—the fields of expertise of faculty and graduate students. The moment was the late 1980s, when a new awareness of the importance of the history of institutions and professions encouraged reexamination of assumptions that had generated these discourses, ordered relations among them, and given us our identity as a Department of English.

In its simplest form, the most pronounced shift in the curriculum has been to move the primary site of inquiry from reading to writing, considered as a linguistic, educational, historical, and political act. This relocation has had many ramifications, but because the impetus for instituting change did arise from local conditions, I need first to describe briefly the history of graduate study in English at SUNY-Albany.

In 1975, Albany's Ph.D. in English, very much a traditional program in literary study, was deregistered by the State Department of Education. In the years following, the faculty worked hard to expand and enrich the doctor of arts degree, which had been offered along with the Ph.D. since 1971. By affirming the doctor of arts' emphasis on pedagogy, and by combining it with the department's strong interest in creative writing and rhetoric and composition, SUNY-Albany developed a national reputation for producing students who had strong credentials in writing and teaching. In addition, throughout the late 1970s and 1980s, faculty increasingly examined the intersection of literary theory and pedagogy; hallway conversations often shifted from mythopoetics to Hélène Cixous to Jacques Derrida to Frederic Jameson.

In 1987, the department concluded that the viability of the doctor of arts degree was in jeopardy, primarily because many Ph.D. programs had incorporated its emphasis on pedagogy into their own programs. After a year-long consultancy with David Simpson, we decided to formulate a new Ph.D. program that would be based on the strengths of the current doctor of arts.[1] The curriculum that resulted has been in place since 1990; the Ph.D. was reinstated in 1992.

In light of this history and in the wake of experience with the new program, one might well ask what new departmental identity, if any, has emerged? Of course, the very idea of an institutional identity can seem a not-so-innocent oxymoron. In the space that joins interests and practices that are if not contrary then at least particular and various, we read the suppression of different histories of methods and convictions by a politics of power. In our department, we have begun to agree enough about the program to begin to understand the nature of our disagreements. We want our graduates to be able to inquire into the movement between theory and practice, the making of knowledge, the history and institutionalization of the profession, and the pervasive presence of ideological positions in English studies. Yet even if this is the critical (and cultural) work for which the program was designed, few of us would venture to say with authority what constitutes the department's programmatic identity. Indeed, the pivotal issue that engages us, and has become the proper site of protracted critique, is the idea of the program's cohesiveness, or integrity, precisely because it is in this idea that faculty must question who they are individually and what the nature of the polity is that joins them.

In the first part of this essay, therefore, I will quote from the program's foundational document, which was prepared by a department committee with the help and advice of a number of outside advisors, and offer a few comments about its description of programmatic coherence. In the second part, after a brief listing of the seven sections of our new curriculum, I will recount some of my own experiences in teaching a class called "Problems in the Development of Literary Language," which is our rewriting of the traditional "History of the English Language" course. The transformations from the old to the new version of this course, I think, exemplify the purposes and effects of our program.

Programmatic Coherence in the Ph.D. Program

Rather than privilege one area or another of English studies, the department has sought to give the curriculum its integrity by creating an environment in which the claims of "writing, rhetoric, criticism, pedagogy, language study, and literary history constantly intersect and are called into question." According to the proposal for the program,

> every course, whatever its focus, explores its subject from the perspectives which creative writers, students of rhetoric and composition, and literary critics bring to bear on it. This interplay of responses will inevitably challenge the belief that literature is discrete and neatly classifiable into periods or that any one approach to it is unproblematically more valuable than another. Ultimately it will make the traditional distinctions between composition, creative writing, and literary criticism difficult to maintain. In this way, the integrity of the curriculum is assured, because the dialogue between similarity and difference in the discourses the students bring to any one class will encourage them to ask whether any subject can exist apart from the implications of theory, ideology, and institutionality that underwrite the methods by which they are investigated. Thus the interrogative stance that results from asking prior, destabilizing questions extends across the curriculum and becomes a principle of its cohesiveness. It prepares students to read the literature and other discourses of any age in a sophisticated manner.... Writers, rhetoricians and literary critics will find the assumptions and practices of their discourses in turn privileged and placed in unfamiliar contexts. Thus they will gain a better understanding of their own practices by seeing the extent to which each writer is also a literary critic and rhetorician, every rhetorician both writer and reader of literature, all literary critics rhetoricians and writers as well.

One colleague declared on reading this last sentence that we evidently wished to call integrity into being purely by virtue of chiasmatic injunction. To him, the phrase "the extent to which" was the merest sop to rhetorical moderation; the force of the sentence clearly enjoins writers to be critics, critics to be writers. He asked, quite legitimately, whether either necessarily benefits by being the other.

Underwriting my colleague's point is a request to take seriously the belief that writing as a praxis is an extension of the nature of those who practice it, that the qualities of discourse can find the ground for their potential unity not exclusively by difference from other discourses but in the constructing consciousness that articulates the discourse. Certainly, the appeal to the interests and perspectives of the constituents of the program would seem to support this reading. The position my colleague advances is not naively humanistic. The fact that he accords writers a certain intractable autonomy beyond the inscription of language and society is enunciated not in ignorance of theories about the interpellative politics of power or the performative sociality of discourse, but as a deliberate provocation to them.

It is equally possible, of course, to maintain, as a number of my colleagues do, that it is precisely in the space of the chiasmus—and in the vacillation of "the extent to which"—that our status as autonomous writers is transformed. No longer unique, experiencing souls who make meaning, we emerge as discontinuous and aleatory subjects on whose bodies the discourses of race, gender, and class already have written their local histories. We become texts: The languages of creative writing, rhetoric and composition, and literary criticism—what we call our proprietary discourses—own and write us more than we do them. In this reading, the program enacts its integrity by attending to the unruliness of our own textuality. By looking to the blind spot that forever haunts the facticity of knowledge, by acknowledging the randomness of the social orderings that this knowledge has produced, we stake our coherence on the practice of an ongoing, self-reflexive critique of the ways and kinds of knowing we have made.

In my opinion, we fully intended to tie our cohesiveness to a commitment to a pedagogy that brings both positions into contestatory dialogue. As our constituting document continues:

> From the above discussion it will be seen that programmatic coherence is dynamic. Each part of the program interacts with and interrogates the others. Such interaction has the twofold effect of keeping the program open to changing relations between subjects and making the program continually aware of its own assumptions and practices. The areas of writing, pedagogy, and literary criticism are thus interwoven by a sustained critique of the nature of understanding and of the history by which such understanding comes to be.

Pedagogy itself, however, is a social transaction; what goes on in classrooms is not free of ideological commitments. But a pedagogy that merely unmasks assumptions in the name of disinterested inquiry, or that scrutinizes ideologies as if they were only texts, without regard to ethical action, strikes some of us as making the actual politics of teaching and learning a spectral affair. Is it enough to ask our students and ourselves whether our writing is creative or critical, not only to articulate but also to historicize our poetics? Can a program achieve a consensus that is dynamic merely by asking its poets and literary historians to put their proprietary discourses at risk? If we seriously entertain the idea of an autonomous writing self, is it possible to avoid recasting participation in the program in the mystifications of an enlightenment politics based on a bourgeois sense of individuality, which preserves selfhood by convincing citizens that they enter into community by obeying the laws they have given themselves? Or, if the self is displaced into the discourse it writes and by which it is written, is it possible to escape reifying language and manufacturing out of it a fictitious coherence based on an imaginary system of exchange? For if we do reposition ourselves as discrete and aleatory subjects, the excluded other that Derrida says enables us to enter into textual relations will always be contingent. And the knowledges we make, and the subjectivities we fashion to accommodate them, will be equally contingent. In such a dispensation, textuality affords only the ghostliest materiality, which is not much on which to form a community. Unless we see writing subjects as sites of knowing already constructed by the social struggle for meaning, what possibility is there for wide-ranging social intervention?

By asking these questions, which a number of colleagues see the curriculum as authorizing the faculty to ask, a third position becomes evident through which the politics of the making of knowledge and the formation of subjectivities become visible. This aspect of our institutional identity brings us closest to contemporary culture studies. It is also an aspect that the faculty has attempted to write across its entire range of course offerings. But neither this third position, nor either of the others, gives the Ph.D. program its coherence. Rather, its cohesiveness and identity are constructed on acts of oppositional pedagogy in an investment in what Mikhail Bakhtin would call the heteroglossia of the image of our languages, in the pragmatic redescriptions of textual communities. The program offers no synthesis; the chiasmus remains between those who write and the forces that write us. But no position will stand unchallenged by others; fair grounds, it seems to me, on which to base an education in English studies.

Problems in the Development of Literary Language

The instrument devised to realize the program's intentions is an entirely new curriculum divided into seven branches of study. Except for writing in history, which has two, each branch has one core introductory course that explores the basic theory, pragmatics, and problematics of that aspect of English studies, as well as its relationship to the overall curriculum. The seven branches, along with their core courses, are Writing in History ("History of English Studies from 1800 to the Present" and "Gender, Race, and Class in English Studies"); Writing Theory and Practice ("Poetics and Literary Practice"); Rhetoric and Composition ("Composition Theory"); Critical Theory and Practice ("Literary Criticism and Theory since 1950"); Leaching Theory and Practice ("Teaching Writing and Literature"); Language and Language Theory ("Theories of Language"); and Literary History ("Models of History in Literary Criticism").

Each branch of the curriculum contains a number of courses in addition to the core courses that examine aspects of the central topic. Merely from branch and course titles, it is apparent that the curriculum attempts to relate the discourses of creative writing, rhetorical theory, and literary criticism. Catalog copy, however, can at best give only a schematic sense of how a program might work. A description of a course I teach, "Problems in the Development of Literary Language" (included under the Language and Language Theory rubric), might provide an idea of one actual experience in the new order of things.

"Problems in the Development of Literary Language" grew out of the sense that although a course in the history of the English language was certainly relevant to the purpose of the program, history, English, and language needed to be rethought. As a first step to such a reformulation, I wrote a preliminary course description:

> By examining certain moments of linguistic conflict in the history of English literature, this course will ask what literary language is, what qualities constitute it, whether these qualities are objectifiable (as theorists such as Jakobson would hold) or inseparable from a historical set of social conditions that produced them (as any number of socio-linguistic or neo-Marxist writers would contend), and how language was recognized as literary both at the time it was produced and retrospectively according to the politics of canon formation.

My plan was to spend some four to five weeks discussing Old and Middle English. The rest of the time would be divided between the Renaissance and the early modern period. The questions we would ponder, however, would have application beyond the particular texts and epochs that prompted them. For the Anglo-Saxon age, we would ask what constitutes literary language in an oral culture; how does literacy affect literary language; and what are the social implications of literary language in a vernacular when the accepted repository of learning and culture exists in a different language (Latin).

During the later Middle Ages, England had become a trilingual nation. The Church was still the repository of learning, and its language still was Latin, but culture was the provenance of the aristocracy, who spoke French. Late in the period, however, an influential, literate, middle class arose that spoke chiefly English and had a large appetite for literature. Moreover, the aristocracy increasingly spoke only English. At this time as well, Lollards and Wycliffites were trying to demystify the Church by translating its protocols and institutions into English, which had become the exclusive vehicle of social reform. The period was a crucible; all the questions that marked our reading of Bede's version of Caedmon's hymn and *Beowulf* became at once more pressing and more complicated. The nearly simultaneous appearance of Chaucer's works and Langland's *Piers Plowman* shows just how complex and visible the negotiations were among the linguistic, social, and political forces that produced literary language.

In my discussion of the Renaissance, I planned to focus on Shakespeare and the language of drama, especially in light of the new historical work by Stephen Greenblatt and others that situated the language of the plays amid competing social and political discourses. We would reformulate earlier questions in light of the tetralogy of *Richard II, Henry IV, Parts I and II,* and *Henry V,* plays of politics presented as history, and ask why drama became the privileged art form during the Renaissance.

Finally I wanted to discuss some literature with which the students might be more familiar. I had originally thought of texts from the early modern period but decided to let the class itself decide. The choice was Toni Morrison's *Beloved,* which we discussed in conjunction with Bakhtin's *Dialogic Imagination.*

Throughout the course, but especially at the beginning, we would read heavily in theory. We would read Leo Spitzer on "linguistics and literary history," Erich Auerbach on "literary language and its public," and Brian Stock on "the implications of literacy." We would read Ferdinand de Saussure, some Russian Formalists, J. Mukarovsky, Roman Jakobson, and other members of the Prague School, and critiques by Mary Pratt and Derek Attridge. We would read essays by Paul de Man and Derrida, excerpts from Michel Foucault, and Hayden White on "the historical text as literary artefact," along with two more sustained theoretical works, Bakhtin's *Dialogic Imagination* and Terry Eagleton's *The Ideology of Aesthetic.* Finally, we would read an institutional history of the History of the English Language course in Britain, Tony Crowley's *Standard English and the Politics of Language.*[2]

As one might suspect, this mixture proved to be supersaturated. The inaugurating premise of the course, announced as such, was to posit that the concept of literary language was primarily either a local phenomenon—that is, a set of qualities that result from an author's choice of words or manipulation of conventions—or an objectifiable set of linguistic operations that transcend historical instantiation, or a socially and politically constructed ideology. I chose theoretical texts, therefore, that might clear a space for positions that roughly corresponded to the three subjectivities I saw the program bringing into dialogue; in the event, they certainly did locate allegiances by dislocating prior assumptions.

But when we read the literary works and tried to determine what made them literary, we all began to feel what I will call the "uncanny distance of history." All along, students had been asked to discuss the "literariness" of their own creative and critical work in light of the ideas that had been discussed. Because we were similarly situated, in Hans-Georg Gadamer's sense, in time and place as well as by the reading we did in common, the contiguity of the texts we produced and the qualities or forces we invoked to explain them were never in question. Whether we argued that it was a describable orientation toward metaphor (in Jakobson's sense) that made a student's poem literary, or that it was the way another's prose description called attention to the social construction of its apparent genre, communication seemed free and easy. The same was true even of a contemporary work set in a different time, like *Beloved,* whose crafted styles challenge both white and black traditions of literary language and in whose languages race, gender, and class write a history of their oppression and refusal in this country.

But what about a text such as *Beowulf,* which insists not only on its alterity in relation to us but also seems to inscribe in itself, in self-consciously high poetic form, an unbridgeable distance between the events it describes and the attitude according to which they should be judged (the heroic actions of a pagan described by a Christian contemplating his own doomed ancestors)? Words that attend to their own historicity, as do the words of *Beowulf*—participating in a living heroic tradition and eulogizing its obsolescence at the same time—are at once evidence of the linguistic nature of literary language and the evident site of cultural and political struggle to control meaning and effect.

Yet however much we wanted to make the literary synthetic—to see it as the product of continued negotiations among the formal qualities of a text, the unifying intelligence that reformulates them, and the cultural contexts that underwrite both text and intelligence—the darkness of history made us uncomfortable. Once one position or another had been argued and the argument had made the politics of allegiances visible, we sensed that all we had touched of the past was our impositions on it. The language of *Beowulf* marks the scene of transition from oral to written; in it we hear the Church rewriting the esthetic of the oral heroic so that it might become its own ideological instrument to recuperate the past. But when we read this recuperation, did we escape practicing the same kind of solipsistic appropriation that rewrites the past in our own image? We are history's other; our distance from history, our absence from it, is what enables us to represent it. That re-presentation, however, mediated by constructions of time and place, erases the texture, the materiality of the events it would make perceptible. And in the space of that erasure we saw ourselves as the human, textual, and political creatures we are. But our distance and absence from the past also made visible the darkness of what we cannot know of the past, an opaqueness that called into question the making of knowledge as a result of unifying consciousness, or as the consequence of our textuality, or by virtue of our social construction.

Or so, at least, it seemed in the class. History itself as a discourse of knowing the past became as much a focus of discussion as the literariness of language; it caused us to rewrite the premises that began our inquiry. It was the resisting force that gave the course its cohesiveness. The chiasmus remains; I have called it history. It allowed me, a teacher of medieval literature trained to know the history of language, to join the dynamic polity that the Ph.D. program would create.

Notes

1. Because the reputation of the Albany doctor of arts is so strong, the department felt it still might be the degree of choice for a significant number of students. We therefore continue to offer the degree. It shares the same curriculum with the Ph.D. program, but its requirements differ.

Simpson's consultancy was extremely productive. Now chair of the English department of the University of Colorado at Boulder, he supplied the impetus to create a program that systematically investigated how creative writing, rhetoric and composition, and literary history could intersect and interrogate one another; he produced the basic configuration of the curriculum as well. Knowing Simpson's experience at Cambridge University during the turmoil of the early 1980s, as well as the influence of Raymond Williams on his thought, we had guessed at some of the convictions that did indeed drive his work at Albany. What we could not have guessed, but discovered to our immense profit, was his extraordinary ability to honor differences of temperament, praxis, and principle among us by channeling them into fruitful dialectic in the program itself (see Simpson, "Teaching English: What and Where is the Cutting Edge?" and the reply by Knoblauch).

2. The texts for the course are: Derek Attridge, *Peculiar Language: Literature as Difference from the Renaissance to James Joyce* (Ithaca: Cornell University Press, 1988); Attridge, "Closing Statement," in *The Linguistics of Writing: Arguments Between Language and Literature,* ed. Nigel Fabb et al. (New York: Routledge, Chapman and Hall, 1988); Erich Auerbach, *Literary Language and Its Public in Late Antiquity and the Early Middle Ages* (Princeton: Princeton University Press, 1957); M. M. Bakhtin, *The Dialogic Imagination,* ed. M. Holquist (Austin: University of Texas Press, 1981); Tony Crowley, *Standard English and the Politics of Language* (Urbana: University of Illinois Press, 1989); Paul de Man, *Allegories of Reading* (New Haven: Yale University Press, 1979); Terry Eagleton, *The Ideology of the Aesthetic* (London: Blackwell, 1990); Victor Erlich, *Russian Formalism: History-Doctrine* (The Hague: Mouton, 1969); Stanley Fish, *Is There a Text in This Class?* (Cambridge: Harvard University Press, 1980); Michel Foucault, *The Archaeology of Knowledge* (London: Tavistock, 1972); Roman Jakobson, "Closing Statement: Linguistics and Poetics," in *Style*

in Language, ed. T. A. Sebeok (Cambridge: MIT Press, 1960); J. Mukarovsky, "Standard Language and Poetic Language," in *A Prague School Reader on Esthetics, Literary Structure and Style,* ed. Paul Garvin (Washington, D.C.: Georgetown University Press, 1964); Mary L. Pratt, *Toward a Speech Act Theory of Literary Discourse* (Bloomington: Indiana University Press, 1977); Ferdinand de Saussure, *Course in General Linguistics,* trans. W. Baskin (New York: Philosophical Library, 1959); Leo Spitzer, *Representative Essays,* ed. A. Forcione et al. (Stanford: Stanford University Press, 1988); Edward Stankiewicz, "Poetic and Non-Poetic Language in Their Interrelation," in *International Conference of Works-in-Progress Devoted to Problems in Poetics,* ed. Donald Davie et al. (Warsaw: Panstwowe Wydawnictwo-Naukowe, 1961); Brian Stock, *The Implications of Literacy* (Princeton: Princeton University Press, 1983); and Hayden White, *Metahistory: The Historical Imagination in Nineteenth- Century Europe* (Baltimore: Johns Hopkins University Press, 1973).

☐ Burning the Commodity at Both Ends: Cultural Studies and Rhetoric in the First-Year Curriculum at Carnegie-Mellon University

Kristina Straub

The English department at Carnegie-Mellon University has been characterized for more than a decade by its departures from traditional literature curricula. Graduate programs in literary and cultural studies and in rhetoric have helped shape a graduate and undergraduate faculty and curriculum that have expanded the repertoire of methodologies and the objects of study beyond what is usually associated with English departments. Cultural studies has been an integral part of the undergraduate curriculum since 1984, when the Literary and Cultural Studies Program began developing theory-driven classes on canonical and noncanonical literature, film, video, and a wide variety of cultural practices.

Within the context of this short history, I have collaborated with Chris Neuwirth, a colleague in rhetorical studies, to design and implement first-year writing and reading courses that integrate cultural theories of meaning production and reception with writing and reading skills acquisition. The experience has led me to perhaps not very startling but nonetheless lived and, hence, hard-won insights into the position of cultural studies within academic institutions.

The Commodification of Cultural Studies

Cultural studies is constituted within a site of production that gives material and ideological value to specific kinds of curricula. The metaphor of the capitalist marketplace helps clarify how certain kinds of learning become commodified as Armanis, designed for an academic elite, whereas others are packaged as off-the-rack goods for the consumption of the undergraduate masses. Within these marketing practices, cultural studies is frequently positioned as a privileged body of knowledge and methodology taught to graduate students. It is not easily seen as the "right stuff" for the first-year nonmajors, who are viewed as the market for rhetoric, which, however falsely and reductively, is often conflated with composition and relegated to the task of giving undergraduates the "tools" they need for their work across the college curriculum. Although this process of academic commodification generally occurs very quietly in the curriculum, it needs to be confronted and analyzed if, in the institutionalizion of cultural studies, we are to avoid replicating traditional hierarchies and specializations.

Since the beginnings of the Literary and Cultural Studies Program at Carnegie-Mellon, we have tried to avoid the containment of cultural studies within the graduate curriculum by the thoroughgoing inclusion of cultural theories and the study of a broad range of cultural practices within undergraduate course offerings. We offer a major in literary and cultural studies that explicitly challenges traditional English curricula. The catalog description spells out this challenge:

> Our Literary and Cultural Studies program is nationally renowned for having taken a decisive stand in the debate about what should constitute the current subject matter of English Studies. Our position . . . has been to expand the "objects" of study beyond the range of canonical "literature" and narrowly circumscribed (normative and aesthetic) views of literary traditions. These narrower views have been criticized for excluding what many internationalist English Departments are now recognizing the need to include: the work of English and American women and minorities, non-Western, non-Anglophone and postcolonial literatures, as well as nonliterary texts such as television, film, advertising, popular writings, and so on. While our Literary and Cultural Studies program has been a leader in expanding the objects of study, it has also led in pioneering the analytic approaches taken to them. Semiotic, historical, social, and cultural approaches to "texts" have opened new directions and implications for the future of literary studies.

The literary and cultural studies major is one of five tracks available to undergraduates; they can also major in professional writing, rhetorical studies, technical writing, or creative writing. These diverse majors grew out of the historical development of three very different programs in creative writing, rhetoric, and literary and cultural studies. Students are not, however, locked within courses specific to their respective majors. Typically, all English majors take an evenly dispersed mix of courses in rhetoric, creative writing, and literary and cultural studies. They all also take a core of three courses, taught by literary and cultural studies faculty, that privilege cultural analysis: "Discursive Practices," "Reading Twentieth-

Century Culture," and "Discourse and Historical Change." Although I certainly cannot claim an unproblematic integration of cultural studies within the diverse curriculum, I can say that the study of cultural theories and practices is integral to undergraduate English education at Carnegie-Mellon University.

Like most English departments, Carnegie-Mellon's provides, in addition to courses for majors, writing instruction for the university's first-year students. "Reading Texts" and "Strategies for Writing," the required first-year courses from 1984 to 1990, were our boldest counter to the elitism of steeping the "in" group of graduate students in Marxism, feminism, and poststructuralist theory while giving the "outsider" first-year students the practical tools of reading and writing. The work of Kathleen McCormick and Gary Waller (the designers of "Reading Texts") and Linda Flower (the designer of "Strategies for Writing") began the task of subverting notions of a skills-oriented first-year curriculum as the polar opposite of "sophisticated" rhetorical and cultural theory.

The courses paired the rhetoric faculty's expertise in writing skills acquisition with the literary and cultural studies faculty's emphasis on cultural theories of reception and production. "Strategies for Writing" called for a focus on "the process of discovery (who one is and what one has to say) and the process of communication," and "Reading Texts" laid the stress on "some of the complex theoretical and methodological issues of reading." Our first-year curriculum was on a continuum with our majors and graduate curricula, not a separate commodity only for the consumption of nonexpert outsiders. The courses initiated the critical step of bringing theory out of its polarized relation to the practical work of training first-year readers and writers and taught us the basic premise that curriculum should be thought of in terms of how it is shaped—commodified—by specific institutional demands.[1]

Defining and Transgressing Boundaries

Cultural studies, as it is thought of and practiced in academic institutions, is probably necessarily caught within contradictions between boundary definition and boundary transgression. Although the term *institution* suggests a stability and centrality that hardly seem applicable to the sort of work that we do at Carnegie-Mellon University, we seem to be continually formulating expectations and conventions—tribal rites, as it were—that govern the very forms taken by constant reassessments and revisions of the curriculum.

Some of the pressure to revise comes from teaching at an institution that tends to value innovation over tradition in the curriculum. Carnegie-

Mellon University is a model postmodern capitalist institution in its allowance for resistance to dominant ideologies and practices within an intellectual and curricular marketplace dominated, but not totally defined, by those ideologies and practices. Counter to hegemonic practices, some of the impetus toward fluidity and change comes from a departmental commitment to what bell hooks has defined as a cultural studies that attends to and supports political efforts to fight the oppression of, for example, people of color, poor people, women, and gays and lesbians (8). Although all of the faculty does not share and value this principle equally, or understand it in the same way, it continues to shape curricular development. Courses in feminism, gay and lesbian studies, African-American studies, and Arabic studies, to give a few examples, are as central to our curricular concerns as are courses in poststructuralist theories or Renaissance literature and historiography.

This revisionary curricular practice, part institutional habit, part political commitment, nonetheless instantiates categories of intellectual importance and moral value even as it challenges them. However wary one is of the institutional practices of curricular commodification, the production of a curriculum results in a commodity that must be sold to instructors and students. As such, it reconstitutes definitions of canon, methodology, and discipline even as it dissolves them.

Positivist Pedagogy

In order to avoid the commodification of cultural studies as a product by and for the elite, I see the need for pedagogical methods that would seem to be at odds with cultural studies' critiques of positivist epistemology. Cultural studies is not reducible to either interdisciplinarity or the mere expansion of the range of cultural objects that should be studied, although it might certainly entail both. Central to the teaching of cultural studies at Carnegie-Mellon is the careful scrutiny of epistemological methods. Students are asked to be critical not only of the objects of their study but also of their methods of learning and interpretation. This self-consciousness means being critical of methods of interpretation while students are in the process of learning such methods. Such a critical stance can lead, in turn, to some pedagogical contradictions: Learn this method of reading but question its importance, we implicitly tell students.

Under the pressure of this contradiction, we worked to foreground rather than efface the methodological processes of reading and writing. To teach cultural studies in introductory reading and writing courses, Neuwirth and I needed to account for how students acquire knowledge and skills. It was not realistic to ask them to perform a feminist critique of advertising or to deconstruct the institutionalization of racism within some cultural context without giving them access to verbal skills of interpretation and argument that we implicitly or explicitly demand they exercise. Asking students to emulate our critiques seemed inadequate to getting the job done. Although many students do learn this way, emulation may or may not teach them how to work outside the specific frame of our examples. This method of instruction depends on what Paulo Freire calls a "banking" model of learning that does not empower a range of students—other than the professorial wannabes—as speaking subjects. Neuwirth and I sought a pedagogy that accounted more carefully for the acretive process that nonexperts use to take in an unfamiliar body of knowledge and gradually master new ideas and skills. We needed, in short, to give first-year students access to methods of writing and reading that were, in turn, predicated on aready-made set of decisions about what kinds of knowledge and skills to privilege.

As a result of this need, we found ourselves in the contradictory position of privileging some epistemological methods and, thus, challenging some hegemonic assumptions about culture and the nature of representation. Cultural studies, particularly the field that most informs the work I do, feminist cultural studies, calls into question positivist ways of knowing, which tend to empower white, male, straight subjects exclusively. As Evelyn Fox Keller has argued, Western scientific "objectivity" is a historically specific ideology that encodes a gendered split between a masculinized objective observer/researcher and a feminized object of study. The Enlightenment construction of objectivity as a mode of philosophical and scientific inquiry is, then, not surprisingly, suspect within feminist cultural studies analysis and criticism. Teaching inexperienced readers and writers to speak for themselves, however, seems to entail privileging this method of interpretation and argument by the very act of using it to train students to read and write.

The First-Year Classes: "Argument" and "Interpretation"

Neuwirth and I wanted a pair of courses that embodied the integral relation between reading and writing, between interpreting texts and making them. Our goal was to develop a single methodology to enable students to improve their skills in both reading and writing. To achieve this, we took a semiotic as well as rhetorical approach to the term *argument*. We reasoned that all texts—expository essays, autobiography, fictional narratives, and experimental videos, for example—are arguments in the sense that they make certain claims by giving evidence. Reading is a process of assessing that evidence, whereas writing is its expression and arrangement. Interpretation makes an argument about a text; argument is, in turn, inescapably interpretive. The two activities are dependent on a shared set of methods. Hence, we decided we needed a pair of classes that taught two sides of the same coin: "Argument" and "Interpretation." We wanted to stress, in the course description, that both courses taught, with different emphases, the same skills:

> These courses are companion pieces that will give students who take both a comprehensive and deeply inter-related grounding in communication processes. Either class taken alone (for 9 units) will serve as a Designated Writing Class; both teach writing along similar lines and both focus on the way in which the two elements of interpretation and argument work together in the processes of communication and social and personal development. The class "Argument" builds on rhetorical theory and puts more emphasis on the formal aspects of developing an argument so as to make an intervention in a conversation, discourse community, or dispute. The class in "Interpretation" builds on social and cultural studies and puts more emphasis on the processes and problems of making sense of other people's positions and arguments as a central part of producing one's own position. Each class is self-contained. They can be taken singly or together, and there is no preferred sequence.

Like their precursors "Strategies for Writing" and "Reading Texts," "Argument" and "Interpretation" draw from both rhetorical and cultural approaches to writing and reading. Unlike the earlier courses, they share a set of methods by which students learn both processes. A concrete and specific methodology for making meaning, either through argument (as a writer) or interpretation (as a reader), is both the main strength of the curriculum and its greatest danger. Through this adherence to method, institutional and disciplinary boundaries between reading and writing, argument and interpretation, and cultural studies and rhetoric are violated productively and creatively. At the same time, an epistemologically loaded methodology risks becoming an unexamined, unselfconscious form of disciplinary regimen.

The first transgression against institutional boundaries was the way in which Neuwirth and I worked together to design the curriculum. Collaboration was not new between the Program of Rhetoric and the Literary and Cultural Studies Program at the first-year level: Flower, McCormick, and Waller had set the precedent years earlier. This time, however, we were asked by Alan Kennedy, our department head, to approach the collaboration on somewhat different terms. Instead of designing a writing class based on rhetorical principles and a reading class based on cultural studies, we were asked to think about two courses that would teach both reading and writing in different but complementary ways and that would include both cultural studies and rhetorical assumptions about the nature of meaning production and consumption.[2]

An obvious result of this merger, given our institutional history, would have been a rhetorical methodology and a cultural studies-defined content. This result would have reinscribed the disciplinary boundaries between reading as the business of cultural studies and writing as that of rhetoric. We did not want those boundaries in place, however; for the reasons explained earlier, we were convinced that teaching writing should not be positioned in the academy as the work of a professorial proletariat while the reading of texts was seen as the more advanced and glamorous (but perhaps ethereal) practice.

The problem, then, was to design content and methodology that were deeply informed by the cognitive understanding of what individuals do when they read and write and by a social understanding of meaning's reception and production as cultural and political. The cognitive work of our rhetoric program seemed to address the problem of knowledge and skills acquisition in practical, workable ways; literary and cultural studies seemed to provide theories and reading practices for explaining the acquisition in terms of power and positionality.

After consultation with other colleagues, Neuwirth and I decided that we needed a common vocabulary for describing a method of reading and writing that opened into the cognitive and the social. A precursor for such a discursive model came to hand in the argumentation methodology designed by Neuwirth, David Kaufer, and Cheryl Geisler in *Arguing from Sources*. This method teaches reading and writing by taking students through a carefully staged acretive process of skills acquisition. Students begin with learning to summarize texts, to read closely, be accountable to the text, and offer a plausible interpretation of that text. Next, they learn synthesis, which involves bringing texts into a conversation with each other by identifying and articulating common and divergent points on an issue. Finally, students move to the stage of analysis and begin to posit problems not fully accounted for in the texts and assess the texts in relation to the demands of those problems.

What was underdeveloped in this methodology was a language that explicitly connected the cognitive process of meaning reception and production with an understanding of meaning as an inevitably political cultural practice. *Arguing from Sources* provided a term for making this connection: *mapping* is used as a metaphor for how one understands the relationality of different texts speaking to an issue. To write was to take a position on a discursive map; to read was to learn the spot where someone else stood. This model kept us close to the cognitive and led almost no distance into the cultural, however, because it operates on the assumption that positionality is a simple matter predicated on individual choice.

We needed pedagogical means of reinforcing the social dimension of argumentation, the ways in which institutionalized differences structure power relations. One measure we took was to strengthen the emphasis given to culture in the course topics. Neuwirth chose to adhere to the topic of literacy, very broadly defined, in "Argument." She framed the topic in a cultural analysis through specific readings on the relationship between power and language. "Interpretation" focuses on how the human body is represented in a variety of popular discourses: fashion photography, AIDS education, and other specific discourses on race, class, gender, and sexual identity. The other measure to give emphasis to the cultural dimension of argumentation came from the methodology itself. Paradoxically, the cognitive method of argumentation seems to have the potential to deconstruct the individualism on which it is based.

The methodology we developed offers a highly task-oriented approach to teaching argumentation as a set of social exchanges in which individuals must operate. The students' first job is to read and understand an argument that may or may not represent a position that is familiar and comfortable. We begin "Interpretation" one semester with a section ("Hard Bodies") from Stuart Ewen's *All Consuming Images* on how work and ideologies of labor shape body image and experience in advanced technological, capitalist cultures. The first assignment is summary, only not so simply understood as paraphrase. It is, rather, understood and taught as a form of interpretation. Rather than expecting students to agree or disagree with an essay informed by cultural theory (let alone comprehend it immediately or completely), the class works through it point by point, transition by transition, until students are able to produce a version of its content. I ask them to think in terms of three different accountabilities: their accountability to the text, to a hypothetical reader who has not read the text, and to their own positionality. In summary, the first two accountabilities take priority.

The process of the assignment may take a period of three to four weeks, a time when the students will also study other readings, critical and autobiographical, that will help them envision a community of diverse thinkers on the issue of how representation affects and is affected by the human body. Argumentation is understood temporally as a process by which one articulates a viewpoint (a sort of conversation model) and spatially as a position that only makes sense in relation to other positions on a map that represents a particular discursive territory (the model of mapping).

The second assignment further emphasizes the relationality and positionality implicit in the metaphor of mapping arguments and in the more rhetorical metaphor of argument as conversation. The class works on developing a synthesis essay that articulates connections and disjunctions between several different arguments on a topic. As with summary, the point is not to get the students to "swallow" an argument so much as to understand how it works and to grasp its relation to other positionalities, other arguments. The task is conceptual and skills-oriented at the same time. Students must be able to articulate a range of opinions and understand their relatedness and differences by bringing different texts into conversation.

Both assignments carry the contradiction between transgression and redefinition to which I have referred. The methodology breaks down the disciplinarily enforced barriers between reading and writing. To read is to construct an interpretation that is also an argument. A reading is a hypothesis about the text that can be supported with evidence from that text, and the method that drives the construction of that reading also structures students' written assignments. But it does so by privileging a particular cognitive method that draws, willy-nilly, new boundaries around what is understood to be the discipline of English studies.

Another, more serious contradiction here is both troubling and liberating, although I am inclined to emphasize the latter. The methodology insists that students produce detailed, concrete arguments toward which they may well feel uneasy, even hostile. Here is the paradox in our use of argumentation methodology: By insisting on adherence to a hermeneutic model that privileges a specific epistemology, we open the possibility of accessing ways of knowing that may be other to what dominant ideology validates in students' experience. The method does not ask students to dig down within their personal experience for the political knowledge of difference and power; it does not assume that students will be converted to heightened social awareness by identifying with otherness. Rather, it holds that cultural differences are, like other forms of knowledge, learned slowly and acretively, with the gradual accumulation of familiarity with others' arguments.

Initially in the course, the students' possible hostility to—or unfamiliarity with—feminism, Marxism, and other analyses of class, race, gender, and sexual difference are confronted with demands for accountability rather than conversion. Yet, the methodology of cognition as purely individual work is privileged, even overprivileged, in the task of learning to produce arguments that articulate social and cultural differences that challenge the ideology of individualism upon which the methodology is based. A utopian goal implicit in the course's design is to reach the point at which methodology deconstructs itself within the student's recognition of its ideological limits.

Like most utopian goals, this point may not be reached within the confines of individual classes, or it might not be reached at all. In the process, however, the students in my institution, who are typically afraid of what is not "American," mainstream, and "safe," are familiarized with what may well have been other to their experience. They can easily get through a class unconverted to a multicultural sensitivity, but it is difficult, I hope, to work through the reading and writing tasks without learning how to be intellectually accountable to cultural positions other than their own.

With analysis, the third formal assignment, students are asked to work into their map of a discursive territory explicit definitions of their own positions. The skills that are emphasized, with the help of Hilary Masters, my colleague in creative writing, are story-telling and narrative development. It is possible that student writing and class discussion at this part of the course might disintegrate into chaotic, unselfconscious opinionizing or anecdotal self-indulgence. To try to circumvent this danger, the class frames the articulation of individual positions within the task of analyzing the strengths and weaknesses of the arguments that have been mapped. Hence, students are asked to think of "troublesome" stories as points of entry into thinking through and evaluating various arguments they have been reading. Does their experience with dieting or bodybuilding, for example, complicate the problems or solutions offered by essays on body image and gender roles, body image and labor? In other words, their experience must be represented in order to account for other arguments, other representations, and, in turn, to hold those arguments accountable. As Michel de Certeau argues, stories "organize walks" over discursive terrain (116). Stories allow students to move among fixed positions and negotiate differences between positionalities in the very act of helping define where they are at a given moment.

Critical, then, to the analytic work that students perform are case stories they develop out of their personal experience, experience with a community, or even with a text. These are what Neuwirth, Kaufer, and Giesler call "troublesome narratives," stories that point to a problem or problems that may be incompletely articulated or suppressed in readings students encounter in their mapping exercises of summary and synthesis (189–95). For example, a student might narrate a problem case that gestures toward an issue for which Ewen's article may not account, such as how class or racial difference complicates the relationship between technology and the body. Narratives work for both reading and writing to develop students' awareness of differences among themselves and between themselves and others.

For their final assignment, students are asked to draw on a pool of "argumentative" sources—their own "problem cases," the stories of other students, and the narrative and expository readings that they have used in the course—to create an analytic narrative that sums up, at the moment at least, their best sense of a particular discursive terrain and their place within it. Personal narratives are, then, deromanticized as individual expression and placed on the social and cognitive terrain of argumentation. Both plot line and imagery are arguments that an individual may skillfully build, but that are always accountable to the other arguments they engage.

Conclusion

I hope we have designed a first-year curriculum that challenges disciplinary boundaries between reading and writing as linguistic practices. This constructive confusion has benefits that work both cognitively (for the individual students) and institutionally (for the academic contexts in which the course takes place). The methodology of argumentation, as we use it, calls on students to engage in systematic practices that foreground the interpretive, meaning-producing qualities of both reading and writing. The boundaries between the two are challenged on the cognitive level as students learn a particular method of consuming a text (summary) that can be enacted, in turn, as writing, the production of meaning. Students often walk into first-year classes assuming that reading is the consumption of a commodity and that as such it needs no more method or structure than eating a bag of popcorn. Most see writing, on the other hand, as a task that they are more or less able to perform but that involves some work. Both "Argument" and "Interpretation" demand that students see reading to be just as much of a task as writing in that it calls for systematic methods that produce meaning. Institutionally, reading and writing become confused because there is no longer a reading course in which students learn to consume texts and a writing course in which they learn to produce them.

These courses enact other transgressions against distinctions traditional to the department at Carnegie-Mellon, distinctions common—although perhaps not so well defined—in other institutionalized English-language programs. The concepts of writing as cognitive, cultural, or expressive practices are undergoing some rethinking among those of us who teach these courses. Carnegie-Mellon's rhetoric program, although diverse and broad-based in its approaches and interests, has perhaps been best known for its emphasis on writing and cognition. Creative writing has given pride of place to individual expression, while the Literary and Cultural Studies Program holds ground on the cultural and social nature of meaning production and reception. Our programmatic differences are in no way becoming blended into a homogeneous whole, nor do we desire that end. Nor are we engaged in what Gerald Graff calls "teaching the conflicts" to students. Rather, we find ourselves bartering for useful theoretical and practical models for the production and reception of meaning. Nobody is bridging any gaps that I can see, but some of us are beginning to do a brisk business in pedagogical theory and practice across territorial lines. I hope that in doing so we are subverting the very commodity structure in which we participate as academicians.

This transgression of disciplinary, institutional, and cognitive boundaries puts pressure on students as well as teachers to reexamine and revise conceptions of personal and cultural practices within the university. As teachers, we find ourselves consciously mapping the territory of our institutionalized space in much the same way that students map differences among texts. At the same time, however, the commerce across various borders pressures us to acknowledge the boundaries that do not get transgressed, the institutionalizing effects of practices that work against institutions. Although the methodology of argumentation calls into question boundaries between reading and writing, consumption and production, between a variety of disciplinary practices and theories, it also instantiates specific linguistic practices and theories as the norm. We expect students to read in certain ways. We expect them to produce sentences, paragraphs, and essays that conform to certain tribal patterns. The constructive confusion between skills and theory results in a specific method of argumentation that seeks to bypass students' knee-jerk reactions to unfamiliar ideas by insisting that they keep to certain tasks. In order to map a cultural terrain, students learn the rules by which a particular game is played; that game, in turn, constitutes another set of boundaries.

The interprogrammatic commerce that has taken place in the English department at Carnegie-Mellon University makes it clear that cultural studies is in the contradictory position of instantiating institutional boundaries even as it challenges them. De Certeau's "Reading as Poaching" and Robert J. Tierney and P. David Pierson's "Toward a Composing Model of Reading" argue the shared nature of reading and writing as active processes; de Certeau characterizes reading as a fluid and inherently rule-breaking practice; and Tierney and Pierson implicitly assume a right versus a wrong way to read. Although the language of mapping and positionality opens writing and reading to a cultural critique of meaning as both malleable product and dialectical process, culturally produced and never natural, it is drawn from a theory and practice that are necessarily restrictive and exclusive. It may be necessary to foreground precisely this contradiction if cultural studies is to avoid becoming just one more institutionalized practice, blind to its own oppressive and exclusionary mechanisms.

Notes

1. For an interesting discussion of some theoretical work that went into shaping our first-year curriculum, see McCormick.

2. There were institutional and theoretical reasons for this merger of method and purpose that Kennedy, David Kaufer, Neuwirth, and I have developed at length elsewhere. For an account of these and of the institutional process of conceptualizing and launching these courses, see Kennedy, Neuwirth, Straub, and Kaufer.

☐ *The Heath Anthology* and Cultural Boundaries

Paul Lauter

To sketch the development of *The Heath Anthology of American Literature* is in some sense to produce a small-screen version of American cultural history since the mid-sixties. The *Heath* emerged from a project initiated in the late 1970s at The Feminist Press and modestly called—in the ebullient spirit of the previous decade—Reconstructing American Literature (RAL). RAL was engendered by the questions raised by the sixties movements for social and political change: Looking at textbooks, curricula, and academic research priorities, we asked "Where are the blacks?" "Where are the women?" Initially, the project was an effort to answer such questions by providing resources like changed syllabi, bibliographies, theoretical grounds, and, above all, the sense that those working to redefine academic study were not isolated but part of a spreading movement.

It seemed obvious in the late sixties that most existing curricula, and the textbooks on which they were were based, displayed and perpetuated traditional, exclusionary definitions of "American literature"—not to speak of "Western civilization." College curricula—so it seemed to us college-focused educational rebels—played a central role in defining and maintaining what we were only beginning to call the "literary canon." If we not only taught differently—as many had learned to do in such projects as the 1964 Mississippi Summer Freedom Schools (see *Radical Teacher* 41 [1991], which reprints much of the 1964 Freedom School curriculum and includes a number of comments about it)—but also introduced different works, we believed we could change the conception of what was valuable to read and also transform students' attitudes toward reading and, it might be, their ideas about social change and their roles in it. We had experienced how exciting freedom school classes on *Native Son* and on works by Langston Hughes, Gwendolyn Brooks, and e. e. cummings could be. Why not try to reconstruct our everyday classrooms along lines directed at once by a radical pedagogy *and* a revisionary conception of literary value?

Toward such ends, alternative publishing enterprises were established, among many others The Feminist Press, KNOW, Inc., Mnemosyne, and Arte Publico. More commercial ventures like Arno were also designed to provide students and other curious readers with previously "lost" or discarded texts, usually in the form of individual volumes containing single works such as Rebecca Harding Davis's *Life in the Iron Mills* or William Wells Brown's *Clotelle*. Without these, faculty had no way to depart significantly from established curricula or the limited criteria of value New Criticism had established as literary gospel.

But by the mid-seventies, it had begun to seem that carrying this work from what were the fringes to the curricular core of the academy required not only individual volumes of "new" texts—becoming too expensive for many students—but also an anthology. The anthology form, moreover, could serve a broader cultural function. As had earlier been the case, an anthology could be used to stake out cultural boundaries different from those previously marked by such terms as *American literature*.

That has, I think, happened. Not solely because of *The Heath Anthology*, to be sure, but because the movement in which the *Heath* has played a role—especially among younger academics—has so changed what goes on in today's classrooms that there is no going back to the monocultural curricula of the 1950s. I would not diminish the *Anthology*'s role in that process. In many kinds of classrooms, simply by placing between the same covers the work of Alice Cary and Edgar Allan Poe, that of Frances E. W. Harper alongside that of H. D. Thoreau, Charles Chesnutt beside Stephen Crane, the *Heath* has helped legitimate ideas not only of "American" but also of "literature" certainly distinct from those on which I was brought up during the fifties. But to focus, even so briefly, on the effects of *The Heath Anthology* is to pass much too quickly by the complex and interestingly contradictory processes of its creation. I want to emphasize two elements here: the relationship of the original RAL project to its commercial realization and the composition of the editorial board that brought the project to fruition.

Reconstructing American Literature as Commodity: Esthetics and Politics

Reconstructing American literature was an ambitious project, and it was apparent even at the beginning that resources quite beyond those available to The Feminist Press would be necessary to carry it out. Initially—and ironically, some might say, in view of the recent culture wars—the source of money was a creation of the Nixon administration, the Fund for the Improvement of Post-Secondary Education (FIPSE). As one of the founders and a staff member of The Feminist Press, I had originally seen the project not as a cultural venture with commercial potential, but as a progressive tool for encouraging and supporting curricular change by my peers and thus for pressuring creators of existing anthologies to alter their books, which they had been doing marginally, at best. In fact, one key part of the project—for which The Feminist Press was actually funded—was compiling, editing, and publishing a collection of syllabi of significantly "reconstructed" courses (*Reconstructing American Literature,* 1983). Such syllabi, we had found in the early days of the academic women's movement, were critical in supporting the development of a new discipline, women's studies, as well as in fostering feminist change within existing disciplines like English, history, and psychology.

Not surprisingly, once D. C. Heath had taken on the project in the mid-eighties, I was apprehensive that our goals could be compromised by a publisher's commercial priorities. The FIPSE program officer, Richard Hendrix, was far more optimistic than I about the possibility of actually creating and successfully marketing a serious revisionist anthology. I saw the project as expressing and helping implement a cause; he recognized that, especially as we turned toward the 1980s, causes needed to be sold as systematically as Ben and Jerry's ice cream.

I viewed my role—at least in the beginning—as organizing other faculty members; I had been doing that for years, but this time the goals involved curricula and culture, not unions or peace or, at least directly, civil rights. Hendrix perhaps saw that there might be less conflict between our organizing objectives and the commercial interests of a textbook house. And that is how it turned out. Or, more accurately, the processes of organizing the field became virtually indistinguishable from those of creating a market for the book. At the same time, the commercial interests of the publisher became virtually indistinguishable from the promotion of our cause, which I would loosely characterize as multiculturalism.

That anything—perhaps short of overthrowing the power relationships of class in America—can profitably be sold is a cliché of contemporary capitalism. Yet one of the more interesting features of the project for me remains the rapidity with which the borders between commerce and cause became indistinct. How to understand that? One might argue that the *Heath*'s departures from the norms of anthologies, that its "reforms," are so minor that they have easily been co-opted.[1] It is true that one *could* use the *Heath* to teach a perfectly traditional course in American literature. Very unlikely, to be sure, but possible. The anthology is, of course, a commodity. But in the real world where it is bought, sold, and used, it is also more than that. The book has emerged not only as a practical revisionary tool and a successful commercial enterprise, but also as a cultural symbol. Within the academic world, choosing to teach from the *Heath* has become a statement, not only that one is reasonably conversant with the new scholarship, but also that one values the authors and texts it has brought to light. The anthology's very existence helps legitimate a variety in American literature classrooms literally unthinkable in the early eighties—as the limits of the syllabi included in *Reconstructing American Literature* illustrate.

But, one might ask, so what? Is the kind of American literature course one teaches a matter of significance? Will it rebuild community in Los Angeles, much less diminish the cultural fissures daily widening across American society? Will it even promote literacy among those who get to college, much less among those daily pushed out of schools into the streets of the 'hood? No serious person could answer such questions with a simple "Yes." And yet, as attacks on *The Heath Anthology* from the right suggest, something more is at stake here than publishing profits or minor rearrangements of the cultural landscape. The question of what we teach cannot be separated from what we value, and therefore, I would argue, from our values. To value writers who have largely been marginalized is at some level to call into question the cultural order, and thus the social boundaries, upon which that process of marginalization has been based.

These connections were imprinted upon my consciousness one searing afternoon in July 1967. I was directing the first functioning community school project in the country, at the Morgan Elementary School in Washington, D.C. We were halfway through an intense and conflicted institute for the teachers and interns who would be staffing the school that fall when I was called in to explain the purposes of the troublesome institute to white and black parents active in the Adams-Morgan Community Council. Well-intentioned and seriously concerned with the education of all the kids in that 99 percent black and poor school, whites in particular feared that we were embarked on what was then called a "black power" curriculum. The argument about our educational and political strategies heated even more rapidly than the storefront in which our folding chairs were circled. Finally, one of the white mothers, her voice pitching higher and higher, said, "But if you teach the students to be proud of the fact that they're black, where does that leave my child?"

Where, indeed? The arguments that particular authors and texts propound certain values inherent in their race or gender is absurd, as the weekly news photographs of Justice Clarence Thomas hardly need to remind us. But to give Langston Hughes equal billing with T. S. Eliot has nothing to do with some mythical essence each might be supposed to have. Rather, it calls into question established power relationships, at least as these are played out in the arena we name "culture"—one among many areas (the voting booth and the abortion clinic entryway are others) where groups of people contest for authority.

Conservatives have claimed that the standards used to promote Eliot and Ezra Pound are "apolitical." Indeed, some reviewers of the *Heath,* like Mark Edmundson in *TLS* and Richard Ruland in *American Literary History,* construct dichotomous models of culture wherein political and esthetic values are held to be utterly separate and decidedly unequal. Edmundson, for example, erects a supposed "discrepancy" between what he calls "traditional literary values" and "'political' conceptions of the origins and purposes of literature" (1133). Indeed, his review of the *Anthology* can be schematized sentence by sentence and paragraph by paragraph within that antinomy:

"conventional aesthetic standards" ----- political standards
"artistic achievement" -------------------- political image
"writing well" ---------------------------- adopting a politically progressive stance
"sophisticated formal concerns" -------- readily accessible narrative
"intensity of verbal invention" ---------- thematic intensity
James Merrill et al. ----------------------- Garrett Hongo et al. (1133)

This absolute cleavage between the realms of the esthetic and the political seems to me theoretically naive—and sort of uninteresting. Indeed, one of the main problems that vexes the question of art is precisely its conflicted intersections with politics—as the careers of such contemporaries as Clement Greenberg, Hilton Kramer, and André Malraux—not to speak of Shelley, Wordsworth, and Pound—should remind us. Art is not politics, nor politics art. Nevertheless, esthetic standards are constructed *by* people *in* history—as the violent shifts in taste, sales, and the price of art amply demonstrate. Standards therefore express, in part, political values—not to speak of commercial interests. Indeed, as my two lists may suggest, Edmundson's own construction of a discrepancy constitutes a political argument for certain kinds of art and certain groups of artists—all white, incidentally—and against others. But that is not surprising. For we learn to value what is valued in "our civilization" (to use Eliot's interesting formulation) and not those things that seem to challenge the order upon which our own status is erected.

The Heath Editorial Board: Reconstructing Standards of Value

This ideological issue of the political and the esthetic was at the center of our problems in shaping the *Anthology*. It was clear to me from the beginning of the project that for both intellectual and political reasons RAL would have to involve a far wider spectrum of participants—especially in terms of race or ethnicity and sex—than that contained in any previous anthology editorial board. American literature as a field of study had exploded during the 1970s, and no small group of academics, and certainly no one individual, could command more than a fraction of the new scholarship, much less that and the existing tradition. I therefore organized an editorial board of fourteen members. The board had equal numbers of white and minority, male and female participants—essential to our intellectual objectives rather than responsive to some abstract notions of affirmative action, as superficial right-wing critics have charged. It was simply a fact of life that the overwhelming majority of those specializing in African-American literature were black, those specializing in women's writing were female, and so forth. If things have changed somewhat today, that is probably as much a function of the contracting job market and the consequent need for applicants to diversify their credentials as it is of the diffusion of progressive politics among academics.

Be that as it may, even a diverse editorial board did not seem adequate to the project's goals. Thus I welcomed a proposal made at the RAL institute in 1982 by Margaret O'Connor that we invite participation by as many scholars in the field as we could reach. Instead of asking the editorial board to come up with the texts we might include, she suggested, why not ask everyone who taught American literature what they would want to see in a collection and, moreover, give them the opportunity to commit themselves to the project by editing the writers they proposed. If this idea had the seeds of a bureaucratic nightmare—especially after some 750 of our colleagues had responded—it was also an ingenious approach to the project's objectives of implementing diversity and organizing the field.

Although I had not realized that editing an author for an anthology would constitute an academically significant credential for these individuals, it was apparent from the outset that having hundreds of colleagues working on the *Anthology* would go a long way to ensuring that hundreds of colleagues would use it. On the other side, so to speak, D. C. Heath devised a series of marketing initiatives, especially a semiannual *Newsletter*. The *Heath Anthology of American Literature Newsletter*, even before the *Anthology* itself was published, became a significant means for promoting educationally progressive ideas as well as for transmitting concrete information about the implementation of multicultural literary curricula. In fact, the *Newsletter* has become the most widely circulated journal in the field, going to more than eight thousand faculty, and its focus on pedagogy and syllabi is itself a significant comment on what defines that field.

But even with the enormous diversity of input, and with the significant differences of training and priorities that characterized the editorial board, we found that our primary task involved reconstructing our own standards of value. Whatever else we were, we were academics, products of a form of specialized training that validated certain ways of thinking about, indeed, of responding to, texts. We were also relatively privileged members of American society, invested in ways barely discernible to us in the system of values and power relationships which—happily for us—sustained the work we did and therefore the jobs we held. We *had* jobs, networks of preferment, and valuable reputations, any of which might conceivably be threatened—or at least eroded—by participation in a culturally radical project. I want to be clear here that I am not attributing bad faith or critical blindness to the other editors. Quite the contrary, I am trying to articulate the limits of my own practice, for I doubt that anyone on the editorial board had been so thoroughly imbued with the spirit of New Criticism as I, whose formative study was with Cleanth Brooks, John Crowe Ransom, and others at Indiana and Yale in the 1950s. I do believe, however, it is useful to make explicit the difficulties our positions in academe presented, as well as those of the anthology genre and what it represents in academic practice.

Even if some diffuse pulses of self-interest were not working obscurely to brake the process of raising our cultural consciousness, we faced the even more difficult problem of not having alternative models from which to work. On what bases, finally, could we make choices among the many, many contenders for place within the limited confines even of two massive three thousand-page volumes? On what basis might we decide—against the recommendations of most of our consultants—to stick with Frances Ellen Watkins Harper and not to include William Gilmore Simms? To keep Alice Cary and, at the last moment, after he had been set in type, excise James Russell Lowell? To include not only the usual Harlem Renaissance minority contingent but also such writers as Anzia Yezierska, John Joseph Mathews, Younghill Kang, and Saunders Redding?

It was a part of Redding's *No Day of Triumph,* selected by Eleanor Tignor, which provided the impetus toward the necessary reexamination of what most of us understood to be the standards defining the American literary terrain. We had gathered for our first meeting, in 1983, at the

Seamen's Church Institute, a sailors' haven in New York near the Battery that had been built on the site of a place in which Melville had lived and was subsequently torn down for a fancy office building during the 1980s. We had read a few potential selections in common in order to begin the process of defining the grounds for making decisions. Now here was Redding's haunting autobiographical and social history, which only one or two of the fourteen of us had known before. Here was his evocation of family culture:

> Consciousness of my environment began with the sound of talk. It was not hysterical talk, not bravado, though it might well have been, for my father had bought in a neighborhood formerly forbidden, and we lived, I realize now, under an armistice. But in the early years, when we were a young family, there was always talk at our house; a great deal of it mere talk, a kind of boundless and robustious overflow of family feeling. Our shouts roared through the house with the exuberant gush of flood waters through an open sluice, for talk, generated by any trifle, was the power that turned the wheels of our inner family life. (*Heath Anthology* 2d ed., 1913–14)

Here was his portrait of Grandma Redding, whose slave master had crippled her ankle by flinging a "hick'ry chunk" at her, who "hated white people," and about whom Redding puzzled: "I do not know how she managed to give the impression of shining with a kind of deadly hard glare, for she was always clothed entirely in black and her black, even features were as hard and lightless as stone" (1914). How was it, we were forced to ask, that we had not known Redding's book? What did that say about our training? And how did it instruct us about what we were looking for in other works, in all of literature?

Answering such questions, constructing new organizational formats, choosing among writers known only to one or two of us, stretched over three years and more, through meetings back at the Seamen's Church Institute, at the Dream Inn in Santa Cruz, at Asilomar on the Monterey Peninsula, and at the University of California at Los Angeles. I recall particularly that circular meeting room at Asilomar, the gentle surf offering a perpetual ostinato, a stray deer peering in at us as we tried to focus on the dozen sheets of newsprint filled with names of writers—famed, marginal, obscure—who might fit into our evolving narrative of the late nineteenth century. "Whoever was Sherwood Bonner," someone asked, "and how did she differ from Gertrude Bonnin?" The question touched off hilarity—not because it was trivial, but because it dramatized how near the furthest boundaries of our knowledge, of academic logic itself, this project was carrying us. And there was heat. "How could we, in good conscience, include someone as dull and racist as Thomas Dixon?" "Well, were we about 'conscience'?" Silence; tension. Were we? Where and how would we draw our lines between the elect and those consigned to whatever limbo remained even after our widespread revival campaign?

We arrived, implicitly and explicitly, at a number of what I hesitate to call by anything as formal as principles. First, we came to think about American culture not in terms of a mainstream into which all the ethnic and minority rills would necessarily be assimilated. Some of us preferred the conception of a salad bowl, others that of a conversation, still others Whitman's image of a chorus. However articulated, what we aimed for in practice was to present American culture as constituted by differing literary traditions, at once overlapping, in part, and significantly distinct, in part. One illustration: African Americans write in English, of course, and many of the most important black poets, like Claude McKay and Countee Cullen, use conventional English forms, like the sonnet. All the same, African-American culture has been decisively influenced both in subject matter and in form by traditions of the African diaspora, as, for examples, the call-and-response style; musical forms like the blues and jazz; the generally serious play implicit in what Henry Louis Gates, Jr., has described as "signifyin(g)"; the impact of platform and pulpit on texts designed more for delivery than for private reading; and the overridingly moral concerns of even the most modernist African-American texts. To read yesterday's or today's African-American literature with richness and precision—not to speak of historical perspective—thus requires learning about at least two social and literary traditions. What is distinctive to the *African-*American tradition, moreover, is not to be learned only by reading the texts of Herman Melville, Mark Twain, and William Faulkner, however influential they are. Thus, even if the long histories of African-American popular and formal cultures were not of great interest in themselves—as they are—we would want to provide students with opportunities to study the differing literary forms and voices that have helped shape work like that of Hughes or Sterling Brown or, today, Toni Morrison, Alice Walker, and John Wideman: Harper as well as Herman Melville, Chesnutt as well as Twain.

Voices *and* forms. We also came to see the need to extend textual boundaries not only to many previously marginalized writers, but also to forms like tales, legends, spirituals, *corridos,* letters, and exhortations—forms often seen as falling outside the perimeters of our discipline. Such boundaries had historically been extended only to encompass the cultural productions of certain privileged groups, like Puritan divines or the

Founding Fathers, whose religious or political tracts and social narratives had always constituted a part of American literature since that cultural entity was first invented. Not all of these new texts are, to be sure, masterpieces—whatever that means. Nor were those, like "The Day of Doom" or *Swallow Barn,* which had conventionally been studied. Still, no museum—and an anthology is a kind of literary museum—hangs nothing but masterpieces. Works are included for many reasons, including historical importance, influence, and perverse originality. What we had to recognize was that no single standard—not even the elusive esthetic merit that conservative critics forever pose and never define—is absolutely decisive.

For example, to return to the *TLS* review, Edmundson poses "surprise" as a critical element in determining esthetic merit (1133). Surprise may indeed be essential to those forms of poetry that emphasize what he calls "intensity of verbal invention" (1133). But do such formal standards constitute the full measure of esthetic value? Leni Riefenstahl creates surprisingly intense visual images in *Olympiad,* but does that make her film glorifying Nazi culture great art? And if it does, what does that say about theories that pose the creation of great art as the supreme accomplishment of human beings? Can we surrender the social values that produce nausea at that technically brilliant film, at antebellum racist writing, or at the anti-Semitism of Eliot and Pound?

We came to feel, as I see it, that there were no clearly demarcated boundaries between what might be called "literariness" and politics or ideology. We were not, finally, willing to forego either. Still, in practice, we might need to err on the side of the social values before we could come to balance formal and ideological criteria. We were not the first into that territory, but we found surprisingly few guideposts to tell us where we had arrived. Like the others we met out there, we became increasingly suspicious of the markers we uncovered. Who had placed them? Under what auspices? To what ends?

As I suggested earlier, the creation of any anthology—and certainly one as revisionist as the *Heath*—is not a process of academic training guided by detached logic. Rather, it is ringed by uncertainty, speculation, and argument. Like any significant collective project, it deeply engages our convictions as well as our knowledge. The final boundary, which became increasingly permeable in the selection process, was that usually maintained in academe between strong feelings and intellectual training. In at least one respect (and probably only in this one), the hot right-wing attacks on *The Heath Anthology* are not surprising. Boundaries, whether one is talking of neighborhoods, nations, gender, or culture, are not light abstractions, but the stuff of battle.

Note

1. This is essentially the argument made by Glen M. Johnson in "Anthologies and Marketing," delivered at "The Canon and American Literature II: The Anthology," a meeting of the American Literature Section at the Modern Language Association Convention, Chicago, 1990.

☐ Always Already Cultural Studies: Academic Conferences and a Manifesto

Cary Nelson

The Americanization of Cultural Studies

The rapidly increasing visibility of cultural studies in the United States gives us an opportunity to reflect on and debate its articulation to existing institutions in medias res, before those articulations are fixed for any period of time. As part of that debate, I have argued for some time that people who comment on or claim to be "doing" cultural studies ought at least to familiarize themselves with the British cultural studies tradition, beginning with Raymond Williams and Richard Hoggart and moving through Birmingham and beyond. Almost nothing in this tradition, one most note at the outset, is simply and unproblematically transferable to the United States. Williams was partly concerned with defining a distinctly British heritage. British subcultural theory, often focused on entire ways of life, is not well suited to describing quite partial identities or mere leisure activities in the United States. The recent anti-essentialist British work on race must in this country confront an often essentialist identity politics. Thus, while anti-essentialist theories of race have the potential to be quite liberating here, we cannot simply adopt them without asking what Americans of different races have gained and lost from essentialism. The interdisciplinary work at Birmingham was often deeply collaborative, a style that has little chance of succeeding in American departments and of surviving the American academic system of rewards. Yet the struggle to shape the field in Britain has lessons we can learn much from, and British cultural studies achieved theoretical advances that are immensely useful in an American context.

That would be part of my answer to a question Jonathan Culler posed, with an air of whimsical hopelessness, at an October 1990, University of Oklahoma conference called "Crossing the Disciplines: Cultural Studies in the 1990s": "What is a professor of cultural studies supposed to know?" A professor of cultural studies might, in other words, be expected to know the history of the field. Professors of cultural studies need not agree with or emulate all the imperatives of British cultural studies, but they do have a responsibility to take a position on a tradition whose name they are borrowing. Moreover, people with strong disciplinary training who are now feeling their way toward cultural studies have something to gain from encounters with others who have already made such journeys. Leaving open what it will mean to realize cultural studies in America, British cultural studies nonetheless establishes some of what is at stake in theorizing culture in any historical moment.

After I made a similar argument at a regional Modern Language Association conference in 1988, my friend Vincent Leitch, who ought to know better, stood up in the audience, waving his arms as he scaled some Bunker Hill of the imagination, and declared that he "thought we had thrown off the yoke of the British two hundred years ago." More recently again, at an Indiana University of Pennsylvania conference on theory and pedagogy in September of 1990 ("The Role of Theory in the Undergraduate Literature Classroom: Curriculum, Pedagogy, Politics"), I heard James Berlin prophesy, with a solemnity nowhere cognizant that he was predicting coals would be brought to Newcastle, that he was simply giving critical theory a new name, that cultural studies would miraculously turn our attention toward "textuality in all its forms." The claim was hardly new; indeed, this heralded revolution had already taken place under another name. In November 1990, a panel on cultural studies at the Pacific Coast Philological Association unself-consciously offered two models of cultural studies: as an opportunistic umbrella for English professors who want to study film or the graphic arts, and as a terrain of vague, metonymic sliding among all the competing theories on the contemporary scene. Cultural studies in that context was considered interchangeable with semiotics, the New Historicism, and other recent bodies of theory. And at an October 1990, University of Illinois panel on "The Frontiers of Eighteenth-Century Studies," John Richetti, preening himself in the manner of a disciplinary cockatoo, announced with satisfaction that "eighteenth-century people had been doing cultural studies all along."

I could add other anecdotes. But these are enough to introduce the first points I want to make: Of all the intellectual movements that have swept the humanities in America since the seventies, none will be taken up so shallowly, so opportunistically, so unreflectively, and so ahistorically as cultural studies. It is becoming the perfect paradigm for a people with no sense of history—born yesterday and born on the make. A concept with a long history of struggle over its definition, a concept born in class consciousness and in critique of the academy, a concept with a skeptical relationship to its own theoretical advances, cultural studies is often for

English studies in the United States little more than a way of repackaging what we were already doing. At its worst, anyone who analyzes popular culture in any way whatsoever—or makes the slightest gesture toward contextualizing high cultural texts—can claim to be doing cultural studies. Of course, nothing can prevent the term *cultural studies* from coming to mean something very different in another time and place. But the casual dismissal of its history needs to be seen for what it is—an interested effort to depoliticize a concept whose whole prior history has been preeminently political and oppositional. The depoliticizing of cultural studies will no doubt pay off, making it more palatable at once to granting agencies and to conservative colleagues, administrators, and politicians, but only at the cost of blocking cultural studies from having any critical purchase on this nation's social life.

People interested in theory have often been accused by the right of facile opportunism. But the historical record actually suggests a very different and much more difficult pattern of struggle and mutual transformation for those invested in the major bodies of interpretive theory. Consider the deep personal transformation, the institutional changes, the wholesale reorientation of social understanding that accompanied the feminist revolution and its extension into the academy. Compare the series of times in this century when taking up Marxism has meant a comparable reorientation of one's whole understanding of society. Even a body of theory like psychoanalysis, which in its academic incarnations has avoided many of its imperatives toward personal and institutional change, has entailed a good deal more than adopting a special vocabulary. Even for academics, psychoanalysis has meant accepting a view of human agency that isolates them from their traditionally rationalist colleagues. In Britain and Australia, taking up cultural studies has followed the more radical pattern among these alternatives. But not for most disciplines in the United States.

Thus, one regularly hears graduate students and faculty members talk frankly about "repackaging" themselves as cultural studies people. The disastrous academic job market, to be sure, along with most of the daily messages consumer capitalism sends us, encourages that sort of anxious cynicism about how one "markets" one's self. Indeed, the job market in cultural studies—at least in English—gives a pretty good indication of how the discipline is going to take up this new paradigm. In 1989 a graduate student at Illinois—who is a specialist in feminist cultural studies and has a degree in communications—interviewed for cultural studies positions at the Modern Language Association convention. It was quite clear that many departments had not the faintest idea what cultural studies is. It was seen as a way to ask the dean for new money by pointing out an area where departments needed to catch up and a way for interviewers to make a display of ignorance look like canny interrogation: "So what is all this cultural studies stuff about anyway?" What better way to ask uninformed questions than in the role of job interviewer? Who cares what serious cultural studies job candidates might think? If the answers are confusing or slightly threatening, the candidate will be out of the room in twenty minutes anyway. Some departments in effect conducted fake, exploratory cultural studies searches as a lazy way of finding out between cocktails a little bit about what the young people are up to these days. As the Illinois student found out, it all comes down to the final question: "But can you fill in when we need someone to do the Milton course?" Meanwhile, the October 1993 *MLA Job Information List* includes such potentially disingenuous ads as those seeking a "medieval literature/cultural studies" specialist or someone in "literary and cultural studies before 1800." Somehow I suspect familiarity with Stuart Hall's work will not be required of candidates for these positions.

At the Oklahoma conference, surprisingly enough, the only plenary speaker who made a full effort to define the project of cultural studies was J. Hillis Miller. Yet Miller, unfortunately, gave no evidence of having read any previous cultural studies work. The field thus presented no challenges, only opportunities. Apparently, the spread of American power and culture across the globe has led some Americans to believe Disneyland is the origin of the world. As someone who respects and admires much of Miller's early work, especially his elegant phenomenological readings of literary texts, I must in this context say that I just do not see its productive relation to the cultural studies tradition. A concern with ethics, central in his recent publications, is not the same as the long cultural studies engagement with left politics. And the internationalization of technology, which was at the center of his Oklahoma talk, "The Work of Cultural Criticism in the Age of Digital Reproduction," in fact points to the importance of global politics and economics, the global dissemination and localization of cultural power—issues Miller thinks will be swept aside in a McLuhanesque spread of technology creating a common global culture. Indeed, it is only blindness to economics, power, and cultural differences that made it possible for Miller to present as an argument his offensive fantasy that everyone in the world will have a personal computer within a few years. Has he no sense of what life is like in South Central Los Angeles, let alone in Bangladesh or Somalia? I take this as the limit case, false cultural studies at its most ugly—a warrant for privileged American academics who are used to juggling theories to begin making claims about the material world as well, without ever looking at it.

The effect of Miller's appearance at the first plenary session at Oklahoma was to give the program an opening benediction, a benediction warranting a humanized, "transnational," confidently democratized version of cultural studies as the new American world order. His key role in depoliticizing deconstruction was apparently to be repeated for cultural studies. I think it is relevant to recall that Miller once cosigned a letter (published in the *MLA Newsletter*) warning that an official Modern Language Association position against the undeclared Vietnam war might make all thirty thousand MLA members liable to a charge of treason. I bring this up not to question Miller's position on the war, but because the letter pointed specifically to his insistence on the separation between academic and political life, a separation that cultural studies has sought to overcome. What is at stake here is a definition of the nature, limits, and mission of cultural studies. Both in the letter and in his efforts to limit deconstruction to a depoliticized version of textual analysis, Miller has more than once had something to say about the cultural role of English studies. Those views are very much at odds with the heritage of cultural studies. They may well come to dominate the Americanization of cultural studies, but this is not a process that should proceed unremarked.

In this context, I do not think an uncritical argument for liberal diversity has much value. Welcoming the opening of the cultural studies field need not necessitate abandoning a debate about which enterprises do and do not deserve to use the cultural studies name, about what commitments cultural studies entails. That is not to say I think either the British, or the Americans and Australians and Canadians who have learned from them, can police the field. In fact, I think a more open, generous, democratic— but less critical—model will likely win the day. This much more inclusive vision probably *is* the future of cultural studies in the United States. I am merely trying to offer a challenge to that enterprise, even if it is a challenge likely to be swept aside by events.

At a paper presented at the annual Modern Language Association convention in December 1991, Janice Radway argued that attempts to define cultural studies and police its borders risk turning it into a "ghostly discipline." I would argue that cultural studies has always been exactly that— a ghostly discipline with shifting borders and unstable contents—and that it needs to continue being so. It is an ongoing set of traditions, a body of work whose contributors are in dialogue and debate with one another. Attempts to define its aims and limits, regularly overthrown, have been part of its history from the outset. It is also in significant ways antidisciplinary; that is, it responds critically to the exclusive parcelling out of objects of study to individual disciplines, to the way academic disciplines divide up the field of knowledge, and to the social impact of much academic work. To some degree, it puts forward its own contra-disciplinary forms of knowledge. Yet none of these stances comes into being in a universe free of disciplinary histories and constraints. Cultural studies defines its enterprise in part by positioning itself in relation to more traditional disciplines; in the process, it becomes something like a cluster of disciplines under erasure. Its own ghostly disciplinarity unsettles all other humanities and social science disciplines; that ghostly disciplinarity is, thus, a condition to be welcomed rather than feared.

The resistance to *any* effort to define cultural studies—a resistance unique to its Americanization—reflects a widespread and quite warranted dissatisfaction with the constraints of disciplinary knowledge. Especially for students and faculty in reactionary departments, cultural studies seems to offer the only realistic solution to a repressive work environment—literally overthrowing disciplinary knowledge. That cultural studies would then itself be occupied with defining its boundaries and deciding which activities should and should not be included under its umbrella seems a betrayal of the emotional needs cultural studies was counted on to meet. For some people, cultural studies is imagined as a kind of polymorphously free zone for any and all intellectual investments. That some individual or collaborative cultural studies work comes to be more widely recognized or valued than other projects seems in that context a violation of the undifferentiated zone of permission cultural studies was imagined to be. That some people defend their particular practices passionately seems equally suspect.

One can begin to see why some students are distressed at the emergence of cultural studies "stars" in the field. It suggests a field hierarchized by reputation and achievement in much the way traditional disciplines are. But is there any alternative? Actually, there is, but only one: wholesale anti-intellectualism. Some ordinarily canny cultural studies scholars are in fact willing to appeal to just that anti-intellectual strain in American cultural studies. Thus Gayatri Spivak was cheered when she opened her Oklahoma talk by disingenuously declaring how relieved she was to be presenting a lecture that was not destined to be immortalized in a book. Would she be even more relieved to have that state of affairs persist for a few years? Similarly, Radway met with applause when she declared at the Modern Language Association convention that the definition of cultural studies should be expanded to include a whole range of political activities. Presumably one could be "in" cultural studies by virtue of joining campus demonstrations. Obviously, cultural studies allies itself with and helps to theorize political action. Cultural studies writers both inside and outside the academy are often involved in politics and concerned with the contribution their work makes to political action. But political action and cultural studies are not interchangeable. It should not be necessary to say this, but apparently it is: Cultural studies is a set of writing practices; it is a discursive, analytic, interpretive tradition.

Although none of the above was acknowledged openly at Oklahoma, these values churned under the surface. This helps explain the absence of references to the history of cultural studies from more than a few of the talks. Actually, the Oklahoma conference did have an implicit but unstated mission. Although some people were invited to participate, most of the papers were given by people who answered an open invitation to submit topics. Essentially everyone who volunteered to give a talk was placed on the program. The result was about 350 papers given in a hundred sessions over three days. So the conference, in effect, said, "Here is a self-selected group of North Americans who declare themselves to be doing cultural studies. Let's see where they stand." That is an interesting and potentially important mission, although its value was limited by being undeclared and, thus, never an explicit subject of discussion during the conference itself.

A Cultural Studies Manifesto

From my perspective, a good deal of what was presented at Oklahoma simply did not qualify as cultural studies. Indeed, I felt it reflected the widespread dissolution and depoliticization of cultural studies in the United States. My experience at the Oklahoma and other conferences, my experience in co-organizing "Cultural Studies Now and in the Future," a conference held at the University of Illinois in April of 1990, and my experience in co-editing *Cultural Studies,* a collection that grew out of that conference (see Grossberg)—together with teaching seminars in cultural studies and writing a book that tried to map out a cultural studies model of a literary genre—leads me to believe some generalizations about the cultural studies enterprise can and must be put forward. I think it is important to try to say both what cultural studies is and what it is not. Keeping in mind the well-known series of definitional articles written throughout the history of cultural studies,[1] l would like to do so in the form of a series of numbered points, a first draft of one version of a cultural studies manifesto.

1. Cultural studies is not simply the close analysis of objects other than literary texts. Some English departments would like to believe that their transportable methods of close reading can make them cultural studies departments as soon as they expand the range of cultural objects they habitually study. Indeed, cultural studies is usually sold to English departments as part of the manifest destiny of the discipline. Our skills at close

reading need to be extended to other cultural domains, it is often argued, lest these domains be left to the dubious care of student subcultures or the imprecise attention of lesser disciplines like speech communication. Similarly, some scholars like the sense of theoretical prestige that an unspecified cultural studies umbrella gives their close readings of nontraditional objects. Indeed, cultural studies often arrives in English departments in the form of an easy alliance between debased textuality and recent theory. But the immanent formal, thematic, or semiotic analysis of films, paintings, songs, romance novels, comic books, or clothing styles does not, in itself, constitute cultural studies. Perhaps that is why one department in 1993 advertised for a cultural studies specialist in "theory and practice"—to avoid being deluged by writing samples consisting of decontextualized readings of films and popular novels. Of course, it is only in America that cultural studies theory and practice are in danger of being severed from one another.

2. Cultural studies does not, as some people believe, require that every project involve the study of artifacts of popular culture. On the other hand, people with ingrained contempt for popular culture can never fully understand the cultural studies project. In part that is because cultural studies has traditionally been deeply concerned with how all cultural production is sustained and determined by (and in turn influences) the broad terrain of popular common sense. Thus, no properly historicized cultural studies can cut itself off from that sense of "the popular."

3. Cultural studies also does not mean that we have to abandon the study of what have been historically identified as the domains of high culture, although it does challenge us to study them in radically new ways. Because every cultural practice has a degree of relative autonomy, every cultural practice potentially merits attention. But we need to recognize that autonomy is not a function of intrinsic merit and that it is never fixed and never more than relative. The notion of relative autonomy, of course, makes it properly impossible to repeat traditional claims that some cultural production transcends history.

4. Cultural studies is not simply the neutral study of semiotic systems, no matter how mobile and flexible those systems are made to be. There can be a semiotic component to cultural studies, but cultural studies and semiotics are not interchangeable. Cultural studies is not satisfied with mapping sign systems. It is concerned with the struggles over meaning that reshape and define the terrain of culture. It is devoted, among other things, to studying the politics of signification.

5. Cultural studies is committed to studying the production, reception, and varied use of texts, not merely their internal characteristics. This is one of the reasons that cultural studies work is more difficult in periods

when the historical record is either fragmentary or highly restrictive in class terms. So long as the difficulties are foregrounded, however, limited but ambitious and important cultural studies projects can be carried out for earlier periods of history.

6. Cultural studies conceives culture relationally. Thus, the analysis of an individual text, discourse, behavior, ritual, style, genre, or subculture does not constitute cultural studies unless the thing analyzed is considered in terms of its competitive, reinforcing, and determining relations with other objects and cultural forces. This task is also, it should be noted, an impossible one to complete in any given instance. But unless the constitutive and dissolving cultural relations are taken as a primary concern, the work is not, properly considered, cultural studies.

This relational understanding of culture was one of cultural studies' earliest defining goals. Yet just what is meant by the relational study of culture has changed and evolved and abruptly shifted throughout the history of cultural studies, from Williams's efforts to describe culture as a whole way of life to the effort by Hall and others to adapt Antonio Gramsci's notion of a war of position to discursive and political analyses of contemporary Britain. One could, in fact, write the history of cultural studies in terms of how it conceives relationality and puts it into practice.

7. Cultural studies is not a fixed, repeatable methodology that can be learned and thereafter applied to any given cultural domain. It is the social and textual history of varying efforts to take up the problematic of the politics and meaning of culture. Its history mixes founding moments with transformative challenges and disputations. To do cultural studies is to take a place within that history.

8. Taking a place within that history means thinking of one's work in relation to cultural studies work on the politics of race. It means taking seriously the way feminism radically transformed cultural studies in the 1980s. And it means positioning one's work in relation to the long, complex, and often contentious history of cultural studies' engagements with Marxism, from Williams to Hall. To treat that history of engagements with Marxism as irrelevant, as many Americans do, is to abandon cultural studies for a fake practice that merely borrows its name.

9. Cultural studies is concerned with the social and political meaning and effects of its own analyses. It assumes that scholarly writing can and does do meaningful cultural work. To avoid facing this challenge and retreat into academic modesty (asserting that interpretive writing is impotent or irrelevant) or into claims of disinterested scholarship (protesting that political commitments vitiate scholarly objectivity) is to hide from cultural studies' historical mission. A poststructuralist academic liberalism might lead one to argue that, because the political effects of discourse

are indeterminate and unpredictable, scholarship and politics are best kept separate. Cultural studies might counter by arguing that such arguments do not free us from responsibility for the political meaning of scholarly work. Cultural studies typically accepts the notion that scholarship entails an engagement with and commitment to one's own historical context. The choice of what scholarly writing to do involves a decision about what one's most effective cultural and political intervention can be.

10. In much the same way, it must be emphasized that cultural studies does not simply offer students a liberal cornucopia of free choices. Cultural studies seeks to empower students to understand the social and political meaning of what they learn throughout the university. It urges them to reflect on the social meaning of disciplinary work and to decide what kinds of projects the culture needs most. A cultural studies pedagogy, thus, encourages a more critical relationship to cultural and political life. One small but necessary implication is that current debates and social practices need to be far more pervasive elements of many more courses than is now the case. Fields like history and literature that often teach pure period courses need to make detailed and specific analogies to present conditions. It is not enough to establish contexts for and relationships between discourses in earlier periods on the assumption that students will make the contemporary connections and work out the contemporary differences on their own. The Taylorized curriculum needs to be thoroughly undermined with the aim of gaining critical purchase on contemporary life.

11. Cultural studies has a responsibility to continue interrogating and reflecting on its own commitments. In fulfilling this task, however, cultural studies has inevitably had a history that is far from perfect. It needs now to critique its investment in what has been called the left's "mantra of race, class, and gender," categories that are properly considered both in relation to one another and to the culture as a whole. It needs as well to question its recent fetishizing of "fandom." A ritualized, unreflective confession of fandom has become almost a requirement in some American cultural studies circles. Being a fan is not a prerequisite for doing cultural analysis. Invoking fandom without describing or specifying its conditions and its cultural construction has little intellectual value. Being a fan gives potential access to important insights; the challenge is to reflect on fandom and articulate what one learns from it.

12. Cultural studies is not required to approve a struggle for dominance among the disenfranchised. Multiculturalism in America sometimes degenerates into a competitive form of identity politics in which oppressed and marginalized groups work to sort themselves out into a hierarchy based on their record of historical suffering. Cultural studies is not, however, sim-

ply a neutral field in which people can give free reign to their inclinations to play identity politics. Cultural studies is properly an enterprise in which people can explore their race, ethnicity, or gender and articulate its relations with the larger culture. A properly relational and historical analysis suggests that no one group can claim the ultimate site of oppression. The progressive alliances we now need require us to avoid using previously marginalized identities to suppress debate and criticism. At the other end of the spectrum, multiculturalism restricts itself to an unrealistic, liberal ideal of diversity and difference without conflict. Cultural studies needs to maintain a critical relation to both these tendencies. Cultural studies may thus establish alliances with multiculturalism but should resist being absorbed by it. Similarly, if multicultural work is to claim a place within cultural studies, it cannot ignore all the innovative work other cultural studies scholars have done on race, gender, and ethnicity.

13. The historicizing impulse in cultural studies is properly in dialogue with an awareness of the contemporary rearticulation of earlier texts, contexts, and social practices. In literary studies, New Historicism may sometimes succumb to an illusion of being able to address only the earlier historical period being analyzed, but cultural studies properly does not. Being historically and politically here and there—then and now—is part of the continuing, and thus necessarily newly theorized, burden of cultural studies. Nothing we rescue from forgetfulness or distortion stays the same. To study the present or the past is inevitably to rearticulate it to current interests; that is a problem and an opportunity to take up consciously, not to repress or regret. Cultural studies can never be a simple program of recovery; properly speaking, such programs are not cultural studies. Indeed, a conservative tendency to categorize every limited project of cultural recovery as cultural studies usually signals a high cultural contempt for the things being recovered. The tendency, for example, to classify efforts to recover minority literatures as cultural studies sometimes reflects an assumption that these literatures are inherently inferior or that they lack the esthetic importance of the traditional canon.

14. In its projects of historical and contemporary analysis, cultural studies is often concerned as well with intervening in the present and with encouraging certain possible futures rather than others. Thus, as cultural studies people reflect on the simultaneously undermined and reinforced status of the nation-state in different parts of the world, they are often also concerned with the future status of nationhood. An interest in how high technology has changed our lives may be combined with an effort to shape its future impact. The opportunities that fragmented postmodern identities offer are not only to be studied, but also to be exploited. A study of the multiple meanings of gender in a given moment may lead to reflec-

tion on how our lives may be gendered in the future. For many scholars outside cultural studies, such double investments are to be avoided. In cultural studies they can be at the center of the enterprise.

15. Cultural studies accepts the notion that the work of theorizing its enterprise is inescapably grounded in contemporary life and current politics. New social and political realities require fresh reflection and debate on the cultural studies enterprise, no matter what historical period one is studying. Although it is possible to overstate the phenomenon of a local theorizing grounded in current social realities because such a process involves a rearticulation of previously existing theories, it is nonetheless true that major changes in cultural studies have regularly come from an effort to understand and intervene in new historical conditions. From a cultural studies perspective, then, one never imagines that it is possible to theorize for all times and places. Not only our interpretations but also our theories are produced for the world in which we live.

16. Cultural studies within the academy is inescapably concerned with and critical of the politics of disciplinary knowledge. It is not simply interdisciplinary in the model of liberal diversity and idealized communication. This means that the nontrivial institutionalization of cultural studies within traditional academic disciplines is impossible unless those disciplines dismantle themselves. A first step, for a discipline like English, is to make a commitment to hiring faculty members who do not have degrees from English departments. Otherwise there is little chance that English departments will even admit that literature does not acquire its meaning primarily from its own autonomous traditions, let alone take up the general problematics of culture. Yet while English departments have much to gain from expanding their enterprises to include cultural studies, it is less clear what cultural studies has to gain from being institutionalized in English departments. If it is to be institutionalized at all, cultural studies might be better served by a variety of programs outside traditional departments.

Not every individual cultural studies book or essay can fulfill all the conditions in these sixteen points. But a successful cultural studies project should position itself in relation to these concerns. When it does not take them on directly, they should be implicit in the project's interests, terms, and references. These, it seems to me, represent some of the key aims and imperatives growing out of thirty years of cultural work. These points are effectively part of the cultural studies paradigm and part of the cultural studies challenge to the contemporary world. Because they are focused on the ways cultural studies has and is likely to continue to change and develop, they are less rigid than the form of a numbered manifesto may lead some readers to think. Indeed, to take up these points is to write in such a way as to engage in a continual interrogation of what cultural studies is and can be. Thus, I have articulated this manifesto at a level of theoretical generality that does not totalize and synthesize all cultural studies projects. These principles do not attempt to anticipate the specific work of local theorizing. To place oneself in relation to the history of cultural studies is precisely to recognize that the practices of cultural studies are not given in advance. They are always to be rethought, rearticulated to contemporary conditions. That imperative to continuing political renewal and struggle is part of what cultural studies has bequeathed to us.

Cultural Studies Now and in the Future

Such a process of negotiation and debate over what is and is not cultural studies has to take place if cultural studies is to have any intellectual power and political effectiveness. Wider alliances need to be formed, but not every alliance is worth the potential price in dissolution and compromise. Perhaps I sound like a Third Period Stalinist who is not ready to accept the Popular Front coalition of the late 1930s. But we need to remember that the broad, inclusive alliance of the Popular Front had a political mission and a political reason for the compromises it made— the struggle against fascism. Those on the left in America and those committed to progressive projects in humanities departments in universities have a related mission—the struggle against the global inequities inherited from the Reagan-Bush era, the struggle against the New Right's views of American education and American culture, the growing articulation of discomfort and anger over racism and sexism as universities' efforts to become more "culturally diverse" take hold. It is our task to make American institutions nervous about cultural studies. One boundary worth drawing around the cultural studies alliance is between those who will and those who will not join that struggle. The price of depoliticizing cultural studies is not a price we should be willing to pay. If the bargain is that we may have cultural studies so long as we do not criticize the government in our classrooms, we should reject it. Cultural studies does not need to render unto Caesar what Caesar thinks belongs to him.

Caesar, however, is in the midst of having his say in any case. Over the past several years, the phrase *cultural studies* has been taken up by journalists and politicians of the New Right in America as one of a cluster of scare terms—the others include *multiculturalism* and *deconstruction*—that have been articulated together to signal a crisis in higher education and American intellectual life generally. One fair response for cultural studies people would be to work to disarticulate these terms, already effectively welded together in popular common sense. Cultural studies is not multiculturalism and is not deconstruction, we might argue, although cultural studies welcomes some versions of multiculturalism and shares with deconstruction sympathies for the general project of poststructuralism. Unfortunately, it seems likely that the qualifications in the second half of the sentence pretty much undo any useful work the denials in the first half of the sentence might do in the public arena. These are distinctions we need to draw for our students and colleagues, but we are unlikely to be able to do so successfully for the media or the public. These are different intellectual traditions, but their points of partial correspondence are sufficient to convince people they are part of the same general cultural pattern. Our audiences, in other words, will smell a rat. Because we can do little now to resist that moment of recognition, it might be better to welcome it. Cultural studies, in other words, might well set out to *be that rat*.

The creature I have in mind is a largely urban animal who is wary, focussed on local conditions, and willing to eat almost anything—an animal very much like cultural studies. He or she is a political animal attuned to assuring the survival of his or her interests. Now that recent theory as a whole has been accused of being politicized—something many theorists of the seventies and eighties would themselves be hard put to demonstrate—cultural studies can willingly occupy the site of theory as politics. Now that efforts to open up the canon and efforts to expand the cultural reach of academia's field of vision have been scandalized for abandoning the transcendent and eternal standards of Western high culture—something not everyone involved in canon revision or multiculturalism would want to embrace—cultural studies can cheerfully occupy the site of standard-free omnivorousness. Everyone else may choose to respond to the right's assault by filling and backsliding and denying they are now or ever have been political in their aims or interests. Cultural studies can step in and be the very thing the right loves to hate. Indeed, those cultural studies professors who are tenured should do their best to attract the bulk of the criticism about politicized pedagogy and scholarship.

Cultural studies has never meant only one thing, and it is unlikely to mean only one thing in the future. It may, then, be necessary for individuals to adopt different cultural studies identities in different contexts. When strategically useful, they can be deconstructionists or multiculturalists. All the while, however, they should be reiterating that the real villain is cultural studies. That should certainly thin the ranks of cultural studies' fair weather friends. More important, it should focus on a body of work (cultural studies) the political responsibilities and effects the field has traditionally worked to understand.

The time has come when the political meaning of teaching and scholarship can no longer be avoided. Attacks on feminist, minority, multicultural, and theoretical research in the academy are helping to discredit those values and constituencies in the general culture as well. A delegitimated university thus does double duty: It oversees its own increasingly curtailed and embattled mission while serving as an object lesson that undermines progressive thought throughout the culture. Meanwhile, the heyday of free time for research in the humanities and social sciences has past. It was a spinoff of the cold war, and the cold war has ended. If the New Right in America has its way, the only time available for research will be that funded by industry. If universities give up their role of social critique, only conservative think tanks will remain to fund social critique over the long term. At the same time, access to higher education will be steadily restricted to more wealthy families. Public elementary and secondary education, increasingly vocational, will be reserved for the poor. A divisive struggle for power among minorities will only facilitate that agenda. We need relational analyses of the political meaning of the work all of us do, we need careful disarticulations of the elements the right has joined to win popular consent, and we need unsentimental readings of the possibilities for alliances among those with the most to lose spiritually and economically. That is a task historically appropriate for a politicized cultural studies that devotes itself to the kinds of cultural analysis the society needs.

Note

An earlier version of this essay, entitled "Always Already Cultural Studies: Two Conferences and a Manifesto," appeared in the *Journal of the Midwest Modern Language Assocation.* Used by permission of the Midwest Modern Language Association.

1. For other programmatic statements on cultural studies, see Grossberg, "The Formation(s) of Cultural Studies" and "The Circulation of Cultural Studies; Hall, "Cultural Studies: Two Paradigms" and "Cultural Studies and the Center"; works by Hoggart, Johnson, and Morris; and Williams, "The Analysis of Culture" in *The Long Revolution.* For bibliographies of the work of two key figures, Williams and Hall, see O'Connor, "A Working Bibliography" and *Raymond Williams.*

☐ Works Cited

Achebe, Chinua. *Things Fall Apart.* London: Heinemann, 1958.
Althusser, Louis. "Ideology and Ideological State Apparatuses (Notes Toward an Investigation) (January–April 1969)." *"Lenin and Philosophy" and Other Essays.* Trans. Ben Brewster. New York: Monthly Review Press, 1971. 127–186.
Alurista. "'Mitólogos y mitómanos,' Mesa Redonda." *Maize* 4 (1981): 8.
Anderson, Perry. *Considerations on Western Marxism.* London: New Left Books, 1976.
———. *In the Tracks of Historical Materialism.* Chicago: University of Chicago Press, 1984.
Anzaldúa, Gloria. *Borderlands/La Frontera: The New Mestiza.* San Francisco: Spinsters/Aunt Lute, 1987.
Applebee, Arthur N. *Tradition and Reform in the Teaching of English: A History.* Urbana: National Council of Teachers of English, 1974.
Aricó, José. *La Cola del Diablo: Itinerario de Gramsci en América Latina.* Buenos Aires: Puntosur, 1988.
Aronowitz, Stanley. *The Crisis in Historical Materialism: Class, Politics, and Culture in Marxist Theory.* Minneapolis: University of Minnesota Press, 1990.
Austin, J. L. *How to Do Things with Words.* 2nd ed. Ed. J. O. Urmson and Marina Sbisa. Cambridge: Harvard University Press, 1962.
Bagdikian, Ben H. *The Media Monopoly.* Boston: Beacon, 1983.
Baldwin, James. *Blues for Mr. Charlie.* New York: Dell, 1985.
———. *The Fire Next Time.* New York: Dell, 1985.
———. *Nobody Knows My Name.* New York: Dell, 1986.
Balsamo, Anne. "Feminism and Cultural Studies." *Journal of the Midwest Modern Language Association* 24 (1991): 50–73.
Baraka, Amiri. *The LeRoi Jones/Amiri Baraka Reader.* Ed. William Harris. New York: DAW, 1991.
Baudrillard, Jean. *Simulations.* New York: Semiotext(e), 1983.
Belsey, Catherine. "Towards Cultural History—in Theory and Practice." *Textual Practice* 3 (1989): 159–172.
Benavidez, Max. "The Labyrinth of the North." *L.A. Times* "Calendar." 15 September 1991: 6.
Bennington, Geoffrey. "Postal Politics and the Institution of the Nation." *Nation and Narration.* Ed. Homi K. Bhadha. New York: Routledge, 1990. 121–137.
Berlin, James. *Rhetoric and Reality: Writing Instruction in American Colleges, 1900–1985.* Carbondale: Southern Illinois University Press, 1987.
———. *Writing Instruction in Nineteenth-Century American Colleges.* Carbondale: Southern Illinois University Press, 1984.

Bondolfi, Lia Tessarolo. "Ecos de la cultura y de la literatura chicanas en Italia." *Missions in Conflict: Essays on U.S.–Mexican Relations and Chicano Culture.* Ed. Renate von Bardeleben. Tübingen: Narr, 1986. 291–299.

Bontemps, Arna. *American Negro Poetry.* New York: Hill and Wang, 1974.

Bourdieu, Pierre. *Distinction: A Social Critique of the Judgment of Taste.* Cambridge: Harvard University Press, 1984.

Brantlinger, Patrick. *Crusoe's Footprints: Cultural Studies in Britain and America.* New York: Routledge, 1990.

Brooks, Cleanth. "The Heresy of Paraphrase." *The Well-Wrought Urn: Studies in the Structure of Poetry.* New York: Harcourt, Brace and World, 1947. 192–214.

Brooks, Cleanth, and Robert Heilman. *Understanding Drama: Twelve Plays.* New York: Holt, Rinehart and Winston, 1945.

Brooks, Cleanth, and Robert Penn Warren. *Understanding Fiction.* New York: Appleton-Century-Crofts, 1943.

———. *Understanding Poetry: An Anthology for College Students.* New York: Holt, Rinehart and Winston, 1938.

Brooks, Cleanth, Robert Penn Warren, and John Purser. *An Approach to Literature: A Collection of Prose and Verse with Analyses and Discussions.* New York: F. S. Crofts and Co., 1938.

Brooks, Gwendolyn. *Selected Poems.* New York: HarperCollins, 1982.

Buckanaga, Jerome (Minnesota Chippewa). "Interracial Politics: The Pressure to Integrate An Experimental School." *The Schooling of Native America.* Ed. Thomas Thompson. Washington: American Association of Colleges for Teacher Education and the Teacher Corps, United States Office of Education, 1978. 52–71.

Burke, Kenneth. "Marx on Mystification." *A Rhetoric of Motives.* 1950. Reprint. Berkeley: University of California Press, 1969. 101–110.

Butler, Judith. *Gender Trouble: Feminism and the Subversion of Identity.* New York: Routledge, 1990.

Cadova, Eduardo, Peter Connor, and Jean-Luc Nancy, eds. *Who Comes after the Subject?* New York: Routledge, 1991.

Cain, William E. *The Crisis in Criticism: Theory, Literature, and Reform in English Studies.* Baltimore: Johns Hopkins University Press, 1984.

Calderón, Héctor, and José David Saldívar, eds. *Criticism in the Borderlands: Studies in Chicano Literature, Culture, and Ideology.* Durham: Duke University Press, 1991.

Carby, Hazel. *Reconstructing Womanhood: The Emergence of the Afro-American Novelist.* New York: Oxford University Press, 1987.

Carter, Deborah J., and Reginald Wilson. *Minorities in Higher Education: Tenth Annual Status Report.* Washington: American Council on Education, 1992.

Certeau, Michel de. *The Practice of Everyday Life.* Berkeley: University of California Press, 1984.

Cervantes, Miguel de. "El celoso extremeño." *Exemplary Stories.* Trans. C. A. Jones. London: Penguin, 1984.

Chambers, Iain. *Popular Culture: The Metropolitan Experience.* New York: Methuen, 1986. 843–851.

Churchill, Ward (Creek/Cherokee-Metis). "Introduction: Journeying Toward a Debate." *Marxism and the Native Americans.* Ed. Churchill. Boston: South End, 1983. 1–16.

Cicero. *Brutus.* Trans. G. L. Hendrickson. Cambridge: Harvard University Press, 1962.

Clark, Veve A. *Kaiso! Katherine Dunham: An Anthology of Writings.* Berkeley: University of California Press, 1978.

Clarke, Kenneth. *Dark Ghetto: Dilemmas of Social Power.* Middletown: Wesleyan University Press, 1989.

Clifford, James. "Introduction: Partial Truths." *Writing Culture: The Poetics and Politics of Ethnography.* Ed. Clifford and George E. Marcus. Berkeley: University of California Press, 1986. 1–29.

"Collection." East St. Louis: Experiment in Higher Education, 1967–68.

"College Art Association Looks at Ways to Encourage 'Pluralism' in Its Annual Meeting." *Chronicle of Higher Education,* 8 Apr. 1992: A9.

Collins, Patricia Hill. "The Social Construction of Black Feminist Thought." *Signs* 14 (1989): 745–773.

Conference on College Composition and Communication Executive Committee. "Statement of Principles and Standards for the Postsecondary Teaching of Writing." *College Composition and Communication* 40 (1989): 329–336.

Cooper, Martha. "Reconceptualizing Ideology According to the Relationship Between Rhetoric and Knowledge/Power." *Rhetoric and Ideology: Compositions and Criticisms of Power.* Ed. Charles W. Kneupper. Arlington: Rhetoric Society of America, 1989. 30–41.

Corn Tassel (Cherokee). "Let Us Examine the Facts." *Native American Testimony: An Anthology of Indian and White Relations—First Encounter to Dispossession.* Ed. Peter Nabokov. New York: Harper and Row, 1978. 152–155.

Cortez, Jayne. *Coagulations: New and Selected Poems.* New York: Thunders Mouth, 1984.

Crouch, Stanley. *Notes of a Hanging Judge: Essays and Reviews 1979–1989.* New York: Oxford University Press, 1990.

Culler, Jonathan. *Framing the Sign: Criticism and Its Institutions.* Norman: University of Oklahoma Press, 1988.

Cruse, Harold. *The Crisis of the Negro Intellectual: A Historical Analysis of the Failure of Black Leadership.* New York: William Morrow, 1984.

Davis, Robert Con, and Ronald Schleifer. *Criticism and Culture: The Role of Critique in Modern Literary Theory.* London: Longman, 1991.

DeCoy, Robert H. *The Nigger Bible.* Los Angeles: Holloway, 1967.

"'Degenerate Art': The Fate of the Avant-Garde in Nazi Germany." Education Department. Los Angeles County Museum of Art, 1991.

Deloria, Vine, Jr. (Hunkpapa Lakota). "Circling the Same Old Rock." *Marxism and the Native Americans.* Ed. Ward Churchill. Boston: South End, 1983. 113–136.

Denning, Michael. "The End of Mass Culture." *Modernity and Mass Culture.* Ed. James Naremore and Patrick Brantlinger. Bloomington: Indiana University Press, 1991. 253–268.

Derrida, Jacques. *Limited, Inc.* Evanston: Northwestern University Press, 1988.

———. "Structure, Sign, and Play." *The Languages of Criticism and the Sciences of Man.* Ed. Richard Macksey and Eugenio Donato. Baltimore: Johns Hopkins University Press, 1970. 247–265.

———. "Women in the Beehive: A Seminar with Jacques Derrida." *Men in Feminism.* Ed. Alice Jardine and Paul Smith. New York: Methuen, 1987. 189–204.

Dollimore, Jonathan, and Alan Sinfield, eds. *Political Shakespeare: New Essays on Cultural Materialism.* Ithaca: Cornell University Press, 1985.

Doyle, Brian. "The Hidden History of English Studies." *Re-Reading English.* Ed. Peter Widdowson. New York: Methuen, 1982. 17–31.

Drake, Samuel Gardner. *Biography and History of the Indians of North America.* Boston: O. L. Perkins, 1834.

D'Souza, Dinesh. *Illiberal Education: The Politics of Race and Sex on Campus.* New York: Vintage, 1991.

Du Bois, W. E. B. *Souls of Black Folk: Essays and Sketches.* New York: Draus International, 1973.

Dumas, Henry. *Goodbye, Sweetwater.* New York: Thunders Mouth, 1988.

———. *Knees of a Natural Man.* Ed. Eugene B. Redmond. New York: Thunders Mouth, 1988.

Eagleton, Terry. *The Ideology of the Aesthetic.* Cambridge: Basil Blackwell, 1990.

———. *Literary Theory: An Introduction.* Minneapolis: University of Minnesota Press, 1983.

Easthope, Antony. *Literary into Cultural Studies.* London: Routledge, 1991.

Edmundson, Mark. "Dangers of Democracy." *TLS,* 19–25 Oct. 1990: 1133.

Ellison, Ralph. *Invisible Man.* New York: Random House, 1992.

———. *Shadow and Act.* New York: Random House, 1972.

Ewen, Stuart. "Hard Bodies." *All Consuming Images: The Politics of Style in Contemporary Culture.* New York: Basic Books, 1988. 185–199.

Fanon, Frantz. *Black Skin, White Masks.* New York: Grove, 1989.

———. *The Wretched of the Earth.* Trans. Constance Farrington. New York: Grove, 1963.

Farenga, Vincent. "Periphrasis on the Origin of Rhetoric." *MLN* 94 (1979): 1033–1055.

Felman, Shoshana. *The Literary Speech Act.* Trans. Catharine Porter. Ithaca: Cornell University Press, 1983.

———. "Psychoanalysis and Education: Teaching Terminable and Interminable." *Yale French Studies* 63 (1982): 21–44.

Fiske, John, "British Cultural Studies and Television." *Channels of Discourse: Television and Contemporary Criticism.* Ed. Robert C. Allen. Chapel Hill: University of North Carolina Press, 1987. 254–289.

———. *Television Culture.* New York: Methuen, 1987.

Foucault, Michel. "Revolutionary Action: 'Until Now.'" *Language, Counter-Memory, Practice: Selected Essays and Interviews.* Ed. Donald F. Bouchard. Ithaca: Cornell University Press, 1977. 218–233.

Fregoso, Rosa Linda, and Angie Chabram. "Chicana/o Cultural Representations:

Reframing Alternative Critical Discourses." *Cultural Studies* 4 (1990): 203–212.
Freire, Paulo. *Cultural Action for Freedom.* Monograph Series No. 1. Cambridge: Harvard Educational Review, 1988.
———. *The Pedagogy of the Oppressed.* Trans. Myra Bergman Ramos. New York: Seabury, 1973.
Friend, Christy. "The Excluded Conflict: The Marginalization of Composition and Rhetoric Studies in Graff's *Professing Literature*." *College English* 54 (1992): 276–286.
Fuller, Charles. *Soldier's Play.* New York: Farrar, Straus and Giroux, 1982.
Fuss, Diana. *Essentially Speaking: Feminism, Nature and Difference.* New York: Routledge, 1989.
Gallagher, Catherine. "Marxism and the New Historicism." *The New Historicism.* Ed. H. Aram Veeser. New York: Routledge, 1989. 37–48.
———. "Raymond Williams and Cultural Studies." *Social Text* 30 (1992): 79–89.
Gates, Henry Louis, Jr. *Black Literature and Literary Theory.* New York: Routledge, 1990.
Germino, Dante. *Antonio Gramsci: Architect of a New Politics.* Baton Rouge: Louisiana State University Press, 1990.
Gibson, Charles. *The Black Legend: Anti-Spanish Attitudes in the Old World and the New.* New York: Knopf, 1971.
Giroux, Henry, and David Shumway, Paul Smith, and James Sosnoski. "The Need for Cultural Studies: Resisting Intellectuals and Oppositional Spheres." *Dalhousie Review* 64 (1984): 472–486.
Graff, Gerald. "The Future of Theory in the Teaching of Literature." *The Future of Literary Theory.* Ed. Ralph Cohen. New York: Routledge, 1989. 251–267.
———. *Professing Literature: An Institutional History.* Chicago: University of Chicago Press, 1987.
Graff, Gerald, and Reginald Gibbons. "Preface." *Criticism in the University.* Ed. Gerald Graff and Reginald Gibbons. Evanston: Northwestern University Press, 1985. 7–12.
Gramsci, Antonio. *Selections from the Prison Notebooks of Antonio Gramsci.* Ed. and trans. Quintin Hoare and G. N. Smith. 1978. Reprint. Bloomington: Indiana University Press, 1982.
Greenblatt, Stephen J. *Learning to Curse: Essays in Early Modern Culture.* New York: Routledge, 1990.
———. *Marvelous Possessions: The Wonder of the New World.* Chicago: University of Chicago Press, 1991.
———. *Renaissance Self-Fashioning.* Chicago: University of Chicago Press, 1980.
Grossberg, Lawrence. "The Circulation of Cultural Studies." *Critical Studies in Mass Communication* 6 (1989): 413–421.
———. "The Formation(s) of Cultural Studies: An American in Birmingham." *Strategies* 2 (1989): 114–149.

Grossberg, Lawrence, Cary Nelson, and Paula Treichler, eds. *Cultural Studies.* New York: Routledge, 1992.

Habermas, Jurgen. *The Philosophical Discourse of Modernity.* Cambridge: MIT Press, 1987.

Hairston, Maxine. "Breaking Our Bonds and Reaffirming Our Connections." *College Composition and Communication* 36 (1985): 272–282.

Haley, Alex. *The Autobiography of Malcolm X.* New York: Ballantine, 1992.

Hall Stuart. "Cultural Studies and the Center: Some Problematics and Problems." *Culture, Media, Language: Working Papers in Cultural Studies.* Ed. Hall et al. London: Hutchinson, 1980. 15–47.

———. "Cultural Studies: Two Paradigms." *Media, Culture, and Society* 2 (1980): 57–72.

Halloran, S. Michael. "From Rhetoric to Composition: The Teaching of Writing in America to 1900." *A Short History of Writing Instruction: From Ancient Greece to Twentieth-Century America.* Ed. James J. Murphy. Davis: Hermagoras, 1990. 151–182.

Harrington, Michael. *The Other America.* New York: Viking Penguin, 1971.

Harjo, Joy (Creek). "Oklahoma: The Prairie of Words." *The Remembered Earth: An Anthology of Contemporary Native American Literature.* Ed. Geary Hobson. Albuquerque: Red Earth, 1979. 43–45.

Harvey, David. *The Condition of Postmodernity.* London: Basil Blackwell, 1990.

Hebdige, Dick. *Hiding in the Light: On Images and Things.* New York: Routledge, 1988.

———. *Subculture: The Meaning of Style.* London: Methuen, 1979.

"Higher Education for the Disadvantaged: A Commentary." East St. Louis: Experiment in Higher Education, 1968.

Hilliard, Asa. *The Teachings of Ptahhotep.* Atlanta: Blackwood, 1987.

Hinks, D. A. G. "Tisias and Corax and the Invention of Rhetoric." *Classical Quarterly* 34 (1940): 61–69.

Hobson, Geary (Cherokee/Chickasaw). "Introduction: Remembering the Earth." *The Remembered Earth: An Anthology of Contemporary Native American Literature.* Ed. Hobson. Albuquerque: Red Earth, 1979. 1–11.

Hodge, Frederick Webb, ed. *Handbook of American Indians North of Mexico.* 2 vols. Washington: Government Printing Office, 1907.

Hoggart, Richard. "Contemporary Cultural Studies: An Approach to the Study of Literature and Society." Occasional Paper. Centre for the Study of Contemporary Culture. London: Hutchinson, 1969.

hooks, bell. *Yearning: Race, Gender, and Cultural Politics.* Boston: South End, 1990.

Holquist, Michael. "The Politics of Representation." *Allegory and Representation.* Ed. Stephen J. Greenblatt. Baltimore: Johns Hopkins University Press, 1981. 163–183.

Hwang, David Henry. *FOB and Other Plays.* New York: Penguin, 1990.

Jacoby, Russell. *The Last Intellectuals: American Culture in the Age of Academe.* New York: Basic, 1987.

Jameson, Fredric. *Postmodernism: or, The Cultural Logic of Late Capitalism.* Durham: Duke University Press, 1991.

JanMohamed, Abdul R., and David Lloyd. "Introduction: Toward a Theory of Minority Discourse." *The Nature and Context of Minority Discourse.* Ed. JanMohamed and Lloyd. New York: Oxford University Press, 1990. 1–16.

Jay, Gregory S. "The End of 'American' Literature: Toward a Multicultural Practice." *College English* 53 (1991): 264–281.

———. "The Subject of Pedagogy: Lessons in Psychoanalysis and Politics." *College English* 49 (1987): 785–800.

Johnson, Barbara. *A World of Difference.* Baltimore: Johns Hopkins University Press, 1987.

Johnson, Richard. "What Is Cultural Studies Anyway?" *Social Text* 6 (1987): 38–80.

Jones, LeRoi. *Black Fire.* New York: William Morrow, 1968.

———. *Blues People: Negro Music in White America.* New York: William Morrow, 1971.

Kardiner, Abram, and Lionel Ovesey. *Mark of Oppression: Exploitations in the Personality of the American Negro.* New York: Dutton, 1990.

Karenga, Maulana. *Introduction to Black Studies.* Los Angeles: Kawaida, 1982.

Keller, Evelyn Fox. *Reflections on Gender and Science.* New Haven: Yale University Press, 1985.

Kennedy, Alan, Chris Neuwirth, Kris Straub, and David Kaufer. "The Role of Rhetorical Theory, Cultural Theory and Writing in Developing a First-Year Curriculum in English at Carnegie-Mellon University." Unpublished essay.

Kim, Elaine H. *Asian American Literature: An Introduction to the Writings and Their Social Context.* Philadelphia: Temple University Press, 1982.

Kingston, Maxine Hong. *Tripmaster Monkey: His Fake Book.* New York: Knopf, 1989.

———. *The Woman Warrior: Memoirs of a Girlhood among Ghosts.* New York: Knopf, 1976.

Knoblauch, C. H. "The Albany Graduate English Curriculum." *ADE Bulletin* 98 (1991): 19–21.

Ladner, Joyce. *Tomorrow's Tomorrow.* New York: Doubleday, 1968.

Larsen, Nella. *Quicksand* and *Passing.* Ed. Deborah McDowell. New Brunswick: Rutgers University Press, 1986.

Lauter, Paul, et al. *The Heath Anthology of American Literature.* 2 vols. Lexington, Mass.: D. C. Heath, 1990.

———. *Reconstructing American Literature: Courses, Syllabi, Issues.* Old Westbury: Feminist Press, 1983.

Lee, Mary Paik. *Quiet Odyssey: A Pioneer Korean Woman in America.* Ed. Sucheng Chan. Seattle: University of Washington Press, 1990.

Lentricchia, Frank. *After the New Criticism.* Chicago: University of Chicago Press, 1980.

———. "Foucault's Legacy: A New Historicism?" In *The New Historicism.* Ed. H. Aram Veeser. New York: Routledge, 1989. 231–242.

Locke, Patricia (Mississipi Band Chippewa/Hunkpapa Lakota). "An Ideal School System for American Indians: A Theoretical Construct." *The Schooling of Native America.* Ed. Thomas Thompson. Washington: American Association of Colleges for Teacher Education and the Teacher Corps, United States Office of Education, 1978.

Lomax, Louis E. *The Negro Revolt*. New York: Harper and Row, 1971.

Lyotard, Jean-François. *The Postmodern Condition: A Report on Knowledge*. Minneapolis: University of Minnesota Press, 1984.

Mailloux, Steven. "Misreading as a Historical Act: Cultural Rhetoric, Bible Politics, and Fuller's 1845 Review of Douglass' *Narrative*." *Readers in History: Nineteenth-Century American Literature and the Contexts of Response*. Ed. James Machor. Baltimore: Johns Hopkins University Press, 1993. 3–31.

———. *Rhetorical Power*. Ithaca: Cornell University Press, 1989.

Maltby, William S. *The Black Legend in England: The Development of Anti-Spanish Sentiment 1558–1660*. Durham: Duke University Press, 1971.

Marcus, Greil. *Lipstick Traces: A Secret History of the Twentieth Century*. Cambridge: Harvard University Press, 1989.

Marx, Karl, and Frederick Engels. *On Colonialism*. New York: International, 1972.

M'Biti, John S. *African Religions and Philosophy*. London: Heinemann, 1990.

McCormick, Kathleen. "Theory in the Reader: Bleich, Holland, and Beyond." *College English* 47 (1985): 836–849.

McDowell, Deborah. Introduction to *Quicksand* and *Passing*. New Brunswick: Rutgers University Press, 1986. ix–xxxv.

Melville, Stephen. *Philosophy Beside Itself: On Deconstruction and Modernism*. Minneapolis: University of Minnesota Press, 1986.

Mo, Timothy. *The Monkey King*. Garden City: Doubleday, 1980.

Modern Language Association. "Modern Language Association Statement on the Use of Part-Time Faculty." *Profession 82*. New York: MLA, 1982. 52.

Modleski, Tania. *Feminism without Women: Culture and Criticism in a "Postfeminist" Age*. New York: Routledge, 1991.

Monsiváis, Carlos. *Amor perdido*. Mexico City: Era, 1982.

———. *Entrada libre: crónicas de la sociedad que se organiza*. Mexico City: Ediciones Era, 1987.

———. *Escenas de pudor y liviandad*. 6th ed. Mexico City: Grijalbo, 1981.

Morínigo, Marcos A. *América en el teatro de Lope de Vega*. Buenos Aires: Revista de Filología Hispánica, 1946.

Morris, Meaghan. "Banality in Cultural Studies." *Discourse* 10 (1988): 3–29.

Mouffe, Chantal, ed. *Gramsci and Marxist Theory*. London: Routledge, 1979.

Mutwa, Vusamazulu Credo. *Indaba, My Children*. Johannesburg: Kohn and Avrill, 1966.

Neal, Larry. "Malcolm X: The Autobiography." *For Malcolm: Poems on the Life and Death of Malcolm X*. Ed. Dudley Randall and Margaret Burroughs. Detroit: Broadside, 1967.

———. *Visions of a Liberated Future: Black Arts Movement Writings*. New York: Thunders Mouth, 1989.

Nelson, Cary. "Always Already Cultural Studies: Two Conferences and a Manifesto." *Journal of the Midwest Modern Language Association* 24 (Spring 1991): 24–38.

Nelson, Cary, and Lawrence Grossberg. *Marxism and the Interpretation of Culture.* Urbana: University of Illinois Press, 1988.
Neuwirth, Chris, David Kaufer, and Cheryl Geisler. *Arguing from Sources: Exploring the Issues through Reading and Writing.* San Diego: Harcourt, Brace, Jovanovich, 1989.
Newton, Judith, and Deborah Rosenfelt. "Introduction: Toward a Materialist-Feminist Criticism." *Feminist Criticism and Social Change: Sex, Class and Race in Literature and Culture.* Ed. Newton and Rosenfelt. New York: Methuen, 1985. xv–xxix.
N'Gugi, James. *The River Between.* London: Heinemann, 1965.
Niane, Djibril Tamsir. *Sundiate: An Epic of Old Mali.* Essex: Longman, 1986.
Norris, Christopher. *What's Wrong with Postmodernism? Critical Theory and the Ends of Philosophy.* Baltimore: Johns Hopkins University Press, 1990.
Nussbaum, Felicity A. *The Autobiographical Subject: Gender and Ideology in Eighteenth-Century England.* Baltimore: Johns Hopkins University Press, 1989.
O'Connor, Alan. "The Emergence of Cultural Studies in Latin America." *Critical Studies in Mass Communication* 8 (1991): 60–73.
———. *Raymond Williams: Writing, Culture, Politics,* 128–75. New York: Blackwell, 1989.
———. "A Working Bibliography: Writings of Stuart Hall." *Journal of Communication Inquiry* 10 (1986): 125–129.
Odets, Clifford. *Six Plays of Clifford Odets.* New York: Modern Library, 1939.
Ohmann, Richard. *English in America: A Radical View of the Profession.* New York: Oxford University Press, 1976.
Okada, John. *No-No Boy.* Seattle: University of Washington Press, 1979.
Palmer, D. J. *The Rise of English Studies: An Account of the Study of English Language and Literature from Its Origins to the Making of the Oxford English School.* New York: Oxford University Press, 1965.
Pareles, Jon. "Pageant Flips Tradition on Its Ear." *New York Times,* 23 Dec. 1991: C11.
Parker, William Riley. "Where Do English Departments Come From?" *The Writing Teacher's Sourcebook.* Ed. Gary Tate and Edward Corbett. 2nd ed. New York: Oxford University Press, 1988. 3–15.
Petalesharo (Skidi Pawnee). "It Is too Soon, My Great Father, to Send Those Good Men among Us." *Indian Oratory: Famous Speeches by Noted Indian Chieftains.* Ed. W. C. Vanderwerth. Norman: University of Oklahoma Press, 1971. 79–83.
Phelps, Louise Wetherbee. "Developmental Challenges, Developmental Tensions: A Heuristic for Curricular Thinking." *Developing Discourse Practices in Adolescence and Adulthood.* Ed. Richard Beach and Susan Hynds. Norwood: Ablex, 1990. 386–414.
———. "The Institutional Logic of Writing Programs: Catalyst, Laboratory, and Pattern for Change." *Politics of Writing Instruction: Postsecondary.* Ed. Richard Bullock and John Trimbur. Portsmouth: Boynton-Cook, 1991. 155–170.

———. "Practical Wisdom and the Geography of Knowledge in Composition." *College English* 53 (1991): 863–885.
Platero, Dillon (Navajo). "Multicultural Teacher Education Center at Rough Rock. In *The Schooling of Native America*. Ed. Thomas Thompson. Washington: American Association of Colleges for Teacher Education and the Teacher Corps, United States Office of Education, 1978. 44–51.
Pratt, Mary Louise. "Arts of the Contact Zone." *Profession 91*. New York: MLA, 1991. 33–40.
"Prolegomena Artis Rhetoricae." Anon. *Prolegomenon Sylloge*. Ed. Hugo Rabe. Leipzig: Teubner, 1931.
Rajan, Gita, and Jessica Munns, eds. *Cultural Studies: An Anglo-American Reader*. New York: Longman, 1994.
Ransom, John Crowe. *The World's Body*. New York: Charles Scribner's Sons, 1938.
Roberts, D. "Mei Mei: A Daughter's Story." Broadcast on "Soundprint," NPR. 27 September 1989.
Rosaldo, Michelle. "Women, Culture, and Society: A Theoretical Overview." *Women, Culture and Society*. Ed. Rosaldo and Louise Lamphere. Stanford: Stanford University Press, 1974. 17–42.
Ruland, Richard. "Art and a Better America." *American Literary History* 3 (1991): 337–359.
Russell, David R. *Writing in the Academic Disciplines, 1870–1990: A Curricular History*. Carbondale: Southern Illinois University Press, 1991.
Ruthven, K. K. *Feminist Literary Studies: An Introduction*. Cambridge: Cambridge University Press, 1984.
Ryan, Michael. *Marxism and Deconstruction*. Baltimore: Johns Hopkins University Press, 1982.
Sagoyewatha [Red Jacket] (Seneca). "We Never Quarrel about Religion." *Native American Testimony: An Anthology of Indian and White Relations*. Ed. Peter Nabokov. New York: Harper and Row, 1978. 69–70.
Said, Edward. *Orientalism*. New York: Pantheon, 1978.
———. *The World, the Text, and the Critic*. Cambridge: Harvard University Press, 1983.
Saldívar, José David. "The Limits of Cultural Studies." *American Literary History* 2 (1990): 251–266.
Sarris, Greg. "Storytelling in the Classroom: Crossing Vexed Chasms." *College English* 52 (1990): 169–185.
Schantz, Nancy Borkow. *Trends in Racial/Ethnic Enrollment in Higher Education: Fall 1980 through Fall 1990*. Washington: U.S. Department of Education, 1990.
Schell, Marc. "Marranos (Pigs); or, From Coexistence to Toleration." *Critical Inquiry* 17 (1991): 307–335.
Schiller, Herbert I. *The Mind Managers*. Boston: Beacon, 1973.
Schleifer, Ronald, Robert Con Davis, and Nancy Mergler. *Culture and Cognition: The Boundaries of Literary and Scientific Inquiry*. Ithaca: Cornell University Press, 1992.

Shumway, David, and Paul Smith. "Off Our Backs!" *In These Times,* 18–24 Nov. 1987: 15.
Simpson, David. "Raymond Williams: Feeling for Structures, Voicing 'History.'" *Social Text* 30 (1992): 9–26.
———, ed. *Subject to History: Ideology, Class, Gender.* Ithaca: Cornell University Press, 1991.
———. "Teaching English: What and Where Is the Cutting Edge?" *ADE Bulletin* 98 (1991): 14–18.
Slevin, James. "Connecting English Studies." *College English* 48 (1986): 543–550.
Smith, Barbara Herrnstein. *Contingencies of Value: Alternative Perspectives for Critical Theory.* Cambridge: Harvard University Press, 1988.
Smith, Paul. "A Course in 'Cultural Studies.'" *Journal of the Midwest Modern Language Association* 24 (1991): 39–49.
Sowande, Fela. *The Africanization of Black Studies: From the Circumference to the Center.* Kent: Kent State University Press, 1970.
Spivak, Gayatri Chakravorty. *In Other Worlds: Essays in Cultural Politics.* New York: Methuen, 1987.
———. "'The Making of Americans,' the Teaching of English, and the Future of Culture Studies." *New Literary History* 21 (1990): 781–798.
Steele, Shelby. *The Content of Our Character: A New Vision of Race in America.* New York: HarperCollins, 1991.
Stewart, Donald. "Two Models and the Harvardization of English Departments." *The Rhetorical Tradition and Modern Writing.* Ed. James J. Murphy. New York: MLA, 1982. 118–129.
Tan, Amy. *The Joy Luck Club.* New York: G. P. Putnam's Sons, 1989.
Tatanga Mani [Walking Buffalo] (Stoney). "The Hairy Man from the East." *Touch the Earth: A Self-Portrait of Indian Existence.* Comp. T. C. McLuhan. New York: Simon and Schuster, 1972. 45–110.
Tecumtha [Tecumseh] (Shawnee). "We Must Be United." *Native American Testimony: An Anthology of Indian and White Relations.* Ed. Peter Nabokov. New York: Harper and Row, 1978. 118–121.
Thomas, Brook. "The New Historicism and Other Old-Fashioned Topics." *The New Historicism.* Ed. H. Aram Veeser. New York: Routledge, 1989. 182–203.
———. *The New Historicism and Other Old-Fashioned Topics.* Princeton: Princeton University Press, 1991.
Thurgood, Delores H., and Joanne M. Weinman. *Summary Report 1990: Doctorate Recipients from United States Universities.* National Research Council. Washington: National Academy Press, 1991.
Tierney, Robert J., and P. David Pierson. "Toward a Composing Model of Reading." *Language Arts* 60 (1983): 568–580.
Torgovnick, Marianna. "Meet the Press: Cultural Criticism in the 1990s." *ADE Bulletin* 100 (1991): 4–8.
Trimbur, John. "Cultural Studies and Teaching Writing." *Focuses* 2 (1988): 5–18.

Turner, Graeme. *British Cultural Studies: An Introduction.* Boston: Unwin Hyman, 1990.

Tutuola, Amos. *The Palm-Wine Drinkard.* Glenview: Greenwood, 1954.

Tyack, David. *George Ticknor and the Boston Brahmins.* Cambridge: Harvard University Press, 1967.

Tylor, E. B. *Primitive Culture: Researches into the Development of Mythology, Philosophy, Religion, Language, Art, and Custom.* 2nd ed. London: John Murray, 1873.

Urrea, Luis Alberto. *Across the Wire: Life and Hard Times on the Mexican Border.* New York: Anchor, 1993.

Valenzuela, José Manuel. *A la brava ése!* Tijuana: El Colegio de la Frontera Norte, 1988.

Vega, Lope de. "El premio del bien hablar." *Obras completas.* Vol. 13. New edition. Madrid: Galo Saez, 1930.

———. "La Doretea." Ed. and trans. Alan S. Trueblood and Edwin Honig. Cambridge: Harvard University Press, 1985.

Vizenor, Gerald (Ojibwa). *Griever: An American Monkey King in China.* Minneapolis: University of Minnesota Press, 1987.

Walker, Margaret. *For My People.* New York: Ayer, 1969.

Wallace, Michele. *Invisibility Blues: From Pop to Theory.* London: Verso, 1990.

Ward, Douglas Turner. *Two Plays.* New York: Okpaku Cmmunications, 1971.

Warren, Bill. *Imperialism: Pioneer of Capitalism.* London: Verso, 1980.

Wayne, Valerie, ed. *The Matter of Difference: Materialist Feminist Criticism of Shakespeare.* Ithaca: Cornell University Press, 1991.

Wellek, René, and Austin Warren. *Theory of Literature.* New York: Harcourt, Brace and World, 1942.

Wess, Robert. "Notes toward a Marxist Rhetoric." *Bucknell Review* 28 (1983): 126–148.

West, Annette Arkeketa (Otoe/Creek). "salt man." *That's What She Said: Contemporary Poetry and Fiction by Native American Women.* Ed. Rayna Green. Bloomington: Indiana University Press, 1984.

Whiteman, Henrietta V. (Cheyenne). "Native American Studies, the University, and the Indian Student." *The Schooling of Native America.* Ed. Thomas Thompson. Washington: American Association of Colleges for Teacher Education and the Teacher Corps, United States Office of Education, 1978. 105–116.

Wilcox, Stanley. "Corax and the *Prolegomena.*" *American Journal of Philology* 59 (1943): 1–23.

Wilentz, Gay. *Binding Cultures: Black Women Writers in Africa and the Diaspora.* Bloomington: Indiana University Press, 1992.

Wilkerson, Margaret. *Nine Plays by Black Women.* New York: National-Dutton, 1986.

Williams, Raymond. *Culture and Society, 1780–1950.* New York: Columbia University Press, 1983.

———. "The Future of Cultural Studies." *The Politics of Postmodernism.* London: Verso, 1989. 151–162.

———. *Keywords*. New York: Oxford University Press, 1976.
———. *The Long Revolution*. New York: Columbia University Press, 1961.
———. *Marxism and Literature*. New York: Oxford University Press, 1977.
———. *The Sociology of Culture*. New York: Schocken, 1981.
Williamson, Judith. "The Problems of Being Popular." *New Socialist* (Sept. 1986): 14–15.
Wimsatt, W. "The Intentional Fallacy." *Sewanee Review* 54 (1946). Reprint. *The Verbal Icon*. Lexington: University Press of Kentucky, 1967. 3–18.
Wimsatt, W. K., and Cleanth Brooks. *Literary Criticism: A Short History*. New York: Random House, 1957.
Women's Studies Group. *Women Take Issue: Aspects of Women's Subordination*. Centre for Contemporary Culture Studies. London: Hutchinson, 1978.
Wu Ch'eng-en. *Monkey*. Trans. Arthur Waley. New York: Grove, 1943.
Young, Robert. *White Mythologies: Writing History and the West*. New York: Routledge, 1990.
Zavarzadeh, Mas'ud, and Donald Morton. "The Nostalgia for Law and Order and the Policing of Knowledge: The Politics of Contemporary Theory." *Syracuse Scholar: An Interdisciplinary Journal of Ideas Published by Syracuse University* (Spring 1987): 25–71.
———. "Theory Pedagogy Politics: The Crisis of 'The Subject' in the Humanities." *Theory/Pedagogy/Politics: Texts for Change*. Ed. Morton and Zavarzadeh. Urbana: University of Illinois Press, 1991.
———. *Theory, (Post)Modernity, Opposition: An "Other" Introduction to Literary and Cultural Theory*. PostModernPositions, vol. 5. Washington: Maisonneuve, 1991.
———. "War of the Words: The Battle of (and for) English." *In These Times* 11, no. 41 (28 Oct.–3 Nov. 1987): 18–19.
Zebroski, James T. "Keywords of Composition: A Discipline's Search for Self." *Thinking Through Theory*. Portsmouth: Boynton/Cook, 1994.
Zizek, Slavoj. *The Sublime Object of Ideology*. London: Verso, 1989.

☐ Contributors

PATRICK BRANTLINGER is chair of the Department of English at Indiana University. His books include *Rule of Darkness: British Literature and Imperialism* (1988) and *Crusoe's Footprints: Cultural Studies in Britain and America* (1990).

PAMELA L. CAUGHIE is an associate professor of English at Loyola University Chicago, where she teaches twentieth-century literature and literary theory. She is the author of *Virginia Woolf and Postmodernism: Literature in Quest and Question of Itself* (1991) and has published essays on Woolf, postmodernism, and feminist theory in journals and collections, including *Writing the Woman Artist* (1991), *Rereading the New: A Backward Glance at Modernism* (1992), and *Making Feminist History: The Literary Scholarship of Sandra M. Gilbert and Susan Gubar* (1994). She is writing a book tentatively titled *Passing and Pedagogy: Postmodern Theories and Cultural Politics*.

ROBERT CON DAVIS, associate professor at the University of Oklahoma, has published widely on cultural studies, American studies, and theory. He has edited several collections on modern literary theory, coedited textbooks such as *Contemporary Literary Criticism: Literary and Cultural Studies* (1993), and coauthored *Criticism and Culture: The Role of Critique in Modern Literary Theory* (1992). He is also the author of *The Paternal Romance: Reading God-the-Father in Early Western Culture* (1993).

LEE FRANCIS (Laguna/Chippewa), national director of Wordcraft Circle of Native Writers, is the author of *The Path of the Brave: Dissolving Ethnocultural Barriers* (1992) and guest editor of *Native American Literatures,* a special issue of *Callaloo* (Winter 1994). His *Native Time: An Historical Timetable of Native America* is in press. He is engaged in research on post-traumatic stress disorder as it applies to cultural groups.

WARREN GINSBERG, associate professor of English and chair of the English department at the State University of New York at Albany, is the author of *The Cast of Character* (1983) and numerous articles on Ovid and on medieval English and Italian literature, especially Chaucer and Dante. He has also edited *Wynnere and Wastoure and the Parlement of the Thre Ages* (1992) and a volume of essays, *Ideas of Order in the Middle Ages, ACTA 15* (1990).

GERALD GRAFF is George M. Pullman Professor of English and Education at the University of Chicago and author of *Professing Literature: An Institutional History* (1987) and *Beyond the Culture Wars: How Teaching the Conflicts Can Revitalize American Education* (1992).

PAUL LAUTER is Allan K. and Gwendolyn Miles Smith Professor of Literature at Trinity College and president of the American Studies Association. He is the general editor of *The Heath Anthology of American Literature* (1990) and the author of *Canons and Contexts* (1990).

SHENG-MEI MA is an assistant professor of English at James Madison University in Virginia. His publications include "Obsession and Oblivion: Jewish and Chinese Genocide Literature" in *Vision in History* and "Contrasting Two Survival Literatures: On the Jewish Holocaust and the Chinese Cultural Revolution" in *Holocaust and Genocide Studies*. He has also published "Orientalism in Chinese American Discourse: Body and Pidgin" in *Modern Language Studies* and "Interracial Eroticism in Asian American Literature: Male Subjectivity and White Bodies" in the *Journal of American Culture,* both of which are chapters in his book-in-progress, *Immigrant Subjectivities in Asian American and Asian Emigré Literatures*. His collection of Chinese poems, *Thirty, Left and Right* (1989), was published in Taiwan.

STEVEN MAILLOUX is a professor of English at the University of California at Irvine. He is the author of *Interpretive Conventions: The Reader in the Study of American Fiction* (1982), *Rhetorical Power* (1989), and several articles on rhetoric, critical theory, and cultural studies. He has also edited a collection titled *Rhetoric, Sophistry, Pragmatism* (in press) and coedited *Interpreting Law and Literature: A Hermeneutic Reader* (1988).

GEORGE MARISCAL, an associate professor at the University of California at San Diego, teaches Chicano and Spanish literature. His book *Contradictory Subjects* (1991) was awarded the MLA's Katherine Singer Kovacs Prize. He serves on the board of directors of Project YANO, a volunteer organization of Vietnam veterans and activists who speak to high school students about the realities of military service.

CARY NELSON is Jubilee Professor of Liberal Arts and Sciences and professor of English and criticism and interpretive theory at the University of Illinois at Urbana-Champaign. He is the author of *The Incarnate Word: Literature as Verbal Space* (1973), *Our Last First Poets: Vision and His-*

tory in Contemporary American Poetry (1981), and *Repression and Recovery: Modern American Poetry and the Politics of Cultural Memory, 1910–45* (1989). His edited and coedited books include *Theory in the Classroom* (1986), *Marxism and the Interpretation of Culture* (1988), *Cultural Studies* (1992), and Edwin Rolfe's *Collected Poems* (1993). He is preparing a volume of his theoretical essays, writing a book on modern poetry, and completing a biography of Edwin Rolfe.

JANICE RADWAY, professor of literature at Duke University, is the author of *Reading the Romance: Women, Patriarchy, and Popular Literature* (1984). She is completing a book titled *The Book-of-the-Month Club and the General Reader: On the Nature of Middlebrown Taste.* She is also coeditor of the volumes on the twentieth-century history of the book in the American Antiquarian Society's collaborative project on the history of the book in the United States.

GITA RAJAN, an Andrew Mellon Scholar at the University of Pennsylvania, is carrying out research on the interstices of art and politics in Indian culture. She has published essays on colonial adaptations of literary/cultural theory and the esthetics of Walter Pater and is coeditor of *Cultural Studies: An Anglo-American Reader* (1994) and *A Handbook of English Postcoloniality: Literary Texts and Cultural Contexts* (1994).

EUGENE B. REDMOND, a professor at Southern Illinois University at Edwardsville, is a specialist in African-American literature. He is the author of *Drumvoices: The Mission of Afro-American Poetry* (1976), the editor of *Drumvoices Revue: A Confluence of Literary, Cultural, and Vision Arts,* and the coeditor of *Literati Internazionale* and *The Original Chicago Blues Annual.* He has also written several volumes of poetry, including *The Eye in the Ceiling: Selected Poems* (1991), winner of the Before Columbus Foundations's 1993 American Book Award. He is working on an epic: *The Dance of the Intellect: A Poetic Memoir of Katherine Dunham.*

NANCY RUFF, an associate professor at Southern Illinois University at Edwardsville, teaches in the English department and the women's studies and classics program. She has published articles on Renaissance literature and neo-Latin studies and served as acting editor of *Victorian Periodicals Review.* Her research centers on the Dido legend in medieval and Renaissance literature.

ISAIAH SMITHSON is an associate professor teaching in the English department and women's studies program at Southern Illinois University at Edwardsville, where he directs the writing program, oversees the M.A. program in the teaching of writing, and teaches seminars on women and language and modern literary theory. He has published articles on seventeenth-century literature, modern literature, literary theory, writing across the curriculum, and composition theory. He is coeditor of *Gender in the Classroom: Power and Pedagogy* (1990).

KRISTINA STRAUB is an associate professor of literary and cultural studies at Carnegie-Mellon University and has directed the university's first-year writing program. She has published work on eighteenth-century English literature, feminist theory, and on how the eighteenth-century English theater contributed to cultural assumptions about sexuality and gender identity. She is working on a book on criminality and bodily excesses in eighteenth-century British popular narratives.

☐ Index

Adorno, Theodor, 51
African-American studies, 57, 170, 185; see also black studies
Alarcón, Norma, 64
Althusser, Louis, 9, 12, 22n, 43, 50, 51, 55; Althusserian thought, 66
Alurista, 65
American culture, 188
American studies, 17, 18, 25, 28, 100
Anderson, Perry, 44
Angelou, Maya, 124n
Anzaldúa, Gloria, 62–63, 105
Applebee, Arthur, 3
Arabic studies, 170
Arnold, Matthew, 35, 36; Arnoldian paradigm, 54
Aronowitz, Stanley, 44
Asian-American studies, 19, 133–39
Asian studies, 138–39
Austin, J. L., 93n
Avila, Teresa de, 62
Aztlán, 65, 74n

Bagdikian, Ben, 53
Bakhtin, Mikhail, 161
Balsamo, Anne, 93n
Barrera, Mario, 105
Baudrillard, Jean, 44, 55
Belsey, Catherine, 54
Bennett, William, 31, 34
Bennington, Geoffrey, 57n
Bergson, Henri, 66
Birmingham Centre for Contemporary Cultural Studies, 2, 6, 30, 45, 66; Women's Studies Group of, 93n
black culture: in college classrooms, 111–21; institutionalized study of, 108; in the streets, 109–11
black feminist criticism, 8, 93n
Black Legend, 59, 60
black power, 113, 183
black studies, 19, 101; /culture studies, 121–24; movement, 112–21

Bondolfi, Lia Tessarolo, 74n
Bourdieu, Pierre, 53
Brantlinger, Patrick, 19, 21, 83, 91, 96, 98
British cultural studies movement, 2, 52, 66, 191–92
Brooks, Cleanth, 10, 11, 186
Buckanaga, Jerome (Minnesota Chippewa), 106n
Butler, Judith, 93n

Cadova, Eduardo, 58n
Cain, William E., 11
Canasatego (Onondaga), 95–96
canon, 2, 4, 8, 9, 18, 29, 38, 54, 57, 68, 98, 101, 103, 124, 127, 131, 132, 162, 167, 168, 170, 180, 201, 204
Carby, Hazel, 8, 9
Casas, Bartolomé de las, 61
Caughie, Pamela, 19, 21
Certeau, Michel de, 53, 176, 178
Cervantes, Miguel de, 70–71
Chabram, Angie, 64
Chambers, Iain, 51
Chan, Sucheng, 136
Cheney, Lynne, 31, 34
Chicano studies, 62
Child, Francis J., 22n
Churchill, Ward E. (Creek/Cherokee Métis), 95
Clifford, James, 29, 80–82, 84, 89, 91, 93n
Collins, Patricia Hill, 93n
converso, 69, 70
Corn Tassel (Cherokee), 102
Croce, Benedetto, 66
Culler, Jonathan, 1, 4, 191
cultural activism, 110
cultural analysis, 5, 14, 25, 174, 200, 205
cultural critique, 2, 28, 29, 31, 41, 67, 82, 92, 178
cultural diversity, 12, 18
cultural feedback, 72

Index

cultural history, 54; as related to pedagogy, 55
cultural identity, 9
cultural inquiry, 25, 42; and pedagogy, 34
cultural intertextuality, 5, 9, 11, 12, 14, 165
cultural nationalism, 62
"cultural poetics," 45–50
cultural politics, 148
cultural popularization, 27
cultural reductionism, 41
cultural rhetoric, 144, 151, 152, 153, 154, 155n
cultural studies, 2, 13, 20, 21, 62, 63, 65, 68, 74, 144, 193; Americanization of, 191–97; and rhetoric, 167–79, 172–73; as double bind for feminist teachers, 77–96; as link to populist individualism, 52; as oppositional tradition, 29, 30, 32, 33, 34, 39, 78, 80, 83, 86, 90, 161, 193; depoliticizing of, 193, 197, 203; false, 194; future of, 203–5; ghettoization of, 34; institutionalization of, 25–42, 54, 62, 83–85, 161, 167–69, 202; interdisciplinary approaches, 40, 77, 170, 196, 202; manifesto, 20, 197–203; model, 77, 89, 192; paradigm, 78, 92, 202; practitioners, 27; relationship to feminism and feminist criticism, 76–92, 93n; versus New Historicism, 43–58
culture, 6, 17, 26, 27, 28, 32, 44, 54, 184, 199; and text, 133; discourses of, 8; politics of, 35, 199; study of, 13
culture studies, 1–2, 6, 8, 9, 12, 13, 14, 16, 17, 18, 19, 20, 21, 133, 136; African-American view; 108–26; as oppositional stance, 3, 13, 17, 20; dissent within, 19–21, 25–140, 32, 34, 36, 42; institutionalization of, 1–22, 31, 95, 105; Native American, 94–107; roles of teachers, 16–17; self-critique, 17

Davis, Natalie Zemon, 58n
Davis, Robert Con, 19, 21
Debo, Angie (Choctaw), 95
deconstruction, 44, 53, 79–80, 131, 203–4

Deloria, Vine, Jr. (Hunkpapa Lakota), 95, 98, 101, 105, 106n
Denning, Michael, 44, 55
Derrida, Jacques, 6–7, 9, 47, 57n, 91–92, 93n, 105, 158, 161
disempowered groups, 63, 64, 68, 98, 78
Dollimore, Jonathan, 45
Doyle, Brian, 3
Du Bois, W. E. B., 122
Dunham, Katherine, 115, 119, 121, 122, 125n, 126n

Eagleton, Terry, 3, 4, 7, 9, 11, 34–35
Easthope, Antony, 46, 54, 89, 90
Edgerton, Samuel Y., Jr., 101
Edmundson, Mark, 184
English studies, 1–3, 10, 11, 12, 13, 14, 17, 19, 20, 21, 22n, 25, 37, 130, 131; and politics of canon formation, 162, 180–90; and politics of power, 158, 160, 174; and textual studies, 148–51, 153, 154, 160–61, 168; as cultural text, 157; cultural role of, 195; /culture studies, 1, 2, 3–6, 14; curricular reform in, 143–56; 157–66, 167–79; ideological position in, 158, 163; institutionalization of, 8, 151, 153
Entartete Kunst (Degenerate Art), 76–79, 80
essentialism, 8, 10, 21n, 42, 191
esthetic formalism, 62
ethnic studies, 2, 13, 14, 26, 95, 98–99; and gender studies, 19
Experiment in Higher Education (EHE), 115–21, 123, 125n, 126n

Fanon, Frantz, 133
Felman, Shoshana, 82, 93n
feminism, 2, 6, 55, 60, 64, 80, 169, 170, 175; and cultural studies, 76–93, 171, 199
feminist theory, 7
Fiske, John, 51, 53
Foucault, Michel, 9, 12, 43, 44, 46, 48, 50, 105
Francis, Lee, 19, 21
Fregoso, Rosa Linda, 64
Freire, Paulo, 27, 32, 35, 73, 105, 171
Friend, Christy, 22n
Fuss, Diana, 21n, 93n

Gallagher, Catherine, 48
Gates, Henry Louis, Jr., 8, 9, 93*n*, 136, 140*n*, 188
gay and lesbian studies, 19, 34, 170
Gibson, Charles, 59
Ginsberg, Warren, 20
Giroux, Henry, 8, 9, 17, 27, 32
Graff, Gerald, 3, 4, 14, 17, 19, 21, 91, 178
Gramsci, Antonio, 52, 65, 67, 74*n*, 199
Greenblatt, Stephen, 44, 45–50, 51, 52, 54, 58*n*, 61–62, 163
Grossberg, Lawrence, 54, 205*n*

Habermas, Jurgen, 44
Hairston, Maxine, 14, 22*n*
Hall, Stuart, 29, 37, 38, 44, 51, 52, 53, 79, 194, 199
Harjo, Joy (Creek), 95
Hebdige, Dick, 44, 51, 56, 57, 84
hegemony, 32, 40, 52, 66, 113, 124, 131, 139
Hendrix, Richard, 182
hermeneutics, 92, 123
high culture, 26, 54, 55, 198, 204
Hobson, Geary (Cherokee/Chickasaw), 97
Hogan, Linda (Chickasaw), 95
Hoggart, Richard, 51, 191, 205*n*
Holquist, Michael, 44
hooks, bell, 16, 34–35, 93*n*, 170
Horkheimer, Max, 51
Hughes, Langston, 105
humanist tradition, 32, 36, 54
humanistic study, 60, 159
Hunt, Lynn, 58*n*
Hurston, Zora, 105, 122
Hwang, David Henry, 137

indiano, 69–70, 73
interdisciplinary programs, 2, 6, 14, 29, 77, 40, 119, 138, 191, 202
intertextual relations, 12

Jay, Gregory, 17, 86
Johnson, Barbara, 93*n*
Johnson, Glen M., 190*n*
Johnson, Richard, 43

Kantian critique, 6
Karenga, Maulana, 125*n*
Kawaida, 113

Keller, Evelyn Fox, 171
Kingston, Maxine Hong, 136
Kimball, Robert, 34

Lacanian critique, 28
Laqueur, Thomas, 58*n*
Lauter, Paul, 20
Larsen, Nella, 78, 85–89
Lentricchia, Frank, 48
Lévi-Strauss, Claude, 6–7
liberal pluralism, 62, 63
literary language, 161–65
Locke, Patricia (Mississippi Band Chippewa/Hunkpapa Lakota), 96
Lord, Betty Bao, 105
Lyotard, Jean-François, 44, 58*n*

Ma, Sheng-mei, 19
Mailloux, Steven, 20
Mainardi, Patricia, 101
Malcolm X, 113–15, 124*n*
Maltby, William S., 59
Marcus, George, 80
marginalization: as source of political resistence, 51; of groups, 62, 67, 91, 101, 127, 130, 138, 183, 188, 200–201; within cultural studies, 36, 39; within English departments, 14–15, 22*n*, 127–40
Mariátegui, José Carlos, 66
Mariscal, George, 19, 21
Marxism, 2, 6, 28, 43, 44, 46–50, 56–57, 65, 98, 99, 100, 169, 175, 193, 199
Marxist cultural theory, 45
McDowell, Deborah, 88
Miller, J. Hillis, 194–95
Modleski, Tania, 78, 91, 93*n*
Momaday, N. Scott (Kiowa), 95
Monsiváis, Carlos, 75*n*
Montes, Roberto Gil de, 73
Montrose, Louis, 44
Morton, Donald, 8, 9, 21*n*, 149, 156*n*
Mouffe, Chantal, 74*n*
multiculturalism, 2, 6, 18, 27, 57, 63, 77, 111, 119, 124, 129, 133, 176, 182, 200–201, 203–4

Native-American studies, 19
Native People, 94–107
nature: and essence, 6, 8, 9, 33; and culture, 7

Nelson, Cary, 20, 21, 39, 54
neo-pragmatism, 50
New Criticism, 1, 3, 10–12, 17, 18, 46, 54, 132, 181, 186; institutionalization of, 11
New Historicism, 43–58, 61, 131, 192, 201
Norris, Christopher, 44

O'Connor, Alan, 66, 205n
O'Connor, Margaret, 185
Ohiyesa [Charles A. Eastman] (Santee Dakota), 95
Ohmann, Richard, 3, 4
Okada, John, 138
Open University, 37, 45
oppositional critics, 35

Parker, William Riley, 3
passing: as pedagogy, 76–93
pedagogy: in cultural studies classroom, 1, 19, 33, 34, 73, 76–92, 105, 153, 160–61, 200, 204; performative, 78, 89–92, 93n, positivist, 170–71; radical, 27, 149
Peñalosa, Benito de, 70
Performing Arts Training Center (PATC), 115–21, 123, 125n, 126n; see also Katherine Dunham
political correctness, 27, 31, 33
political discourse, 163
popular culture, 5, 26, 27, 51, 52, 54, 55, 77, 193, 198; studies, 25
postcolonial: critique, 25, 41; studies, 57, 60; "Yellow Man," 130–33
post-Marxists, 46
postmoderism, 44, 84
poststructuralism, 19, 28, 43, 44, 46, 47, 49, 50–51, 55, 56, 57, 60, 131, 169, 204; French, 64
Pratt, Mary Louise, 75n
Price, Richard, 89

Radway, Janice, 19, 21, 195, 196
Rajan, Gita, 19
Ransom, John Crowe, 11, 186
Reconstructing American Literature (RAL), 180–81, 185
Redding, Saunders, 186–87
Redmond, Eugene B., 19
rhetoric, 3, 14, 15, 54, 74, 101, 151–55, see also cultural rhetoric

rhetorical study, 144, 159, 171
rhetorical theory, 20, 143, 172
Rosaldo, Michelle, 107n
Ruland, Richard, 184
Ruthven, K. K., 9
Ryan, Michael, 44

Sagoyewatha [Red Jacket] (Seneca), 102
Said, Edward, 57, 131–32
Saldívar, José David, 65, 74n
Sartre, Jean-Paul, 28
Schell, Marc, 60–62, 74n
Schiller, Herbert I., 53
Schleifer, Ron, 29
Schlesinger, Arthur, 31
semiotics, 56, 198
Silko, Leslie Marmon (Laguna Pueblo), 95, 105
Simpson, David, 45, 47, 57n, 158, 165n
Sinfield, Alan, 45
Smith, Barbara Herrnstein, 81, 92
Smith, Paul, 83–84, 93n
Smithson, Isaiah, 25
social critique, 205
Sorel, Georges, 66
Spanish studies, 19
Spivak, Gayatri Chakravorty, 2, 4, 21n, 196
Sophist thought, 6
Straub, Kristina, 20
subject/subjectivity, 8, 17–18, 28, 29, 30, 34, 40, 41, 51, 54–57, 63, 64, 68, 73, 77, 84, 89–92, 146, 149, 150, 159, 160, 161, 163, 171

Takaki, Ronald T., 105
Tate, Allen, 11
Tekahionwake [E. Pauline Johnson] (Mohawk), 95
textual communities, 161
textualism, 82
Ticknor, George, 60
Thomas, Brook, 50, 58n
Thompson, E. P., 51, 66
Torgovnick, Marianna, 13
Treichler, Paula, 54
Turner, Graeme, 55
Tylor, E. B., 5, 6, 12

underrepresentation: of women and ethinic groups, 15–16

Valdez, Luis, 68, 75*n*
Valenzuela, José Manuel, 72
Vega, Lope de, 70, 71

Wallace, Michele, 93*n*
Warren, Austin, 11
Warren, Robert Penn, 11
Welch, James (Blackfeet/Gros Ventre), 95
Wellek, René, 11
West, Annette Arkeketa (Otoe/Creek), 103
Whiteman, Henrietta V. (Cheyenne), 95
Wilentz, Gay, 138
Williams, Raymond, 5, 6, 12, 21*n*, 28, 43, 45–46, 47, 48, 51, 66, 96, 105, 165*n*, 191, 199, 205*n*
Williamson, Judith, 51
Wimsatt, W. K., 10, 11
women's studies, 13, 14, 19, 57, 100, 112
"Wyoming Resolution," 22*n*

Young, Robert, 46

Zavarzadeh, Mas'ud, 8, 9, 21*n*, 149, 150, 156*n*
Zizek, Slavoj, 58*n*